Ancient Egyptian Scribes

Bloomsbury Egyptology

Series editor: Nicholas Reeves

Ancient Egyptians at Play, Walter Crist, Anne-Elizabeth Dunn-Vaturi and
Alex de Voogt
Ancient Egyptian Technology and Innovation, Ian Shaw
Archaeologists, Tourists, Interpreters, Rachel Mairs and Maya Muratov
Asiatics in Middle Kingdom Egypt, Phyllis Saretta
Burial Customs in Ancient Egypt, Wolfram Grajetzki
Court Officials of the Egyptian Middle Kingdom, Wolfram Grajetzki
The Egyptian Oracle Project, edited by Robyn Gillam and Jeffrey Jacobson
Foreigners in Ancient Egypt, Flora Brooke Anthony
Hidden Hands, Stephen Quirke
The Middle Kingdom of Ancient Egypt, Wolfram Grajetzki
The Unknown Tutankhamun, Marianne Eaton-Krauss
Performance and Drama in Ancient Egypt, Robyn Gillam

Ancient Egyptian Scribes

A Cultural Exploration

Niv Allon and Hana Navratilova

Bloomsbury Academic
An imprint of Bloomsbury Publishing Plc

B L O O M S B U R Y
LONDON · OXFORD · NEW YORK · NEW DELHI · SYDNEY

Bloomsbury Academic

An imprint of Bloomsbury Publishing Plc

50 Bedford Square	1385 Broadway
London	New York
WC1B 3DP	NY 10018
UK	USA

www.bloomsbury.com

BLOOMSBURY and the Diana logo are trademarks of Bloomsbury Publishing Plc

First published 2017

British Library Cataloguing-in-Publication Data
A catalogue record for this book is available from the British Library.

ISBN:	HB:	978-1-4725-8395-6
	ePDF:	978-1-4725-8398-7
	ePub:	978-1-4725-8397-0

Library of Congress Cataloging-in-Publication Data
Names: Allon, Niv, author. | Navrâatilovâa, Hana, author.
Title: Ancient Egyptian scribes : a cultural exploration / Niv Allon and Hana Navratilova.
Other titles: Bloomsbury Egyptology.
Description: London, UK ; New York, NY : Bloomsbury Academic,
an imprint of Bloomsbury Publishing Plc, 2017. | Series: Bloomsbury Egyptology |
Includes bibliographical references and index.
Identifiers: LCCN 2016057215 | ISBN 9781472583956 (hb) | ISBN 9781472583987 (epdf)
Subjects: LCSH: Scribes–Egypt. | Scribes–Egypt–Biography. | Egypt–History–
New Kingdom, ca. 1550–ca. 1070 B.C. | Literacy–Social aspects–Egypt.
Classification: LCC DT65 .A44 2017 | DDC 493/.1–dc23
LC record available at https://lccn.loc.gov/2016057215

Cover image: Egyptian relief of scribes. Photo by CM Dixon/Print Collector/Getty Images

Typeset by RefineCatch Limited, Bungay, Suffolk
Printed and bound in Great Britain

Contents

Acknowledgements

This book was first imagined in the grounds of the Metropolitan Museum of Art in New York with the kind assistance of several colleagues and friends and many cups of coffee. Through the generosity of the Andrew W. Mellon Fellowship and with the support of the Education Department and the Department of Egyptian Art, the two future authors met in September 2012 and eventually started writing. In the Department of Egyptian Art, our thanks go to Dieter and Dorothea Arnold, then the head of the Department; Marsha Hill, and Diana Craig Patch, who were generous hosts and supporters of our research throughout our fellowship and in the years that followed. We are similarly grateful to Sara Chen, Elizabeth Fiorentino, Adela Oppenheim, Catharine Roehrig, Heather Masciandaro, Isabel Stünkel and other members of the Department of Egyptian Art, as well as to Marcie Karp from the Department of Education at the Museum, for their help and support.

Special thanks for participating in the debate about scribes go to Hans-Werner Fischer-Elfert, Orly Goldwasser, Dimitri Laboury, Richard B. Parkinson, Massimilano Pinarello, Chloé Ragazzoli and whoever agreed to listen and to share their thoughts and comments. Many colleagues and friends from several countries were also helpful and supportive, either in their role as librarians or partners in discussion: Dana Bělohoubková, Diane Bergman, Francisco Bosch-Puche, Benedict Davies, Rob J. Demarée, Elizabeth Fleming, Jiřina Růžová, Deborah Sweeney, Catherine Warsi, Kei Yamamoto, Liana Weindling, Sunny Yudkoff and Adam Stern. Friends and family often stood by us even when our focus on ancient lives became exasperating: Ofer Dynes, Adela Jůnová Macková, Nanette B. Kelekian, Sholmit, Edo, and Nevoh Liberty to name just a few of those we were fortunate to have around us. To them all we owe a debt of gratitude.

We would like to thank Nicholas Reeves for suggesting the project and persevering in the most delicate initial stages. Finally, Anna McDiarmid, Lucy Carroll and Alice Wright of Bloomsbury Publishing were helpful and patient editors and facilitators. Judy Tither and Merv Honeywood guided the book through the editing and typesetting process.

Illustration acknowledgements: we acknowledge the help of institutions who generously allowed use of their copyrighted material. We would like to specifically thank Sinéad Ward, Rights and Reproductions Officer of the Chester Beatty Library, Dublin; Amy Taylor of the Ashmolean Museum, Oxford; Lucie Vendelová Jirásková of the Czech Institute of Egyptology; Emily Dean of the Imperial War Museum; Julie Zeftel of the Metropolitan Museum of Art.

List of Illustrations

Abbreviations

DZA   Digitalisierte Zettelarchiv des Wörterbuches der ägyptischen Sprache.

GMT   Černý and A.A. Sadek, et al., *Graffiti de la montagne thébaine*, Cairo, 1969–74

KRITA   K.A. Kitchen, *Ramesside Inscriptions Translated and Annotated I–*, Oxford, 1996–

LÄ   *Lexikon der Ägyptologie*, Wiesbaden, 1972–92

PM   B. Porter, R.L. Moss and J. Málek et al. 1960–2007. *Topographical Bibliography of Ancient Egyptian Hieroglyphic Texts, Reliefs and Paintings*, 2nd. ed., rev. and augm. Oxford

RITANC   K.A. Kitchen/B.G. Davies, *Ramesside Inscriptions Translated and Annotated. Notes and Comments I–*, Oxford, 1996–

Urk I   K. Sethe, 1932. *Urkunden des Alten Reiches*. Urkunden des aegyptischen Altertums, Band 1. Leipzig & Berlin.

Urk IV   K. Sethe, H.W. Helck et al. 1903–84. *Urkunden der 18. Dynastie*. Urkunden des aegyptischen Altertums, Band 4. Leipzig & Berlin.

Wb   A. Erman and H. Grapow. 1926–63. *Wörterbuch der ägyptischen Sprache*. Leipzig.

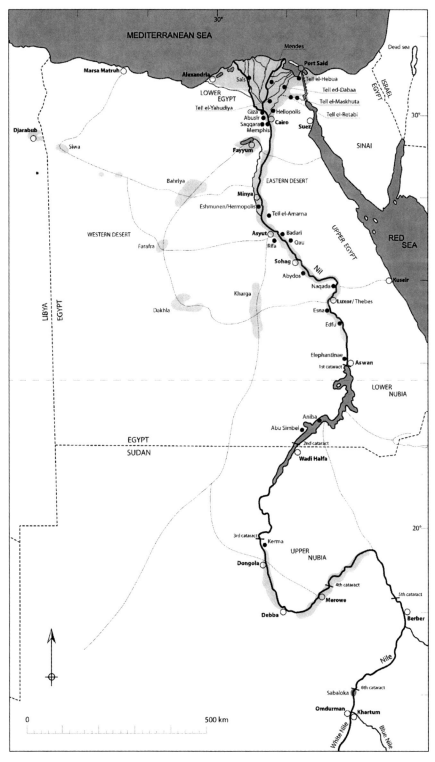

Map of Egypt (© Archive of The Czech Institute of Egyptology. Author L. Vařeková, 2016).

Introduction: Exploring the Social Figure of the Scribe

The book is dedicated to the study of ancient Egyptian scribes of the New Kingdom and to their perspectives on their role and place in society. We will examine ten figures – their lives, their careers and the traces they left behind in the form of texts, objects and monuments – with the aim of understanding how each of them made sense of the term 'scribe' as well as of their standing in the Egyptian society, and how they conveyed it both to themselves and to others. Together, they present a rich portrait of what it was to be a scribe in New Kingdom Egypt.

Already at the outset, the term scribe has a variety of different meanings. The term is most often used in Egyptology in translations of the word $z\underline{h}3.w$ or $s\check{s}$, when it appears in such titles as $z\underline{h}3.w$, 'Scribe', $z\underline{h}3.w$-n-pr-$\underline{h}d$ 'Scribe of the Treasury', or $z\underline{h}3.w$ $nswt$, 'Royal Scribe' (scribe of the king). The Egyptian word derives from the root $z\underline{h}3$ with the semantic field of 'to write, to draw',[1] whose duality of meaning is also apparent in the similarity between the Egyptian words for $z\underline{h}3.w$ and $z\underline{h}3.w$-$\underline{k}dw.t$, 'scribe' and 'draughtsman'. The variety of meanings and of compound titles, in which $z\underline{h}3.w$ appears, points at the diversity of tasks with which different scribes were charged. Already, any monolithic idea of the scribe becomes fragmented into diverse vocations, from a village administrator to a temple accountant or an artist.[2]

At the same time, the term scribe seems to have taken on a life of its own in Egyptology. The rectangular palette, which was the customary writing equipment throughout most of ancient Egypt is often described in the scholarly literature as a scribal palette, and statues that show their owners seated on the ground with papyri on their lap are considered scribal statues. Scribes and these representations became so synonymous that the squatting posture itself began to be considered as an indication that a person is represented as a scribe even where neither a papyrus nor a palette is depicted. The proliferation of the term is also apparent in the textual realm, where those who wrote a text or produced a manuscript are described as their scribes. From $z\underline{h}3.w$ to scribe, the term invites a greater variety of interpretations, including author, copyist, literati and literate.

Recent decades have brought a number of important forays into the conundrum of the scribe. A series of studies by John Baines and Christopher Eyre took aim at the notion of literacy and the importance of documents in ancient Egypt, causing quite a stir.[3] Among a number of important claims, Baines and Eyre point to the disproportionate relations between the prevalence of scribes (and literate men) in ancient Egypt and their attestations in sources available to Egyptologists. Likewise, they warn us against projecting modern conceptions of writing and scribes onto ancient men, which conflate literacy with high status and scribes with elite. The relationships between these terms, Baines and Eyre remind us, are diverse and complex, and they vary from one society to another. They are markedly different in our modern document-oriented society from those in the predominantly oral society of ancient Egypt.

Further developments in the study of literacy contributed to disentangling the term scribe from that of literate. All scribes may be assumed to be literate to some extent, but it is a logical fallacy to assume that all literate people were scribes. Literacy, moreover, covers a wide range of capabilities, ranging from recognizing a few signs to being able to read complex writings, and from signing one's name to being able to produce written texts independently. Building especially on the work of Brian Street, recent years have brought studies that emphasized the multiplicity of literacy, or literacies, that depend on context and society.[4] As scribes and literacy are nevertheless closely related, we explore the relationship between the two terms later in the book.

More recently, the study of scribes was greatly advanced through two important works. Focusing on the corpus of *Late Egyptian Miscellanies*, Chloé Ragazzoli brings attention to the self-fashioning of scribes and to the manner in which they shaped their community through the circulation of texts that reaffirmed their values and their feeling of belonging.[5] Finally, Massimiliano Pinarello's recent publication challenges the very notion of the scribe as a modern construction, ultimately suggesting it should be done away with.[6] Ragazzoli's interest in questions of perceptions and self-representation, and Pinarello's critique of the assumed connotations of the term scribe serve as guidelines and inspiration for the work presented in this book.

Despite the complex and often contradictory aspects at the heart of the term scribe, we see it as indispensable. The term *zẖꜣ.w* is so intertwined with administrative titles that its interpretation often gravitates towards the professional, while the term scribe could at least remind us of the word's other potencies which were evident in ancient Egypt. We do not employ this term without hesitation, as the term scribe arrives on the scene already laden with connotations not fully compatible with ancient Egypt, but unfortunately, no other term could replace it without evoking its own set of associations. Therefore, rather than doing away with it, we would like to build upon its inherent contradictions. As we would like to show, these were evident in ancient times in the different connotations of the word *zḫꜣ.w*. Instead of voiding the term of its meaning, we would like to populate it with the interpretations which were given to it in ancient times. As we focus on different figures and their interpretations, we develop a greater understanding of the term 'scribe', with each figure developing its own character. Often, these views are conflicting; several men have taken it upon themselves to set clear criteria as to who may consider himself a scribe and who may not.

To this end, focusing on the New Kingdom presents a unique opportunity to study the multiplicity of approaches towards the figure of the scribe. Evidence for scribes and their self-perception may be found throughout all periods of Egyptian history.[7] Our decision to focus on a specific period in Egypt's history is intended to avoid adhering to an image of ancient Egypt as a timeless and changeless society. Instead, we wished to try to capture what the term scribe means at a specific moment in time. For this purpose, the New Kingdom provides a plethora of sources relevant to our discussion, including papyri, stelae, tombs and other monuments. This richness of evidence allows us to extend our study beyond the realm of texts and to incorporate iconographical studies and discussions regarding archaeological context. We do not focus on the New Kingdom, however, without hesitation. This period saw great changes in its culture, religion and use of language during its 500 years, and we try to take note of differences between the Eighteenth Dynasty and the Ramesside Period. A growing emphasis on writing and scribes throughout the New Kingdom invites us to at least consider the different voices in this book.

The ten figures, on which we chose to focus, all contribute to a lively discussion on the term scribe. Naturally, we could have looked at other figures,[8] who would have highlighted different aspects of the term scribe. We tried, however, to bring together diverse voices belonging to kings and military men, administrators, draughtsmen and high officials to show a variety of interpretations and their recurring themes.

The book comprises ten chapters organized chronologically. This allows the reader to appreciate several subtle changes that influenced Egyptian elites throughout the New Kingdom. Each chapter is dedicated to the study of one figure and its approach to the issue of scribes. As every figure outlines a different way into the subject, while presenting its own set of challenges, the chapters employ a variety of approaches. Some engage directly with the meaning of the term scribe, while others provide a rich portrait of the lives, careers and social worlds of those men who identified themselves with it. The chapters thus stand independently and can be read in any order. To allow such flexibility, we revisit a few basic notions in different chapters and a glossary has been added at the end of the book. Together with the prologue, they are intended to bridge some Egyptological idiosyncrasies, and appeal to students and readers who are interested in scribes, literacy and the social history of ancient Egypt.

We begin with a prologue, which explores the material aspect of writing through the artefacts connected with writing. The first, seventh and tenth chapters show the great variety of tasks with which the scribes grappled. The second and the fifth chapters bring to the fore the question of literacy and scribes, one through a prominent official who saw himself as an educated man, but not as a scribe; the other through the palettes of Tutankhamun and that of his (half)-sister, considering questions of royal and women's literacy. Chapters four and nine show figures who were very much engaged with setting the boundaries around the term scribe, setting criteria to exclude those who are not, to their minds, worthy. The third, sixth and eighth chapters focus on men who saw the role of the scribe beyond the administrative realm. Other threads can be highlighted, such as the boundaries between scribes and draughtsmen in the first and the seventh chapters, or those between soldiers and scribes in chapters three, six and nine. Together, the ten figures present the notion of the scribe as a term in contention, bringing to life the constant shaping and reshaping of social figures and boundaries, with which ancient Egyptian society was engaged–very much like our society today.

The authors, May 2013 to May 2016, on the road.

Prologue – Writing Tools and Hands

Before we embark on the journey, which ultimately should tell the scribe's story, we would like to turn first to the technical side of writing and to introduce an array of written artefacts encountered in New Kingdom Egypt. After all, objects are often the only testimony to the lives of the ancient men and women who once held them; a story of Egyptian scribes cannot omit their implements.[1]

The most visible written artefacts of ancient Egypt are hieroglyphic texts, which were carved and painted by specialist and artists and artisans. The hieroglyphs[2] were a unique monumental script, known thanks to Herodotus as the 'hieratic' script. Herodotus considered it a writing system used for sacred texts (hence its translation, 'of or concerning priests'). In his time, a later form of Egyptian, the Demotic, was the everyday script.[3] However, for a long period, the hieratic was the main script used in administration and, accounting, as well as medical manuscripts and literary texts. A letter as well as a love poem of the New Kingdom would have been written in hieratic.

Hieratic was mostly written with pen and ink, and its production involved a variety of artefacts including writing palettes and ink-containers. The Egyptian rush pen, cut at a slant and chewed to form a brush-like head,[4] was closer to a small hard-pointed brush than to a pen with a nib. Writing with it required dexterity that allowed the creation of clearly written ligatured as well as non-ligatured signs of l cm or less.

It is mostly the implements associated with hieratic that appear in depictions of writing in ancient Egyptian art. Whether in two or three-dimensional depictions – scenes appearing on tomb walls and so-called scribal statues – writing was quite often depicted being performed with a palette and brush-like pens.[5] These depictions show a variety of writing hands, standing, seated, squatting, on top of a pile of grain, or in an office,[6] registering accountants, counting commodities or prisoners of war. Many of those bear scribal titles, and it seems, at least judging from these depictions, that hieratic was the norm.

The New Kingdom (sixteenth to eleventh century BC) left a rich legacy of both literary and non-literary hieratic texts. Among these, three main categories of written artefacts appear: papyri, ostraca and writing boards.

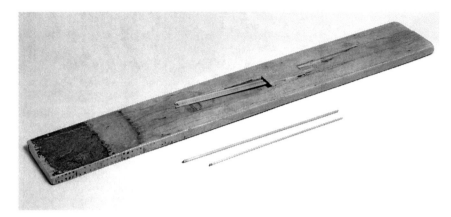

Fig. 0.1 Palette inscribed for Smendes, High Priest of Amun. © The Metropolitan Museum of Art, Harris Brisbane Dick Fund, 1947, 47.123a–g.

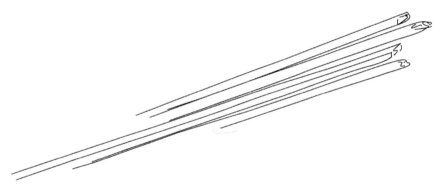

Fig. 0.2 Detail of pens from the palette inscribed for Smendes. © The Metropolitan Museum of Art, Harris Brisbane Dick Fund, 1947, 47.123a–g. Drawing by HN.

A New Kingdom papyrus[7] roll had strips cut from the papyrus stem arranged horizontally on the recto (inside of the roll, usually the first side to be written on) and vertically on the verso (outer side of the roll). The rolls came in different heights – a standard New Kingdom roll with a literary text would have up to 17 or 20 centimetres, certain specialist texts (funerary papyri, formal royal documents, but also technical texts, such as mathematical papyri) were up to double that height or more.[8] That the size of a papyrus sheet or roll was influenced by practical considerations seems to be indicated by the fact that the tallest roll (Papyrus Greenfield, EA 10554.87, British Museum) is a Book of the Dead, which was not to be handled after burial.[9] However, once rolled up, even the large papyrus manuscripts became practical again – one of the foremost early specialists on papyrus conservation and mounting, Dr Hugo Ibscher

(1874–1943)[10] worked out that 'a papyrus of 6 m in length gave when tightly rolled a cylinder 5–6 cm thick, which could easily be spanned by the fingers of a hand'.[11]

The surviving New Kingdom texts on papyri may be arranged in four groups, as proposed by Stephen Quirke:[12] The first is a group of early Eighteenth Dynasty technical texts, including Papyrus Edwin Smith, Papyrus Ebers (i.e. two medical treatises) and the Rhind mathematical papyrus. These are of an unknown provenance and as such cannot be linked to any particular literate community. The second group consist of late Eighteenth Dynasty literary manuscripts containing the texts of *Sinuhe*, *The Eloquent Peasant* and the teachings of Ptahhotep and Merikare. These texts may be connected with either of the capital cities, Memphis or Thebes, possibly as grave goods or parts of someone's private library. The third group are sets of books from Ramesside Memphis[13] which contain papyri Anastasi, D'Orbiney and Sallier, mostly bearing texts subsumed under the heading *Late Egyptian Miscellanies*. The fourth group came from Ramesside, Western Thebes and also contained the Chester Beatty papyri, again with *Late Egyptian Miscellanies*, but also a dream-book and literary and historical texts. Individual hands in some of these text collections can be traced back to individual names, e.g. the Deir el-Medina scribes Kenherkhepeshef or Djehutmose Tjaroy and the scribe of the Memphite collection, Inena. Some copyists – like Inena – added their name to a text collection of their making, underlining thus the importance of good compiler or copyist work in the process of making and continuing the Egyptian written culture.

Ostraca were fragments of pottery or limestone flakes which usually contained a short text or an excerpt from a longer text. There were notable exceptions to this rule, such as the large limestone piece of the Ashmolean Ostracon of Sinuhe.[14] It is the largest preserved limestone ostracon from ancient Egypt (AN1945.40, Ashmolean Museum, Oxford) and is inscribed on both sides in hieratic in black and red ink with most of the text of the story of *Sinuhe*. The ostracon, the gift of A.H. Gardiner to the Ashmolean, probably came from Thebes.[15]

Ostraca seem to be spread across Egypt, with particular concentrations in Western Thebes and smaller finds in Memphis, the oases and elsewhere,[16] probably due to attempts at preservation. Ostraca could have uneven surfaces; although many limestone examples were probably produced purposefully,[17] it was still a stone surface and the writing pen had to be controlled accordingly, which could have caused problems for the writer (as indeed it still does on occasion for modern copyists when tracing the texts).

(a)

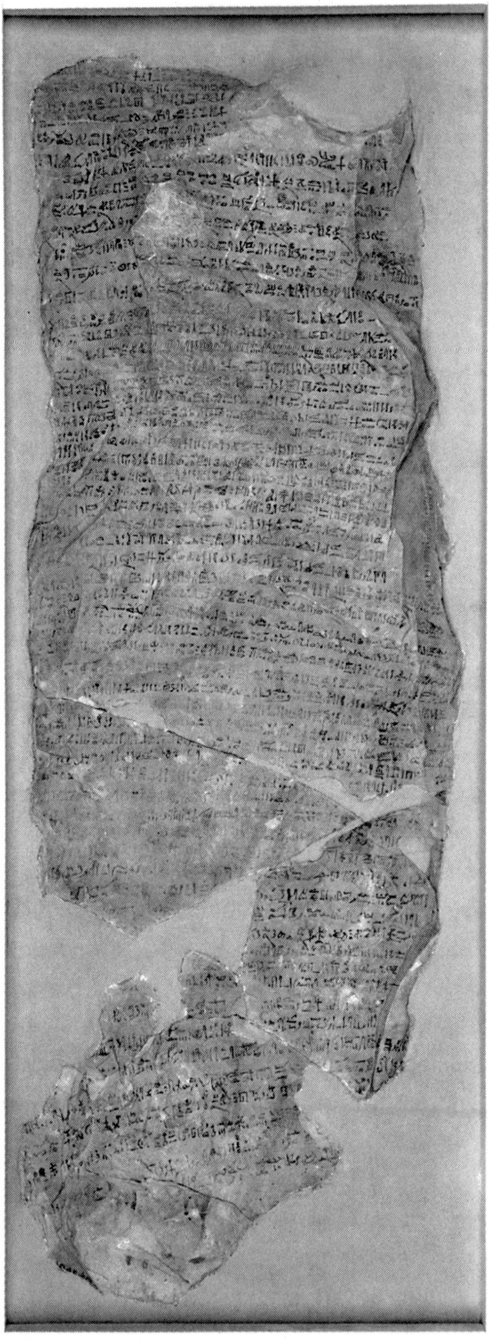

Fig. 0.3a & b The Ashmolean Ostracon of Sinuhe. Ashmolean Museum AN1945.40.
© The Ashmolean Museum, Oxford.

(b)

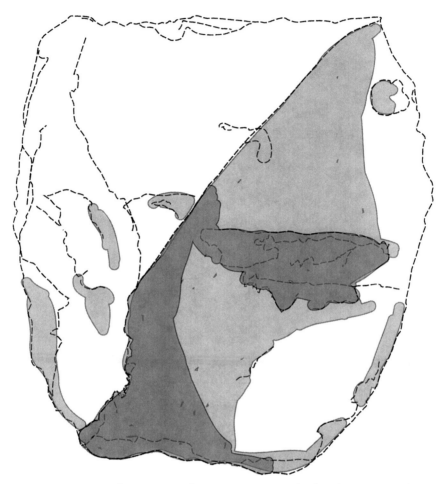

Fig. 0.4 A New Kingdom ostracon showing an uneven ridged surface. Drawing by HN after surface of Ostracon Prague Náprstek Museum P 7216.

A further and distinctive category of a written culture artefact typical of the period was the writing board,[18] usually a stuccoed wooden board bearing training texts and drawings, often re-used, washed and re-stuccoed.[19] The boards consisted of wood covered with stucco with a layer of linen used to even out the wooden surface and support the stucco.[20] A tablet in the Louvre (N 693) had one stucco coat, then a layer of canvas covered by a layer of smooth stucco.[21] Several boards are dated to the late Second Intermediate Period and to the New Kingdom (mostly Eighteenth Dynasty[22]) – e.g. the Carnarvon tablets,[23] the British Museum tablet,[24] the Dra Abu el-Naga board, the Louvre boards (N 693 and AF 497)[25], the MMA board[26] and the Prague board.[27] The Carnarvon and Dra Abu el-Naga boards were found in the area of West Theban non-royal tombs; the exact provenance of the Louvre and Prague boards is unknown, whilst for the Prague specimen, Western Thebes is a likely connection.

The writing boards appear to have been used to train draughtsmen as well as more ordinary scribes employed in non-artistic tasks. The stuccoed boards were practical for an apprentice as they were re-usable and relatively smooth – consequently easy to write on. Their use for trainee artists – with master drawings copied by apprentices – is discussed later in more detail. The texts found on them are of some importance for a prospective literato as well as an administrator – there were classical texts in Middle Egyptian such as the *Satire of Trades* (Louvre N 693) or the *Teaching of Amenemhat* (Prague P 7228) or the text of *Kemit*, possibly a special training text (Dra Abu el-Naga).

Egyptologists have discussed the choice of material for different writing purposes. Ostraca appeared to the Egyptologists as semi-permanent, exercise or draft material, whereas papyri were used for long-term storage, final manuscripts and so on. Due to the demanding manufacturing method, it was also assumed that papyri must have been rather expensive. The cost, however, was a relative matter.[28] Furthermore, real texts contradict categorical divisions of the actual ancient use of papyri and ostraca. Ostraca was used as notebooks, exercise books and so on, but were also used for longer texts or letters.[29] Writers might have also experimented with their new creations or adapted literary texts on ostraca. But the main difference was mostly the size – ostraca (with the above exceptions) usually contained an excerpt or one text, as well as smaller papyri served for letter-writing, and larger rolls contained collections of texts. Formality of the written text might also have played a role – notes for personal use could have been entrusted to an ostracon, a formal letter to a superior to a papyrus.

Thus far, mobile writing surfaces have been considered – pieces of wood, stone, pottery or papyrus. The hieratic script, though, apart from governing on ostraca and papyri, appeared also in rock inscriptions and graffiti, either carved in the surface or written in ink (or indeed both, carved and coloured), as it would have been on ostraca and papyri. The Theban hills are covered with hieratic signatures and remarks of craftspeople and scribes who lived and worked in Western Thebes.[30] Theban tomb chapels, temple corridors and roofs, or Memphite pyramid precincts bear witness to staff and visitors who commemorated their presence with graffiti.[31] Rock surfaces at mines, quarries and desert roads complete the list.[32] These texts were often purposefully left testimonies[33] of the written culture of Egypt and of the men and women who read and wrote them, although the title of a scribe, so frequent in graffiti, belonged mostly to men.

Graffiti thus brings us back full circle to the question of scribes and their perception. Here, however, we meet the limitation of objects in aiding our pursuit. Many of the hands that held pens and palettes to write on papyri and ostraca belonged to scribes – at least it is safe to assume so. When we begin to acknowledge that other hands could hold writing equipment without their owners calling themselves scribes, the picture becomes much more complicated. Making matters worse, once we introduce questions of perception and intentionality, objects turn even more stubbornly mute. Even if a scribe happened to hold them to write, they rarely tell whether he saw himself as doing so, and whether he perceived his action as specifically scribal. How much do our titles as researchers or curators influence the reading and writing of our own texts? Do all readers of these works see themselves as Egyptologists or as scholars? Remaining mute, the objects remind us how patchy the paths we are pursuing could be and how much needs to be considered to uncover perceptions of scribes in New Kingdom Egypt.

1

Paheri

Looking back on his life, Paheri must have felt a sense of satisfaction. He, who was born into a well-to-do family, managed to outdo his ancestors and to become the mayor of two main cities in Upper Egypt, Iuynet (ancient Esna) and Nekheb (ancient Elkab). The royal court entrusted him with even wider responsibilities, appointing him to oversee the administration of an extensive area along the banks of the Nile. In his own success story, Paheri saw himself as both agent and protagonist, in the manner of the narratives of the elite of his time. Setting himself apart, Paheri uses an uncommon turn of phrase in his autobiography, declaring 'it is my pen that made me famous'.

Paheri's praise may read as the hallmark of an educated and well-learned man. Paheri lived in an era that saw a bustling manuscript culture, in which scribes and copyists boasted of their skilful fingers.[1] It was a time of pioneering scholars, who saw great importance in the pursuit of knowledge and who produced written compendia of various sorts.[2] Like many of his contemporaries, Paheri took pride in his knowledge of texts. His statement about the pen may, therefore, suggest he too was actively engaged in the literary and scholarly scene of his day. Unfortunately, no papyrus or ostracon remains to tell of the exploits of Paheri's pen, which might have been put to very different uses.

The context, in which Paheri made his remarkable statement, suggests two further possible interpretations. The autobiographical text, in which this rare self-praise appears, decorates one of the walls of Paheri's tomb.[3] There, scribes are depicted holding pens to produce lists and accounts (see Fig. 1.1), suggesting that Paheri rose to prominence as a talented accountant. And yet, a wider context provides another interpretation. In the tomb of his grandfather, which lies nearby, Paheri depicts penmanship in the context of laying out the tomb and decorating its walls. Thus, while his tomb suggests that his writing relates to accounting and administration, in an adjacent tomb he portrays penmanship in the context of art.

Paheri thereby proposes an alternative Eighteenth Dynasty interpretation to the image of a scribe. Through the texts and the iconography of the two tombs, Paheri portrays a wide array of textual activities. Some that we traditionally associate with writing are absent; others are given unexpected emphasis. His vision of writing points to the prominence of two textual practices in ancient Egypt: the importance of the accountant to the economy of the land, and the work of the artist to preserve the memory of those who governed it. Paheri does not discriminate between the two. For him, apparently, one does not appear to be more valued than the other.

In our quest to understand Paheri's vision of the scribe, we need to look closely at Paheri's world. First, we will turn our attention to Paheri's place among the elite of the Eighteenth Dynasty and to his family's role in the critical moments of its establishment. Furthermore, Paheri left behind texts and images that project his perception of his world and convey his notions of the ideal order of things. His family's tomb-complex at Elkab thus provides an invaluable opportunity to understand both his perception and his views.

A tomb in context

The city of Elkab, where Paheri lived and was buried, is located halfway between Luxor and Aswan, the southern outpost of Egypt before Nubia. Numerous temple ruins, cemeteries and fortifications tell of the rich history of the site, which has its origin in prehistoric times. Its monuments serve as a testimony to the continuation of the settlement at Elkab – or Nekheb in its ancient name – for millennia, through the formative years of the early Pharaonic state up to the days of the Roman Empire.

Like the ancient history of the site, which extends back to the early years of ancient Egypt, its research history goes back to the early days of Egyptology. The site was visited throughout the years, but it first attracted the West's attention with Napoleon's campaign in Egypt. Along with his armies, Napoleon sent an expedition of savants – scholars in different fields – who set out to study and document the riches of ancient and modern Egypt. Both the expedition and the result of its labours, the *Description de l'Egypte* – whose first volume was published in 1809 – were instrumental in fashioning the West's image of Egypt and of the Orient. This early endeavour cultivated the fascination with all things Egyptian that is often referred to as 'Egyptomania'. When Napoleon's savants travelled past Thebes, they came upon the ancient site of Elkab, and on 20

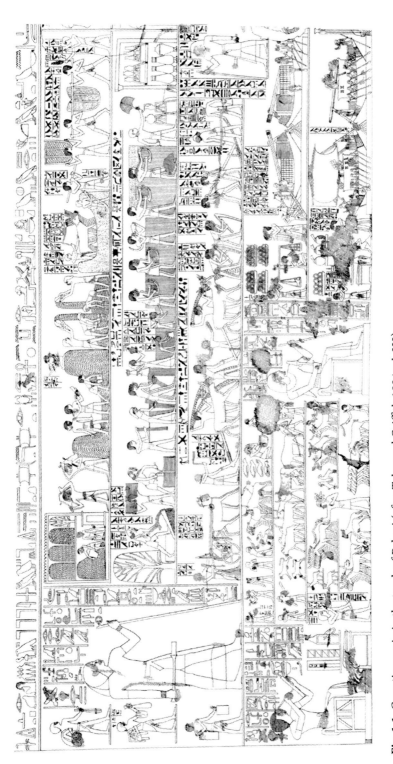

Fig. 1.1 Counting grain in the tomb of Paheri (after Tylor and Griffith 1894: pl. III).

September, 1799 they found the rock-carved tombs of Paheri and of his grandfather, Ahmose, son of Ibana.[4]

The tomb of Ahmose soon proved to be of great importance to the study of ancient Egyptian history. The inscriptions decorating the walls of the tomb tell of Ahmose's service in the navy in an era that saw the end of a divided Egypt and its unification under a Theban dynasty.[5] Accompanying the Upper Egyptian rulers, he fought against the Hyksos who ruled in the north, and participated in the pursuit against them into Syro-Palestine. Ahmose took part in a number of additional military campaigns during the formative years of the New Kingdom and in later decades set out against enemies to the north as well Nubia in the south.

Ahmose's inscription is an outstanding narrative of ascent to prominence through courage and determination. Ahmose, who was himself born to a navy-man, followed in his father's footsteps by joining the service at an early age. It was the navy, he tells us, that taught him to sleep in a net hammock. Soon the military was sent to slaves Avaris, the capital of the Hyksos, where Ahmose showed remarkable bravery. In recognition of his part in the successful campaign, the king rewarded him with slaves and with the gold of honour, the highest distinction of the day. Consequently, many hands were cut and cities conquered,[6] first under Ahmose, the royal namesake of the son of Ibana, and then under his successor, Amenhotep I. In his final years, Ahmose served under Thutmose I and received vast lands in the area of Elkab and its vicinity as well as slaves as workmen, whom he lists in his tomb. The tomb of Ahmose encapsulates a period in the history of ancient Egypt at a crucial moment in time, all told through the life story of this one man.

Ahmose, son of Ibana, was able to maintain and increase the importance of his family. While the kings of the Eighteenth Dynasty continued with military campaigns in foreign territories following the formative years of the New Kingdom, the elite soon shifted its emphasis from military service to state and temple administration. Ahmose probably recognized this trend, since he married his daughter to a courtier who was tutor to one of the princes (see Fig. 1.2). Paheri, the product of this marriage, also married a woman whose family had ties to state administration, her father being chief of transport and her brother a functionary in the service of the king. As a result, Paheri shows himself in his tomb in complete administrative attire – there is no mention of his family's military background. Like his father, he was a prince's tutor, but he ranked higher than anyone else in his family's history, overseeing the administration of great areas of land. Paheri was thus enjoying the fruits of his grandfather's efforts to transform the family's military gains into courtly and administrative symbolic capital.

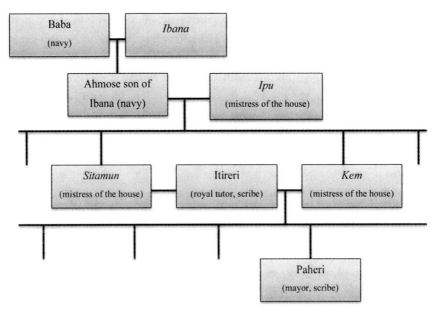

Fig. 1.2 Paheri's family tree (after Davies 2009).

Writing in Paheri's tomb

The importance of Ahmose's inscriptions had to wait until the ancient Egyptian hieroglyphs were deciphered to be fully appreciated. When Napoleon's savants visited the site, it was Paheri's tomb that won their praise. In his memoir, one of the French scholars noted that the tomb seemed like a book, left by the ancient Egyptians to instruct future generations about the work and customs of the civil life and its economy.[7] It is in the context of this 'book' that Paheri provides an answer to the question, 'What defines a scribe?'

The decoration in Paheri's tomb follows the scheme of elite tombs of its time. The tomb complex comprises a forecourt and a main chamber, whose walls are decorated with figures and activities. These depictions include banquet scenes and images that relate to agriculture, commerce and funerary rites for the tomb owner. Others show images of Paheri adoring the gods as well as Paheri himself being worshipped by one of his sons. Similar architectural and iconographic schemes appear in Theban tombs of the early Eighteenth Dynasty, especially in that of an official named Wensu, suggesting a direct borrowing from one tomb to the other. Unfortunately, Wensu's tomb no longer exists, but the iconographic similarity clearly reflects the relationship of Paheri's family with the royal court and with Thebes, one of Egypt's capital cities. This link, furthermore, appears in the roles of three members of Paheri's family, who bear the title *zḫ3.w ḳdw.t n jmn*, 'draughtsman of Amun,' the main deity of Thebes.[8]

The family's ties to the royal court also appear on the back wall of the tomb. Set into a niche, a triad statue shows Paheri seated along with his two wives. The statues are badly preserved and only the outline of their figures survives – all the important detail of their garments and expressions has been lost. Enough remains to show the two wives embracing Paheri, who is seated between them. The walls of the niche itself are also coloured and decorated. On one side, they show Paheri seated with one of his wives before a son, who performs the *ḥtp-di-nswt* rite for his father. On the other side, Paheri performs a similar ritual before two dyads. One shows his parents, and the other shows Wadjmose and Amenmose, sons of Thutmose I. The scene thus emphasizes Paheri's ties to the court in his role as the royal tutor, which appears again in another image in the tomb. The scene, which is set on the east wall, depicts Paheri sitting on a chair, with a figure seated on his lap. The latter appears naked and wears a curl of hair, the two main signs for youth in ancient Egyptian art; it probably depicts one of Paheri's royal charges.

Apart from the statues, the decoration of the back wall of Paheri's tomb is remarkable in its own right. The wall is inscribed throughout with a text set between red lines and on a yellow background. The text, which opens with praise and wishes for Paheri, shifts in its midst to a first-person narration by the tomb owner himself. Paheri enumerates his virtues in the service of the king as a just judge and as a loyal servant, who carried out all the king's commands. Attentive and wise, he knew when to speak, when to keep silent, and – even more importantly – which words to avoid:

> I did not speak in order to deceive another . . .
> I did not alter a message upon reporting it
> Neither did I speak with words of the ignorant (*ḫ3.w-mr*)
> Nor did I repeat those which are without character.[9]

The interpretation of *ḫ3.w-mr* is not without doubt. Scholars have translated it as referring to 'the masses' or 'the commoners', thereby seeing Paheri's statement as referring to his eloquence and to his sophisticated choice of words. The term appears, however, in a fragmentary passage in another text in which it may be equated with 'the ignorant'.[10] This interpretation, which emphasizes the trustworthy nature of one's words, might better fit the preceding and following lines in Paheri's biography, in which he speaks of the accuracy of his report. To be a scribe – in this context – was to reliably collect and pass information within the administration of the land.

A similar ambiguity might appear later in his autobiographical text, when Paheri refers to his knowledge of texts:

I am a noble who is beneficial for his lord,
wise and free of negligence
    having gone on the path, which I advised,
    having learned that which comes forth of life . . .
I reckoned (*ḥsb*) the ends of books
  the boundaries of all the king's concerns
  (of) all things of the palace *ỉpḥ* . . .[11]

At first glance, Paheri's statement seemingly refers to his extensive knowledge of the written corpus, in a similar manner to other scholars of his time. Instead, he immediately clarifies the extent of his statement. The knowledge pertains to the affairs belonging to the palace and to the king. Rather than a scholar, Paheri emerges in this statement as a competent administrator.

The images decorating the walls of the tomb further enhance the administrative aspect of the scribe's work. Paheri represents in his tomb a few instances in which writing plays an important role. When Paheri sits to receive and inspect gold, the precious metal is weighed on scales with scribes present (see Fig. 1.1). When grain is collected and brought to the granary, a scribe sits on top of a pile of grain and notes down the amounts. Here, it would appear, writing had come into its own – to support the running of the country's economy. To be a scribe in this context was to be a capable accountant. Yet, even here, the pictures have more nuance.

Assuming responsibilities over the grain and the administration of such vast areas was no small matter. Grain occupied a central place in the ancient Egyptian economy, in which food production was first and foremost agrarian with wheat and barley as the principal food crops.[12] Moreover, grain functioned as a common measure of value in the exchange of commodities. Every town, village and important institution maintained grain storage facilities, from which wages and rations were distributed.[13]

The role of writing and documents within the administration of food production, its storage, and its distribution might nonetheless be more a matter of symbolic value. Our knowledge of the administration is often influenced by its ideal depiction in tomb art, in which documents often accompany the work of the official. Yet it remains rather difficult to assess the true prevalence of documents due to the arbitrary nature of preserved sources. These tomb owners, moreover, were constructing and maintaining the administration of the land while establishing new ways of interacting with texts and documents. Their own relationships with writing were bound to affect the representations of texts and writing in their tombs. The quest for the reality behind tomb art is not without its problems, forming part of the elite's constructed image of itself and of its surrounding. Rather than mirroring reality, these texts and images were aimed at recreating and negotiating society's central concepts.

The message was never monolithic. Concepts were adapted by people, not only according to what was a shared set of values, but also to their own personal interpretation. Paheri, for instance, differs from most of his contemporaries, in that he represents himself writing, not just employing other people to write. In one image, he takes out his pen and conducts the inventory himself. The wall painting shows him seated (see opposite) before a scribal kit, a papyrus holder and a palette. Below, there is a chest for storing papyri. An inscription accompanies the image that reads:

> Reckoning (*ḥsb*) the number of cattle by the mayor of Esna, the overseer of fields of the southern district, the excellent confidant of his lord, from Dendera until Elkab, the scribe Paheri.

The same verb *ḥsb*, 'reckoning', appears here and in the aforementioned passage from Paheri's autobiographical text. This verb may be rendered here and in other occurrences as 'to count' and 'to distribute' – two main activities of the administration. Paheri thus promotes accounting as part of his self-representation. In doing so, he emphasizes this aspect of the scribe's work over other possible conceptualizations prevalent in his time. A scribe, according to his tomb, is one who writes lists and accounts; the penmanship, which made Paheri famous, would then relate to these very skills. But this is not the whole story of Paheri's pen.

In a wider view: Writing in the tomb complex

When Paheri chose to cut his tomb into the southern side of the cliff at Elkab, he probably chose the location due to its proximity to the tomb of his grandfather, Ahmose, son of Ibana. The two tombs show more than accidental similarities. They were constructed with a similar plan in mind, with one main chamber and

Fig. 1.3 Paheri engaged in writing (after Tylor and Griffith 1894: pl. III).

a vaulted ceiling. The neighbouring tombs even resemble one another in their artistic style and in their iconography. Paheri may have thereby intended that his tomb be viewed jointly the tomb of his grandfather, the great admiral. With this scheme in mind, their similarity appears to convey a sense of stability and continuity.

The two tombs were perhaps even built as a functional unity. The artistic style dates them both to the same era: the reign of Thutmose III, suggesting that they were built around the same time. The two tombs, moreover, complement each other in their presentation of the extended family. Paheri appears in the tomb of Ahmose, but his branch of the family is not elaborated here. The names of Paheri's sons and daughters can be found in his own tomb, suggesting that their absence from his grandfather's tomb was intended to avoid duplication.[14]

In the inscriptions at his tomb, Ahmose, son of Ibana, takes credit for its construction. A large portion of the tomb is inscribed with the biographical text that mentions his battles and victories. At the end of the inscription, Ahmose speaks of his old age: he may have been sixty or even seventy years old, quite an age in ancient Egypt. As he reached old age, he says in the text, he wished to find rest in the tomb that he had created.

One specific scene, however, on the east wall of Ahmose's tomb speaks of Paheri's involvement in its construction.[15] The image shows Ahmose, son of Ibana, holding a staff in a gesture that conveys high status and authority.[16] Paheri stands in front of him, shown on a considerably smaller scale, holding a scribal palette in his hand.[17] The difference in scale indicates the prominence of Ahmose; he is the main focus of the scene. Similarly, Ahmose is the main figure in the long biographical text that runs before him. A shorter inscription above refers to Paheri. It reads:

> It is the son of his daughter who conducted the works in this tomb,
> enlivening the name of the father of his mother,
> the draughtsman of Amun, Paheri, true of voice.

Paheri's statement may serve here as an artist's signature, but whose signature is it? Paheri was not the only one in Ahmose's family to bear this name. Paheri's father also had children with his sister-in-law, Sitamun, and the grandson of the couple was similarly named Paheri. This young member of the family also bore the titles scribe and draughtsman; scholars have suggested that it is his image that appears here.[18]

The façade of Ahmose's tomb suggests otherwise. There, images of Paheri appear bearing titles that clarify that it was *our* Paheri. On one side of the door-jamb, Paheri appears with the title draughtsman of Amun, and the accompanying inscription reads: 'It is the son of his daughter who causes to live his name, scribe, grain accountant of the southern [district], Paheri, true of voice'. An inscription on the left jamb, undocumented until recently,[19] refers to Paheri with the epithet '[confidant of] the treasurer'.[20] The same title appears in the tomb of Paheri, where his responsibilities for grain collection and distribution were thematized, as discussed above. The figure holding the palette in Ahmose's tomb is probably Paheri, holding the utensils with which he carried out the works in his grandfather's tomb.

Paheri's depiction thus offers another interpretation of his earlier statement about his pen. As the decorative programme of Paheri's tomb has much in common with tombs of the Theban elite, it is possible that the very reproduction of these elements outside of Thebes has won Paheri his renown. Here, the pen extends outside the realm of accounting and governing. According to the image of Paheri in the tomb of Ahmose, to be a scribe means to be an artist who creates living memories.

The appearance of both interpretations in the same mortuary complex hints at an important aspect in Paheri's conceptualization of the notion of a scribe. The two tombs, as suggested above, were crafted with a functional unity in mind. Paheri, it seems, chose to emphasize different aspects of a scribe's work according to the context in which it appears in the tomb. In his own tomb, emphasizing his participation in the economic aspect of the country, he picks up a pen to write an inventory. In his grandfather's tomb, the building of which he conducted, he holds a palette and presents his titles as a draughtsman. Paheri does not seem to discriminate between the two, and they seem to complement each other. After all, the term for draughtsman in ancient Egypt, *zḥꜣ.w ḳdw.t*, is based on the word, *zḥꜣ.w*, 'scribe'.

Not all shared Paheri's approach, and a few texts in another tomb at Elkab state the opposite. The owner of the tomb, Setau, held the title of High Priest of Nekhbet – one of the prominent goddesses in this area – in the Twentieth Dynasty, a few centuries after Paheri. Two sub-scenes in his tomb focus, however, on another figure who appears holding writing equipment in one and writing in the other. The inscriptions identify him as priest and scribe by the name of Merire, who directed the work on the tomb and wrote the inscriptions.[21] Claiming authorship, Merire declares that 'it was not a draughtsman. It was his heart that directed it', thereby clarifying that he himself was no draughtsman. A few centuries apart, Paheri and Merire seem to participate in an on-going debate relating the boundaries between draughtsman and scribe – Merire emphasizing a division between the two, and Paheri blurring it.

Concluding remarks

In his tomb, Paheri attributes his tomb agency to his penmanship, stating that it was his pen that made him famous. Such a statement could be read in the context of the Eighteenth Dynasty scribal culture as referring to literary or scholarly endeavours. Images and texts in his mortuary complex at Elkab, within which he was buried, provide two further paths to interpret his statement. The autobiographical text in his tomb and adjacent scenes places his penmanship within the realm of accounting and administration. Nearby representations of Paheri in his grandfather's tomb place the pen in the hand of the artist. They portray Paheri as a draughtsman signing his own artistic creation.

The two interpretations are not mutually exclusive. If we indeed take the tomb of Paheri and that of his grandfather together, then the two interpretations complement each other. Through the decoration of his family's tomb complex at Elkab, Paheri shows his pride in being both a competent accountant and a skilled artist.

2

Senenmut

The Egyptian female sovereign Hatshepsut of the Eighteenth Dynasty, who had styled herself both as a queen and a king, has commanded attention as well as stirred the imagination of most of those interested in ancient Egypt, including Egyptologists. Hatshepsut was a royal wife of Thutmose II and a regent of her nephew and stepson Thutmose III. Within the first decade of her regency, she opted to step in as a full king alongside the juvenile sovereign Thutmose III. Eventually, they reigned together for about twenty-two years, during which time Egypt was thriving.[1] Explaining her exceptional position and her success as a ruler has been puzzling – several historians have chosen to suppress or diminish her successful role,[2] whilst others saw in her the true founder of the Egyptian New Kingdom.[3] The latter opinion reflects Hatshepsut's own approach to the grand building projects which adorned Egypt and Nubia.

The historical narrative of Hatshepsut's reign has often been influenced by a period opinion on women and power, in both the positive and the negative sense. A.H. Gardiner, himself a formidable and multifaceted personality, chose to apply a partisan view: 'It is not to be imagined, however, that even a woman of the most virile character could have attained such a pinnacle of power without masculine support.'[4] Stripped of its gender bias, however, his observation captured one important characteristic of the Dynasty Eighteen kingship – its long-term reliance on trusted supporters, who were often in office from one reign to another. There was a tightly knit band of loyal subjects that each sovereign cultivated and whose support they strove to secure for their successor.[5] Hatshepsut, like her father, Thutmose I, and her nephew, Thutmose III, created a network of people (men as well as women[6]) who supported her both personally and politically.

However, if it was important men around a woman who was king, likened later generations have added to the gender bias and have often Hatshepsut to other women in top positions[7] – Elizabeth I or Catherine the Great. Besides political ties, personal relationships between the ruling woman and her retainers were often looked for. Was there an Earl of Leicester or a Prince Potemkin-like figure also for Hatshepsut?

One man in particular seemed a likely candidate – his name appeared alongside hers on objects from a foundation deposit of the queen's temple and her name again appeared within his tomb, which is indeed exceptional even for courtiers and confidantes of a ruler.[8] Senenmut was a steward of the domain of Amun and of the royal household. His career was explained in personal terms as that of an *éminence grise*, a 'secret king,'[9] or indeed at least an influential lover of the queen. His 'rise' and 'fall', then, was seen in terms of a bitter dynastic struggle between Hatshepsut and Thutmose III.[10] His demise was seen to foretell the downfall of his sovereign.[11] A more careful examination of his monuments, however, indicates a different story.

Besides his actual or imagined personal relationship to his sovereign, his career as a dignitary and a courtier is both typical and unique. Like other men in his network of dignitaries and courtiers, he left extensive written messages. His monuments reveal that he accumulated an extensive collection of titles, none of which refer, however, to his scribal skills. Was Senenmut then

Fig. 2.1a Bead with names of Hatshepsut and Senenmut showing cartouches of Maatkare Hatshepsut. © The Metropolitan Museum of Art. Purchase Edward S. Harkness gift, 1926, 26.7.746.

Fig. 2.1b Drawing of the bead MMA 26.7.746. Drawing by HN.

a scribe in any sense of that word, or were these texts just in service of his well-fashioned self? His figure invites us to explore and appreciate the relationship between literacy and scribehood in the Eighteenth Dynasty corridors of power.

A man of importance

The Metropolitan Museum of Art in New York houses an ostracon which shows sketches on both sides made by a confident hand (see Fig. 2.2a). One side provides a double portrait of a man in a short curly wig and, in one instance, with a short beard; the other, a deftly sketched animal, perhaps a rat or a mouse, or even a fennec.[12] The animals would each have a slightly different meaning, ranging from more negative (a rat) to a more positive (a fennec); certainly the mouse was somewhat ambivalent: a harvest destroyer, but also a rather cute hero of folk tales.[13] It is very tempting to comprehend this little piece as a satirical triple portrait of a powerful, but not universally popular, man.

Although we shall never be sure about the pugnacity or otherwise of the satirical pun, the identity of the man is almost certain, as the ostracon not only

Fig. 2.2a Ostracon with two profiles of Senenmut on one side shown here, and an animal sketched on the other. © The Metropolitan Museum of Art. Anonymous gift. 1931, 31.4.2.

comes from the Deir el-Bahri area, but the face is the same as in named portraits of Senenmut found in his tomb. The remarkable man collected ninety-three titles and ranking epithets,[14] including:[15] Steward of the God's Wife, Steward of the Princess (Neferure), Overseer of the Estate of Amun, Overseer of Amun's Granaries, Overseer of all Royal Works, Treasurer, Overseer of the Works of Amun, Truly Known to the King, Royal Retainer and so on.

Senenmut owned two tombs and left a number of other monuments of personal commemoration. Theban Tombs 71 and 353[16] were built at his behest in Deir el-Bahri. Near Theban Tomb 71, the burial plot of his parents, Ramose and Hatnofret, was identified. Texts in Theban Tomb 71 included a false door stela of quartzite.[17] A number of statues of Senenmut[18] bore his titles, biographical information and other symbols of his status. A large range of formal and informal documents relating to him were found, as the example of the animal-decorated ostracon or his destroyed portraits in the temple of Deir el-Bahri[19] show. Traces of his professional presence were also found outside the capital of Thebes, near Aswan or at Gebel el-Silsila.[20]

Texts were an important means of representation for Senenmut, as was the case with most of his contemporaries. They accompanied to great effect tomb decorations and were also a decisive part of a stela or a statue of a dignitary, often listing not only his titles and epithets, but also his chief achievements. In the case of Senenmut, his titles, his relations, his devotion and his abilities

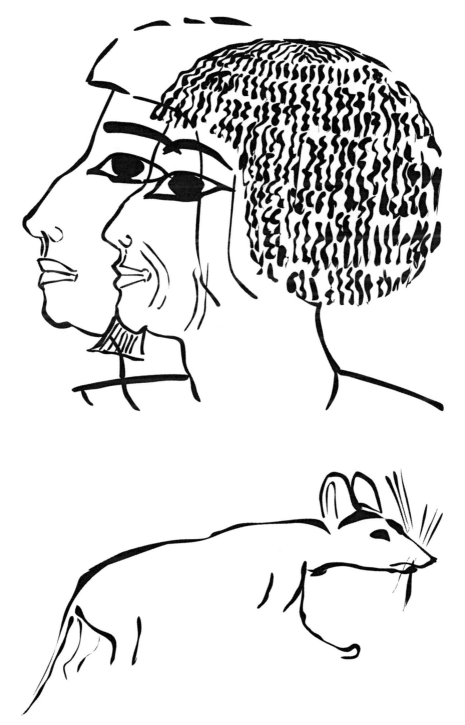

Fig. 2.2b 1 and 2. Three faces of Senenmut? After ostracon MMA 31.4.2. See Fig. 2.2a.

that were of use to the sovereign are all contained in texts adorning his monuments.

It would appear that much more is known about elements of his biography[21] than with most of his contemporaries, with the exception of select dignitaries of a similar status. Yet, as is so often the case, may questions arise.

Senenmut was born to Ramose and Hatnofret. The family does not seem to have been of an elite standing, although it is possible they were among the more important families of Armant (Iuny), the city of warrior god Montu.[22] His mother Hatnofret is titled as a *nb.t pr*, the head of a household, and his father was titled as a *s3b*, a generic designation of a dignitary, in his son's tomb[23] (perhaps he was 'ennobled' thus posthumously).[24]

His father and several other family members were reburied with Hatnofret, who died as an elderly lady at a time when her son was an important man at court. Her burial goods were lavish (including gilded masks) and mummification was carried out with attention and care. It is plausible to assume that Senenmut wished to provide an appropriate burial for his parents and other relatives having attained an elevated status.[25]

How did he attain such a status? Although he rose very high, it was a cursus that was by no means unique. His beginnings are unknown, but he appeared at the court of Thutmose II and his wife, Hatshepsut, as a tutor to the Princess Neferure, as well as a steward of her estate – both the economic and personal well-being of the princess were entrusted to him. Tutors, stewards and nurses were people with very close access to the royal person(s); if they were trusted, they could attain and wield considerable influence.[26] Still, his status was probably first proclaimed by Senenmut with aplomb and on a large scale,[27] although he had contemporaries who already appreciated their involvement in the royal upbringing equally highly – a veteran military man, Ahmose Pennekhbet from Elkab, mentioned that he 'brought up the eldest daughter . . . Neferure'.[28]

When Thutmose II died, Senenmut was in charge of the household of the widowed queen. Hatshepsut must have decided to trust him even further – his responsibilities were at first to organize the cutting and transport of two obelisks of the queen from the Aswan quarries. He was then also required to open further quarry sites at the sandstone quarries of Gebel el-Silsila, where he also dedicated a shrine, as the site was connected to the divine powers of the river Nile.

These tasks no doubt tested his abilities and loyalty. The royal family continued to have faith in him. His position as the royal tutor, which Senenmut was keen to emphasize by his statuary at that time (multiple portraits show him with his princely charge),[29] led to further honours. When Queen Hatshepsut chose to become king in year 7 of the joint reign, Senenmut was named a high steward of Amun, i.e. a person who administered the vast domains of the chief temple of the dynastic patron, Amun of Thebes. His personal monuments again reflected the concentration of titles – and no doubt actual power and influence – in his hands with a number of as yet unconventional statues, including a portrait in the role of a surveyor with a coiled measuring rope.[30] This might reflect his role as a steward of large temple domains, but also his role in his sovereign's building works. He also had the title of Overseer of Works of Amun in Djeser-djeseru, the temple of Hatshepsut at Deir el-Bahri, although his inscriptions do not refer to these works as frequently, unlike his other building tasks that are listed in his texts, such as the obelisks at the temple of Amun at Ipet-sut, or the temple of Mut, Lady of Isheru.[31] Senenmut was, however, not the only man in charge of the royal buildings – overseers of building works included other important dignitaries, such as Hapuseneb, who had a high position in the priesthood of Amun, and Minmose, who continued in the role under Thutmose III.[32]

A deft combination of tradition and innovation was apparently his motto, which Senenmut articulated in one of his texts repeated on several statues – he claimed to have made what was not found in the texts of the ancestors. It would be tempting to see here an attestation of his original architectural solutions; however, these were in no small measure inspired by the past, including the temple of Djeser-djeseru, the outer form of which followed in the footsteps of the temple of Nebhepetre Mentuhotep[33] and the details of decoration and text composition were inspired by Old and Middle Kingdom monuments. Yet, the application of past models was certainly very original.[34] There was very little, if any, direct copying, but much remodelling and inspired creativity. Although the concept of an artist in ancient Egypt is certainly different from the individuality of a modern artist, creativity and the ability to find new solutions is clearly recognized in the ancient production – note also Paheri's pride in his achievements, or later, the emphasis a Ramesside artist, Dedia, put on his works.

Senenmut's originality certainly influenced the making of his own monuments that excel both in quantity and quality, and seem to mirror his career. A number of statues represent him with Neferure, but there are others – sistrophore and naophore statues suggested his allegiance to Hathor and to Renenutet, a goddess particularly connected to Armant, which might have been his family's home town. Some of the statue forms were very innovative such as the above-mentioned example depicting him with the measuring rope,[35] and the same could be said about the cryptic writings of the queen's name that adorned select statuary.[36]

The text on his statue CG 42114[37] asked that his statues were to be 'in the following of the images of your majesty',[38] again an original formulation of the fact that many commemorative monuments of the Eighteenth Dynasty dignitaries were the result of a royal privilege and/or gift. Some of his monuments would further seem to overlap the non-royal/royal divide – his shrine in Gebel el-Silsila was exceptional compared to other dignitaries' shrines on site, as it included images of Hatshepsut and Senenmut himself offering to major deities. The Gebel el-Silsila shrines were located in an area probably understood as a sacred space, dedicated to the river Nile and its nourishing flood, but Senenmut, unlike his contemporaries who focused on a cenotaph-like type of monuments with family portraits and offering texts, approached deities himself and involved his sovereign in his shrine. Given the connection with the Nile floods in Silsila, it is interesting to read the text on one of his statues now found in Chicago.[39] Senenmut, carrying the young Princess Neferure, had included a long text with a *htp-di-nswt* offering formula and a text praising his function as an efficient courtier and tutor to the princess, but also with a sequence claiming special powers for himself: 'It is the steward, Senenmut, who has come from the flood, to whom inundation has been given, so that he has power over it as the Nile flood.'[40] However, teachings and instructions of the time often referred to the Nile also symbolically: 'One must long for the Nile flood, then one profits by it.'[41]

Senenmut's career flourished at least until year 16 of the joint reign of Hatshepsut and Thutmose III. Year 11 shows him – possibly symbolically – at Sinai following his royal charge the Princess Neferure, here titled as the God's wife of Amun, offering to the goddess Hathor, Lady of Turquoise.

His charge, Princess Neferure, might have died around year 11 of the joint rule of Hatshepsut and Thutmose III, and his monuments seem to focus further on his care for the domain of Amun.[42] After year 16 of the joint rule of Hatshepsut and Thutmose III, Senenmut is much less prominent in the records, but by that time he must have served the Thutmoside family for over thirty years.[43] The end of his career and life are seemingly shadowy, but there need not have been any spectacular fall – he may simply have left his exalted position due to any combination of factors, from a power struggle to ill health, the latter being more likely.[44] Recent studies have speculated that he might have predeceased the queen, passing away around year 18–19.[45]

The context of his times may also offer some explanation, though much remains that we may only speculate on. Senenmut became an official and a courtier under a joint reign of two monarchs; he was living in an exceptional era. Being a courtier was never an easy role, although it was prestigious and sometimes it allowed individuals to create history. To live and rise at court in ancient Egypt was as complicated as it was in the Westminster of Elizabeth I or the Versailles of Louis XIV. To get closer to this aspect of Senenmut's life, a visit behind the scenes of a royal court is warranted.

Queen and king, the court and the literato

The courtiers need a sovereign, but then the sovereign also needs an entourage. An attempt at detailed parallels between Louis and Hatshepsut may be naturally misleading, but some principles of a monarchical existence may well be similar. One of them is the process of a fabrication of a king. Peter Burke devised and made the terminology famous by applying it to the above-mentioned French ruler.[46]

To say that a sovereign had to 'fabricate' him- or herself does not mean that they were lying or pretending. It indicates a self-awareness of the concept of presentation of the royal person and office, a royal self-fashioning that has a well-modelled public façade. A cult of problematic 'sincerity' is a modern preoccupation (note the carefully choreographed 'informality' of modern-day politicians), whereas in antiquity the sovereign would have been preoccupied with decorous practices and deeds. Such practices might have also included a claim to exceptional sincerity and lack of exaggeration in the royal texts – as in the case of Hatshepsut as well as of Thutmose III, who included sincerity claims in their rhetoric. The foundation ritual stela by Thutmose III starts with a statement by the king himself to the effect that he ordered this text to be written down:[47]

> The king himself ordered these words to be written, as said in the council about the making of monuments, before the face of those on earth for . . .[ever]

The commemoration, which interests the king, is clear. Moreover, later, the king remarks his words are absolute truth (lines 5–6): 'My Majesty said this in truth, to let it be known to all people, I detest greatly saying lies, there is no word (in it) without verification'.[48]

Also the concept of a body politic[49] – here as an ideal male adult royal figure – was applied by Hatshepsut, represented as a male king, and by Thutmose III, who was presented as an adult king when he was probably still a child or very young man.[50] Both Hatshepsut and Thutmose developed and adapted their statuary to suit the changing demands of a partner kingship, which started as a political companionship of a young child and a still relatively young woman, and ended with a mature or elderly lady and a man in his prime, with his own political agenda.[51]

There are some uncanny resemblances to the later image-making of sovereigns of a more recent age, such as the above-mentioned Louis XIV, the Sun King. 'How well the scholars of the age of Louis XIV knew the oriental tradition of ruler-worship it is difficult to say',[52] but both the ancient and the absolutist monarchy had to operate a complex process of the making of royalty, using various concepts of the royal body[53] and its adequate public presentation in ceremonies as well as in works of art and in architecture.

In the image-making process, the role of a royal entourage is both that of a supporting cast and of helpers and decision-makers in the process. The court interacts with the sovereign and with the society at large. The sovereign needs to convince, control and impress both the court and the society, but the court also gives him backing, being a stage for crucial royal presentations, decisions and large as well as individual audiences. A literary image of some aspects of the process is shown in a royal novel, in Egyptology known as *Königsnovelle*, because the term was introduced into the field by German Egyptologists.[54] Here, the king is usually consulting his court about an important decision. The courtiers offer solutions, but it is the sovereign who makes the right choice, which is often more ambitious – and in case of military decisions more daredevil – than any his court had been suggesting. Thutmose III used this format for a text commemorating his victory at Megiddo.[55]

The rooms of the palace, as well as the dignitaries and entourage of the court, act in many different ways and have many different roles, as barriers, props, mediators and suitable frameworks for the sovereign. Some aspects of the Middle and New Kingdom court are relatively well documented. The Eighteenth Dynasty tombs give us access to an idealized portrait of one of the crucial scenes in the court life – the royal audience. Audiences for foreign vassals and foreign embassies bringing tribute appear to have been staged with special aplomb.[56] The tomb scenes included dignitaries leading the foreign emissaries and chiefs to the king, and a rich pictorial list of precious tribute.[57] Throughout the Eighteenth Dynasty, the emphasis was also increasingly on another court ceremonial, 'gold of honour' awards. The courtly communication had to be maintained and showcased on both sides.

The dignitaries echoed the royal effort – detailed autobiographies of the period abound with descriptions of successfully executed building projects or participating in military campaigns and deeds of bravery as well as responsibility for and on behalf of the king.

Ineni, who was overseer of works (and specifically of construction of the royal tomb) for Thutmose I as well as for Thutmose II, and who lived into the reign of Hatshepsut and Thutmose III, was keen to stress the range of building works – from monuments of Amun of Ipet-Sut (Karnak), to the erection of obelisks to the building of the royal tomb of Thutmose I that 'no one saw and no one heard'.[58] The long list of achievements and epithets, however, culminated in the title of scribe. Hapuseneb, a priest and dignitary, had listed buildings he oversaw in great detail, not dissimilar to Ineni. In a different context, a dignitary Senemiah[59] (with tomb TT 127) also named himself a scribe, and pointed out that his writing tools made him famous (but note nuances that might have been hidden in such a statement, as in the case of Paheri).

In a different area of expertise, military men noted acts of bravery. Amenemhab was a soldier-guard of the king, who participated in the Levantine campaigns of Thutmose III; his fighting and strategic abilities brought him royal recognition. He was keen to register a single act of bravery in which he killed a mare sent to lead the stallions of Egyptian chariotry astray.[60]

Senenmut did not stay far behind in the enumeration of successful work and projects, such as on his statue CG 579, 'all building works in Ipet-Sut, in Thebes, in the temple "Djeser Djeseru" (Deir el-Bahri)'.[61] However, texts on statues, stelae and in tombs testify to royal favour that was bestowed not only for a particular project being well done or for a particular practical skill applied, but for more abstract and continuous qualities – reliability, trustworthiness and steady competence – which had been emphasized from the beginning of the dynasty and throughout its duration up to the Amarna period (q.v. Paheri and Tjanuni). The nature of the service to the king might have differed, from building projects to military campaigning, but the underlying values of loyalty and reliability – whether it was high priest Hapuseneb or the steward Senenmut building for Hatshepsut or a soldier Amenemhab fighting for Thutmose III – remained the same.

Articulating these values was a major matter for a dignitary's (auto-)biography. Hapuseneb, for example, says in an inscription on his statue, 'I did not neglect any matter of the Lord of the Two Lands; I followed tasks set to me. I was not admonished in the palace...'.[62] Senemiah[63] added, 'I listened to no gossip and idle talk on the day of the fight'. Senenmut himself declares: 'I was a noble one, beloved by his lord,' and elsewhere he explains why this was so: 'I was advanced before other courtiers, and having realized my excellence in her (= the king's) heart, she appointed me chief mouth of her household.'[64] Finally, he concluded, 'I was righteous.'[65]

Although a direct overlap in wording of popular teachings and of tomb texts is not easy to prove,[66] communication skills, especially the qualities of discretion and the gift for expression, were praised in both these important New Kingdom genres, as both captured aspects of an ideal elite habitus.[67] The oft-copied *Instruction of Ptahhotep*[68] suggested:

> If you are an excellent man,
> Who sits in the council of his lord,
> Concentrate on excellence . . .
> Only the skilled artist[69] speaks in the council . . .[70]

Altogether, the words of the biographies (q.v. also Paheri, Tjanuni, Dedia) and teachings have a somewhat uncanny resemblance with a much later text by Desiderius Erasmus, who characterised an *omnium horarum homo* – a 'man for all seasons' thus:

> . . . one with whom
> He freely spoke of matters great and small,
> Confiding to him thoughts approved or not,
> If he so wished, and found him trustworthy;
> With whom he took much pleasure openly
> Or privily; a man to whom no thought
> Suggested heedlessness or ill intent,
> A cultured, loyal and a winsome man,
> Contented, happy, learned, eloquent,
> Speaking but little and that fittingly,
> Obliging, knowing well all ancient lore,
> All customs old and new, the laws of man
> And of the gods, who with due prudence told
> What he had heard, or kept it to himself . . .[71]

Was Senenmut just such a dignitary for Hatshepsut and Thutmose III? His texts should lead the posterity – and the deities – to believe so.

A man for all seasons?

Since the Middle Kingdom, an accomplished courtier – indeed a cultured person – was defined as a person with self-control, ability and rhetorical skills.[72]

Although the ultimate goal, if the teachings and instructions are to be trusted, may well have been a better world for all,[73] it may be said that the life at court was not for the faint-hearted, as it included day-to-day dealings with the nominally absolute power of the king of Egypt.

In a recent study, Andrea Gnirs gathered evidence on the exceptional atmosphere at court. She suggests that whilst the king and the ruling elite were interested in presenting the system as an ideal meritocracy, the actual state of mind of many officials was that of anxiety – they not only had to be accurate in executing their tasks, from book keeping to rituals, they also had to excel in the correct presentation.[74] Persuasion and rhetoric training, clear speech and self-control, were capable of saving the day as hinted at in the autobiographies and instructions alike (starting with *Ptahhotep*).

Senenmut also included in his tomb decoration one of the complex scenes that embodied the prestige of the king and the fragility of his dignitaries' position – the royal audience. In Senenmut's case, the meeting included foreign embassies as both participants and audience (a group of onlookers) at the royal audience, where Senenmut had a part to play. It was one of the most prestigious events in the life of the royal residence. He was probably confident of his court role and accustomed to the corridors of power.

This was Senenmut's day-to-day environment: palace corridors, audience halls tutoring the princess, and close contact with his kings, and, other dignitaries, surely not all of them friendly. Power struggles inside the Egyptian elite may be elusive, but their traces are quite clear – tombs or statues defaced. The king might have granted temple statues and privileged scenes, however, once the tombs were accessible as places of memory and cult, they might also have been a target for others.

That Senenmut's cult lived on in his funerary edifices is attested by hieratic remarks with dates and instructions such as 'words to say'[75] by his funerary priests or other personnel, who thus marked the religious texts and spells on the walls (the graffiti are unlikely to have been made by casual, if interested, visitors without a specific purpose). Royal favour or even a posthumous cult, however, did not prevent Senenmut's tomb and other monuments, like many other statues, tombs and stelae, from becoming a battlefield of social memory. This destiny afflicted not only some of Senenmut's depictions, but also many of his near coevals – for example, TT 100, a famous tomb of Rekhmire, vizier to Thutmose III, was attacked also.

Text damage in Senenmut's tomb led to debates about the survival of his memory. Although there were many damaged Eighteenth Dynasty tombs, the fact that Senenmut's images were attacked was seen as proof of his spectacular fall. Senenmut's adversaries might have attacked some of his depictions in the Temple in Deir el-Bahri or even in the Gebel el-Silsila shrine, and later, the Atenist iconoclastic missions under Akhenaten, probably attacked both his shrine at Gebel el-Silsila[76] and his memorial in Thebes. The combined impact of the two generations of attackers, i.e. casual enemies plus one major blow by Atenist persecution of divine names, which included Mut, the consort of Amun (hence Senenmut, the 'man of Mut'), would perhaps suffice as an explanation, without recourse to the image of an intense royal persecution. In addition, monuments of Senenmut were restored in the Ramesside era, which appear to have respected Hatshepsut as a king of Egypt.[77]

Ultimately, however, attacks appear feeble given the dozens of these statues and texts that survive. In fact, a large number of his monuments survived with only slight damage. The sheer quantity of his statues and texts, of course, was a contributing factor.

Texts were a powerful tool of commemoration, applied to statues, stelae and tomb walls. The Eighteenth Dynasty tomb included in its text selection a Call to the Living,[78] which commented on the good services and character of the deceased and asked those capable of doing so to talk about his name and deeds. These were again immortalized repeatedly on statues in temples as well as on tomb walls – one of the main weapons, it would seem, against oblivion. However, only the literate were expected to read them and report the good character of the deceased to others. Texts were there to be read, no doubt, but also to be perceived as powerful memorials even by those who could not read them.

Was Senenmut interested or involved in selecting and composing his own texts? Interested, quite likely, but involved? The man claimed originality and knowledge, making it unlikely he would have not been involved in creating his own historical record.

Historical communication

Considering all the offices Senenmut held in the administration of the estates of Amun and of the queen, one might ask whether he was indeed literate, or whether an imaginary army of pen-pushers did his bidding. Senenmut, however, worked his way up from humble offices to the most important and was personally involved in the administration of the granaries of Amun and the royal households. Literacy and numeracy were essential for most of the offices that he held and –

although there is no definite proof of personal literacy – it is questionable whether throughout his entire brilliant career he had to rely on a personal scribe to read and write the innumerable accounts, bookkeeping, inscription drafts and ultimately text compositions for his sovereign and his own monuments.

To Senenmut, it seems, literacy was more than an administrative tool. It was part of a broader cultural communication that included a gateway to historical memory, a link between past, present and posterity. And one in which he enthusiastically took part. Writing and elite memory are in alliance in Egypt and Senenmut's approach to his own commemoration is a prime example of a widely applied concept which he developed in new directions. What is certain is his use of writing to promote himself and his activities – his trail across the Egyptian memoscape from Aswan to Silsila to Karnak and Luxor to Sinai is remarkable. Whether Senenmut's command of literacy included both hieratic and hieroglyphs must, however, remain a moot point, unlike other makers of memory we will explore in the following chapters.

An original approach to traditional material is shown in his statuary, as well as in his shrine at Gebel el-Silsila.[79] In his tomb, he operates with old texts in new sequences and with entirely new statue forms. He grasped the role of text as a means of communication with the elite for posterity and made sure that his role in history was as firmly recorded as that of his kings. Proof of his own literacy is circumstantial, but strong. One is almost tempted to point out that even workmen at his tomb were literate and Senenmut himself experimented with cryptography.

Senenmut was a loyal top administrator, an inventive artist and quite possibly a successful courtier in the service of Hatshepsut and Thutmose III, a man for whom literacy was essential. Yet, neither his administrative endeavours nor his scholarly pursuits prompted him to describe himself as a *scribe* at any point of his career. To him, it seems, literacy, power, and scribehood were more disparate than almost any other figure among the ten featured in this book.

3

Tjanuni

'You Cannot Be a Man of the World Unless You See the World' read the red bold words on the colourful poster (see Fig. 3.1). Featuring exotic destinations like a Jamaican village or the darkly-lit Sphinx at Giza, the print portrays a world that is both foreign, yet inviting. Only two lines of text at the bottom reveal the advertisement's true aim, announcing 'Join the Army and Travel Round the World for Nothing'. The poster was part of an interbellum campaign of the British Military Service, intended to encourage young men to enlist in the army. Through slogans like 'Join the Army, See the World', it portrayed a military remote from battle cries and gruesome death. The military, it suggests, is a career path that leads to self-realization as a sophisticated and experienced man of the world.

Each period has its own set of ideals, but the military may have held a strong allure in Eighteenth Dynasty Egypt. The kings of this era extended their reach into remote territories, sending their troops as far north as the Euphrates and as far south as the Nile's fourth cataract. Egypt thereby broadened its borders, placing permanent troops in Syro-Palestine, and establishing Nubia as its colony.[1] Even if the idea of alluring travel to exotic places might have had limited application in Egypt, there were opportunities exclusively offered by the military life.

Maintaining this extensive war machine, required the support of a large administration. Along with soldiers, archers and charioteers, scribes and officials accompanied the troops to localities unknown to their predecessors. Their lives, therefore, became exceptionally different from their counterparts in the civil and temple administrations. Though they often shared similar values, like the ideal of *Königsdienst*,[2] the wars in which they fought provided them with a unique interpretation of this value. They fulfilled their aspiration of serving the king by serving his campaign by his side – symbolically, if not physically.

Among these men marching towards Djahi (Syro-Palestine) was Tjanuni, a man of no conspicuous genealogy. He joined the army as a military scribe and

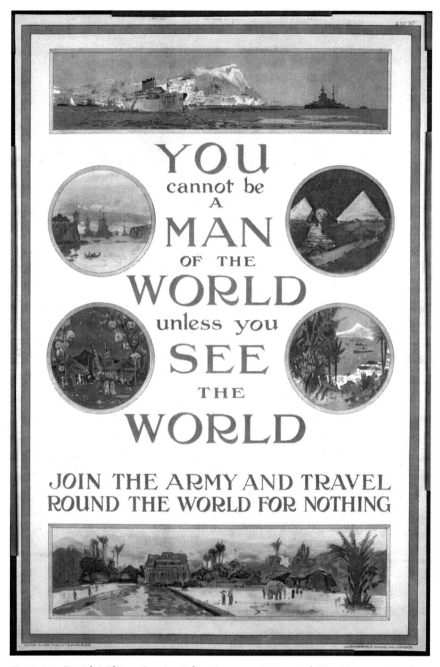

Fig. 3.1 A British Military Service Advertisement. © Imperial War Museum, London. Art. IWM PST 13504.

served no fewer than three kings: Thutmose III, Amenhotep II and Thutmose IV. He accompanied them into battle and received the prominent titles of Overseer of Military Scribes and General. At home, he was given a position in the civil administration and a tomb in the Theban necropolis, the burial ground of the elite of his time.

During his years in the service of the king, Tjanuni may have registered numerous men and counted an abundance of goods and loot, but his name is known today for the remarkable use of his pen. According to his own testimony, inscribed on the walls of his tomb, he employed his pen to record the military achievements of his rulers, thereby memorializing their victories. This separates Tjanuni from most scribes of his time, as he prides himself on writing a special genre of text, one that highlights a sense of history. Tjanuni's retrospective remark at the end of his life brings to the fore the important role of scribes in the military and, in turn, the military's impact on their lives and work.

The New Kingdom war machine

The advent of the New Kingdom was intertwined in wars on two fronts. After the demise of the Middle Kingdom, territories in the south fell under local rulers from Nubia, who reigned from their capital city in Kerma. The site is now known for its impressive fortifications and extensive cemeteries, which testify to the greatness of the kingdom that built them. To the north, in Egypt's Delta, reigned a dynasty of West-Semitic origins, whose population settled in the area as merchants, workmen and mercenaries during the Middle Kingdom, and likewise gained power after its collapse.[3] The Theban rulers of the early Eighteenth Dynasty established their dominance over all of Egypt through the defeat of these two powerful adversaries.

The defeats were not achieved by a single blow, but rather during a long series of campaigns. The tension against the northern Hyksos arose during the reign of Seqenenre Tao, a Seventeenth Dynasty king. This historic moment would be remembered centuries later, in the so-called *Quarrel of Apepi and Seqenenre*.[4] In reality, Seqenenre's mummy revealed that he suffered a fatal injury, probably inflicted at the hands of the enemy.[5] Not even Kamose, his son who succeeded him, was entirely successful in vanquishing this northern enemy; only Ahmose, his second son to ascend the throne, managed to conquer Avaris, the enemy's capital, and to defeat the Hyksos forces.[6] The downfall of the southern Kingdom of Kerma was only attained during the reign of Thutmose I, the heir to Ahmose's successor.

During those years, the military itself grew and took on a new form, partly due to the introduction of new technologies. Bowmen were always a significant part of ancient Egyptian military forces, but with the rise of the New Kingdom, the simple bow was replaced by a composite, whose string was more taut, compared to earlier forms.[7] Similarly, horses had only recently been introduced into Egypt; they soon became a sign of elite status and power. In the military, they were employed to draw chariots, which served as a moving platform, from which archers could shoot at the enemy. Along with the composite bow, Egyptian military chariotry became a force to be reckoned with.[8]

Having defeated the Hyksos and the Kingdom of Kerma, the military machine. Thutmose I fought further campaigns in Syro-Palestine, embarking on a war against the northern Kingdom of Mitanni. On the southern front, he led his forces even further up the Nile, reaching Kurgus, which lies between the fourth and the fifth cataract. Later kings continued to send out forces against foreign lands and nomadic people at Egypt's borders, often early in their reign. These campaigns provided the sovereign with an opportunity to demonstrate his power and dominance before the gods.[9]

Thutmose III, under whom Tjanuni made his first steps in the military, was so prolific in his campaigns that he is popularly referred to as ancient Egypt's Napoleon. Following in the footsteps of his grandfather, Thutmose III's military campaigns reached Kurgus in the south and the Euphrates in the north. Altogether, he is known to have carried out seventeen campaigns during his sole reign, and possibly a few more while he shared the throne with his stepmother, Hatshepsut. When his mummy was examined and found to be of a rather short stature, Egyptologists saw even greater resemblance to the French ruler.[10] Other military campaigns were carried out during the time of his son, Amenhotep II, and of his grandson, Thutmose IV, but to a much lesser extent.

Tjanuni's modest origins

All's well that ends well. Tjanuni returned home safely after taking part in a number of military campaigns and ultimately received a burial fitting for a member of the elite near the valley in which his kings had their eternal resting place. Visitors to his tomb find inscriptions that praise him as his sovereign's eyes and ears, and the one who is his monarch's heart. Of his beginning, however, we hear very little, which suggests that his success was very much his own doing, as well as a sign of his time.

All our knowledge of Tjanuni begins and ends with his tomb. His burial place, which received the modern designation Theban Tomb 74, is located in Sheikh Abd el-Qurna, where many prominent officials and high dignitaries were buried.[11] His tomb neighbours those of seven other officials who served under Thutmose IV, the last king Tjanuni served. The tomb is entered from a small courtyard, leading into a corridor cut into the rock. Another hall was carved to intersect with the corridor to create a T-shape that characterizes many of the area's tombs. Like his neighbouring officials, Tjanuni received the tomb by the grace of the king, who bestowed on him the right to be buried in the vicinity of the Valley of the Kings, where the sovereigns themselves found their final resting place.

The tomb, furthermore, presented its owner with an opportunity to commemorate himself, and indeed the images and inscriptions decorating the walls of Tjanuni's tomb provide us with invaluable information about his roles in life and his beliefs regarding the afterlife. Perhaps the most significant of these inscriptions bears Tjanuni's autobiographical text. Painted in black on a yellow background, the text imitates the shape of a stela, like those, which were carved in stone and placed in niches in similar tombs. Tjanuni's painted inscription tells of his history and achievement in twenty lines, only small portions of which are preserved today. Fortunately, early modern visitors to the tomb, including Jean-François Champollion himself, one of the fathers of modern Egyptology, inspected the tomb and copied what they managed to see of the text. Their copies allow us to reconstruct several sentences that have since become too damaged to read. In these lines, Tjanuni says:

> I accompanied the good god, the ruler of Maat, the king of Upper and Lower Egypt [Menkheperre (Thutmose III) given life] . . . every year . . . [I saw the victories of the king] which [he] did [upon all foreign lands. As captiv]es, he brought the rulers of Syro-Palestine to the [beloved] land (Egypt), [having plundered all their towns and cut down their trees. There is no foreign land, which stood against him.] It was I who made firm (*smn*) the victory which he made upon all foreign lands, being done [in writing like it was done.
>
> I accompanied the good god the King of Upper and Lower Egypt Aa]kheperure (Amenhotep II), for I was the confidant of his Majesty, my favour being firm everyday . . .
>
> I accompanied the good god, the lord of the two lands, Menkheperure (Thutmose IV), given life forever like Re. [I wrote for him numerous troops] . . .[12]

Despite the broken phrases, the text conveys a strong sense of excitement. Tjanuni speaks in admiration of the Egyptian forces and their overwhelming power, which vanquishes all, plunders all and cuts all trees down. The text follows the form of an historical biography, a genre that dates back to the Old Kingdom and which was revived in the early New Kingdom with great vigour, as exemplified by Paheri and Senenmut. Like other examples of this genre, Tjanuni's inscription tells of its patron through narrative sequences interwoven with historical events. A prominent example of this genre was employed by Ahmose son of Ibana, the grandfather of Paheri, who is featured in the first chapter of this book. Like Ahmose who writes on his role in the vanquishing of the Hyksos enemy at the birth of the New Kingdom, Tjanuni speaks of his participation in the military campaigns at the side of his kings. Reign after reign, both men saw their king lead armies and return in victory.

Similar to Ahmose, the military played a significant role in shaping Tjanui's life path. Its impact on his life is palpable throughout the inscription. Victories and captives, plunder and destruction are evident in almost every sentence of the text. The significance of the military is even apparent in the very narration of the events. As Tjanuni relates his autobiography, the phrase *jw šms.n=i ntr nfr*, 'I followed the good god (the king)', accompanies the reader from one event to the other, from the reign of one king to another. This layout structures Tjanuni's life as a sequence of kings and military campaigns, leading towards his burial in great honour.

One piece of the puzzle, however, is still missing, as we learn nothing of his origin. Many of Tjanuni's contemporaries indicate their familial ties, mentioning the names and titles of their parents, their siblings and occasionally of more remote relatives. Paheri, for example, locates his tomb in the vicinity of his well-known grandfather and Rekhmire, vizier under Thutmose III, depicts a dynasty of viziers of whom he was the last. Doing so, they locate themselves within networks of social status and inherited power. Tjanuni, in contrast, makes no mention of his parents, and the lack of genealogy in his tomb may very well suggest that the status of his parents did not merit attention. His origins may indeed have been modest, rather like those of Senenmut; however, he took care to 'ennoble' his parents posthumously with a new burial.

Tjanuni's rise through the ranks seems to suggest great social mobility, but a few words of caution are needed here. The military is indeed often associated with the opportunity given to men of low socio-economical background to risk their lives and in return to obtain status and power. It is noteworthy, however, that despite the similarities in their life stories, Ahmose was a navy warrior, who earned his gold of honour literally in exchange for his enemies' hands. Tjanuni, in contrast, was a military scribe, and thereby must have obtained this profession from his father with possibly some state education.[13] Even if his parents were not among the highest echelons of the elite, he nevertheless belonged to a small and privileged group of literate men. Moreover, the reluctance to mention his parents might be no more than a rhetorical means to aggrandize the royal favour he received thanks to his character. It is not unfathomable that rather than celebrating his genealogy, Tjanuni focused on fashioning himself as a self-made man and a favourite of the king.

Military, scribes and military scribes

Like Tjanuni, many others saw the good in military life. The tombs of Amenemhab in Thebes and of Ahmose, son of Ibana, in Elkab tell of their valour in battle for their kings. Amenhotep, son of Hapu, who was venerated later in history, also started his career in the military, as did Haremhab and Paramessu, the last king of the Eighteenth Dynasty and the first king of the Ramesside Period.

Not all, however, saw the military as a good thing. A genre of texts praising the scribal profession while satirizing other occupations took aim at the military life in the New Kingdom.[14] Profession after profession, such texts describe the misfortunes and the physical hardships that each occupation entails: the hands of the metalworker stink like fish and eggs; the washer sits with crocodiles, and so on.[15] Fortunately for the literate reader, the scribe is his own master. He neither pays taxes, nor does he sully his hands and clothes in the work of the field. The genre, which enjoyed great popularity throughout different periods, has its roots in the Middle Kingdom, where it focused on peasants and craftsmen. In the New Kingdom, however, we find the soldier repeatedly appearing in texts that focus on the in miserable everyday lives and the immanent death that awaits them in battle. More than anything, this negative attitude among the scribal elite may be a response towards the rise of the military and the growing need to compete with its attractions.

Tjanuni, however, was neither a soldier nor an ordinary scribe. As a military scribe, he travelled far from the easy conditions of a village scribe or from those of a scribe of the treasury. Compare, for example, the image of scribes seated in the office inside the tomb of Tjay (Theban Tomb 23).[16] The image is clearly idealized, but the scene depicts scribes with long, bright garments seated in a roofed structure inscribing long papyri (see Fig. 3.2).

Fig. 3.2 An office life according to Theban Tomb 23 (after Borchardt 1907: 59).

In contrast, images of writing in the tomb of Tjanuni present us with very different aesthetics. There, Tjanuni stands with writing equipment in his hands looking over scores of men, in what seems an overcrowded yet orderly hustle. His actions are described in the caption of the image as *snhj*, a verb, which may denote 'marching' or 'registering':

> Writing (*zẖꜣ*) the military before [his Majesty], registering (*snhj*) the troops of recruits, causing that each man knows his doing in the entire military by the true Royal Scribe, whom he loves, the Military Scribe, Tjanuni, true of voice.[17]

The paragraph speaks to Tjanuni's view on the role of the military scribe. A military scribe is one who acts before the king, and who is crucial to the proper running of the military. It is thanks to him that soldiers know their role and place.

A similar emphasis on knowledge appears elsewhere in the tomb in an image that describes Tjanuni's activities outside of the military. The scene shows the tomb owner standing with scribes in front of rows of men, horses, and cattle. In the caption to the scene, Tjanuni ascribes himself quite a remarkable extent of responsibilities:

> Registering (*snhj*) the entire land before his Majesty, viewing all, knowing (*rẖ*) the army, the priests, the royal artisans, and all workers of the whole land by the Scribe [of the military, the beloved] of his lord, Tjanuni, true of voice, who says: 'We have completed (it).'[18]

This paragraph is interesting for a number of different aspects. First, it continues the idea that was raised in the other scene, of associating writing with knowledge.

Similarly, it places the scribe above all other professions; he is all seeing and omniscient. It allows him to speak in a voice that is both plural and singular at the same time, when he says 'we'.

The scene is furthermore unique in portraying the notion of a demographic census. Scholars have debated the feasibility of a national census in ancient Egypt, and the evidence for such an endeavour is indeed scarce. One kind of census was mentioned as early as the Second Dynasty, when a system of biannual censuses seems to have been in place.[19] More probably, however, it was dedicated to the counting of cattle and wealth rather than an attempt to grasp the extent of the human population. Whether this practice was prominent before Tjanuni or even during his time, his representation of the census is singular. Perhaps this notion of the census as counting men is an extension of Tjanuni's military career, where counting enlisted soldiers and captured men were integral parts of his work. If so, then the military had yet another impact on Tjanuni and on the way he thought of his role in society.

Writing history

In his elaborate self-praise, Tjanuni employed many common epithets of his time like 'unique friend', 'close companion', and many others. For most part, his autobiographical text reads like many other narrations of contemporary members of the elite, revolving around exceptional ability and royal recognition. One feature of his activities stands out from to the usual repertoire for its remarkable nature. While Tjanuni was accompanying the king in his successful campaigns, he says, he was the one who made firm the victories, by committing them to writing.

Historiographical texts were neither an invention of Tjanuni nor of his time. As Donald Redford has shown, ancient Egyptian rulers and officials speak of a genre of *gn.wt*, 'Annals', which they perceived as texts that collect the events of a reign or a time.[20] Other inscriptions, appearing on royal and non-royal stelae, as well as on tomb walls, often made use of historical information, like the aforementioned historical biographies of Tjanuni's days. Similarly, royal texts that decorated walls of temples were never quite shy about narrating their king's wars and victories.

Tjanuni, however, was the first to lay such a claim to the authorship of a historiographical text. Direct claims of authorship are quite rare in ancient Egypt, especially during the Eighteenth Dynasty. In the literary sphere, one could find texts, which were ascribed to a specific figure – like the teachings of Ptahhotep or those of Khety – but in those texts, the protagonist is often described as having delivered a speech, rather than writing it down. Tjanuni is the first to claim that he put a text, and a historiographical one, into writing.

Tjanuni wrote, furthermore, in the days of Thutmose III, whose victories were recorded on the walls of the temple of Karnak in the form of annals. Scholars have suggested that Tjanuni might have been involved in the composition of these texts, either directly or indirectly, but in any case through the manuscripts that he produced at his work in the army. Military scribes like Tjanuni are assumed to have kept journals of the daily happenings;[21] these in turn might have been collected and served as the material that allowed the scribes of the monumental annals of Thutmose III to produce a hieroglyphic formal account. Other researchers, like Redford, see a more direct relationship, pointing out correctly that Tjanuni employs the verb *smn*, to convey that he is making the victories 'firm, enduring'.[22] Such a verb accentuates the memorialization of the events suggesting they were written and immortalized on a monumental scale. Tjanuni's text thus suggests that rather than an accessory, he possibly was a direct participant in the process of monumental commemoration.

Concluding remarks

This chapter began with the allure of military life in modern as well as in ancient times. Despite hardships and imminent danger, the military succeeded in attracting men (and, mainly more recently, women) of various backgrounds to join its ranks. Such phenomena were common throughout history, and it might be valuable to evoke here in the closing lines of the chapter another character who accompanied his ruler on the same piece of land as Tjanuni, and who described his contribution with the following words:

> My pen accompanied his sword and helped his dominion: the former provided endorsement, the latter causing death; the former sustaining security, the latter inducing fear.[23]

'Imād al-Dīn al-Kātib al-Iṣfahānī, was Saladin's personal secretary and later chronicler of his reign (1125–1201 AD).[24] Reflecting on his life, he contemplated the role he played in the service of his ruler as a man of the pen. He was no warrior, but rather a prolific writer, scholar and historian. The passage appears in his book dedicated to revive Saladin's memory after his death and to immortalize his deeds.

The statement also rings true with Tjanuni's story. He accompanied his kings in their campaigns beyond the borders of Egypt and he committed his pen to the proper administration of the military, which was a massive organization by the time of Egypt's Napoleonic pharaoh, Thutmose III. Like 'Imād al-Dīn al-Kātib al-Iṣfahānī, he also saw significance in the memorialization of his rulers' victories, and grasped the pen as the appropriate tool for this purpose. This view of the scribe's duty distinguishes Tjanuni from almost any other ancient Egyptian scribe.

4

Amenemhat

Amenemhat was a run-of-the-mill name for an educated Egyptian in the New Kingdom,[1] as it included a major dynastic deity of the time, the Theban Amun. It also used to be a Middle Kingdom royal name that retained its significance, thanks to a popular instruction text, the *Instructions of Amenemhat*.[2] At home, he – like his royal namesake – might have been called Ameni for short.[3] But perhaps no one used a familiar nickname for our writer. He arrived at the necropolis of Saqqara near the city of Memphis either in the fifteenth or fourteenth century BC and left evidence of his literacy as well as of his temperament. We are able to recreate a single scene from his life with a fair degree of accuracy, but most of his life and his professional roles will have to be collated with the help of approximate parallels. Nevertheless, Amenemhat's writing gives some insight, even if speculative, into the thoughts of a New Kingdom educated man, as well as into the profession of a scribe.

Setting the scene: Writing on the wall

Amenemhat found his way into a shaded corner of a stone edifice that used to be a chapel within a pyramid precinct. The sand-blasted, but still elegant little building with high and smooth limestone walls, had a small lobby which led to a narrow inner room. The chapel was part of a large architectural complex, mostly built in limestone, which belonged to an Old Kingdom sovereign, Netjerikhet. Throughout most ancient and modern times, he was known as 'Djoser',[4] the king who was among the first to use stone for his funerary monument. Djoser did so on a monumental scale, and the step mastaba he built continues to fascinate students of Egyptology as it did the ancient Egyptians. Later kings (or rather their architects) were inspired by the architecture. However, our visitor's attention was apparently fully occupied by something else, when he noticed that others had visited the site before him.

Limestone blocks, especially in the chapel lobby, were marked with characters in black ink. These seemed to have appeared on the walls quite a short time ago, and almost looked the same as the handwriting Amenemhat was used to seeing on more formal administrative documents or copies of literary texts he probably dealt with. The writings on the wall were in hieratic script, in 1–2 centimetre-high signs, standing out, shiny and black, on the matte limestone. Egyptology knows these texts as New Kingdom visitors' graffiti.

Our New Kingdom visitor was annoyed at his predecessors and made no secret of his feelings as he wrote on the wall, using the same hieratic script delivered with a rush brush and black ink:

> There came the scribe of skilled fingers, he has no equal in his qualities in the entire city of Memphis, the Scribe Amenemhat. I say – tell me, it breaks my heart as I see the work of their hands. This isn't good skill. It is like a work of a woman who is lacking the knowledge. Were they not allowed entry to see the temple – I saw such sluggishness, they were no scribes enlightened by Thoth.[5]

He signed himself, like most graffiti writers, only as a scribe. His text leaves us in no doubt of his literacy, but with little clue as to his job title. Was he a member of administrative personnel? Was he an 'outline scribe', i.e. a draughtsman, who like many of his contemporaries, shortened his title? As the stories of artists like Paheri or Dedia (q.v.) confirm, the art profession is not to be excluded, but Amenemhat was keen to stress his literacy and writing skills. As this book sets out to explain, the status of a scribe included the essential fact of literacy, but the roles of a literate person in Egyptian society were varied. Amenemhat left only this simple title on the wall. Judged on title alone, he might have been working in any of the above jobs. Perhaps, however, this text highlights – explicitly as well as implicitly – other characteristics of a scribe than literacy or indeed a particular job; there is a social element.

At first sight, the text betrays anger. Amenemhat's anger must have been such as to prevent his adhering to the usual etiquette of graffiti writers – on this occasion, he made no reference to the sacred space he had just visited, nor did he add a date to his text, as most of his predecessors and contemporaries had. If these other graffiti give rise to speculation that they were premeditated acts of personal commemoration in writing.[6] Amenemhat seemingly produces a choleric outburst. But at the same time his angry comments appeal to the ideal skills of the literate culture, which included good writing, and also to an ideal of

Fig. 4.1 The state of Amenemhat's graffito in the 1920s. Gunn Mss. XII.7.2. © Griffith Institute Archive, Oxford.

a scribe as a cultured person – enlightened by Thoth. He too looks for values that deserved to be committed to writing.

What are we looking at, then? Before we consider Amenemhat's text exceptional testimony or otherwise, there is his spatial and temporal background to investigate. Our reconstruction of his background, his training, his appraisal of women and writing, and eventually his motivation for making the graffito in the pyramid complex will have to be derived from the context of the New Kingdom city of Memphis and on information gleaned from other graffiti makers. Amenemhat and his maligned predecessors in that Saqqara chapel were far from exceptional in their desert venture.

An Eighteenth Dynasty collection of Amenemhats

Although the exact date of Amenemhat's trip to Saqqara is unknown, the handwriting suggests it was during the Eighteenth Dynasty. Interestingly, the name 'Amenemhat' appears on a number of monuments at approximately the same time as the angry graffito. For instance, other graffiti in Abusir or

Fig. 4.2 The collection of Amenemhats from a selection of Memphite graffiti of the Eighteenth Dynasty. Above: Abusir; below: Dahshur. Drawing by HN.

Dahshur (again pyramid fields) refer to or were written by an Amenemhat.[7] However, an identification of the choleric Amenemhat from Saqqara with any of the other local Amenemhats is purely speculative, if also very tempting. Had at least some of the other graffiti also been penned by this man, then we would have a visitor who toured several pyramid fields of Memphis. However, even if the identification were likely (and the handwriting is Eighteenth Dynasty in all cases, but not quite in the same hand), we have no other personal data for the man – speculative data must be derived from comparanda.

A graffiti maker's background: The city

As Amenemhat left his temporary retreat within the pyramid precinct, he probably retraced his steps back to the city of Memphis, which he claimed to be his home and himself to be its most excellent educated man. At the time of the Eighteenth Dynasty, Memphis, an ancient site of administration and government of Egypt, was perhaps best described as the 'second capital' of the country.[8] It was a busy city with major temples, royal domains, a palace, administrative offices, military barracks and a port. Its actual appearance, however, is still a matter of guesswork.[9] We know more about institutions and offices, and some officials, than about urban structure, buildings or the look of this major metropolis of the ancient world. It was against this backdrop of offices, accounting work and possibly schools or document storage,[10] that Amenemhat and literate people like him belonged.

In the New Kingdom, members of the royal family often resided in Memphis. The heir to the Egyptian throne was known to reside in the second capital – the eldest sons of Thutmose III, of Amenhotep II, as well as of Amenhotep III probably had an official seat in Memphis. A royal family member had a corresponding entourage. Eventually, kings themselves probably found Memphis a useful and desirable location when mounting the large military expeditions to Asia, which were hallmarks of the reign of Thutmose I and Thutmose III. Diplomatic efforts, characteristic of the reigns of Thutmose IV and Amenhotep III, also required a base from which to start. Further royal institutions in need of literate personnel were called royal domains.[11] Finally, large temples and related establishments employed scribes with various job descriptions.

Memphis was also a seat of the second most important man in Egypt after the king, the vizier. At least from the time of Thutmose III (mid-Eighteenth Dynasty), if not earlier, there were two officials with this title, one of them in Memphis, the other in Thebes.[12] A vizier had a rather large agenda;[13] he was also the king's right-hand man for the royal building projects, in which he was helped by overseers of royal works and by mid-rank administrators, whose titles usually included the designation 'scribe' with a further specification.

Someone like Amenemhat might have been in the service of an official establishment. He might have been a local, or his family might have moved into town from a considerable distance away, possibly even from Thebes, the southern capital and main religious centre in Egypt. Amenemhat himself might have come as a young accountant or administrator in the service of Thutmoside dignitaries. At least two such dignitaries are attested as travelling between Thebes

The New Kingdom Memphis and surrounding necropolis (after KITCHEN 1991)

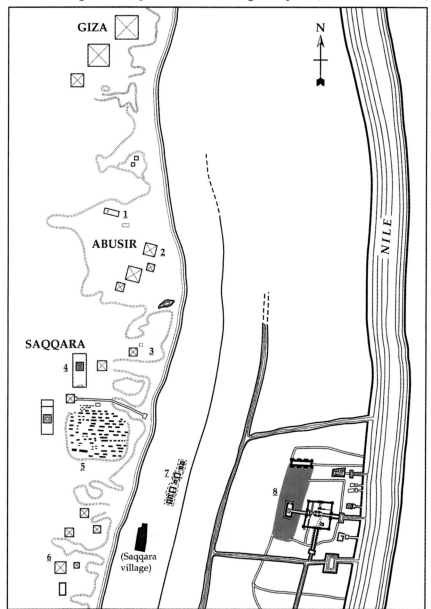

1 – 5th Dynasty sun temples, 2 – Pyramid of Sahure, 3 – Pyramid of Teti, 4 – Pyramid of Netjerikhet Djoser, 5 – area of New Kingdom tombs, 6 – South Saqqara, 7 – possible location of New Kingdom memorial temples, 8 – New Kingdom city of Memphis

Fig. 4.3 Map of New Kingdom Memphis. © Archive of The Czech Institute of Egyptology. Drawing by Jolana Malátková.

and Memphis (which was routine for many members of the upper echelon of Egyptian society[14]), as well as actually visiting the monuments in the desert to the west of Memphis.

One of these was a man of some consequence for the administration of the country during the reign of Thutmose III – Amunedjeh, the overseer of granaries and later a royal herald. Amunedjeh was buried in Thebes (TT 84), but his professional life meant that he travelled to different parts of Egypt and possibly even abroad.[15] The herald may also have had some responsibility for the king's building projects. Amunedjeh left a graffito at the sun temple of King Userkaf in today's Abu Ghurab.[16]

Another dignitary of the same era was Puiemre, the second prophet of Amun. Like Amunedjeh, this man was part of Theban social circles – in his case specifically of the priesthood of Amun. He was also buried in Thebes (TT 39). Yet, Puiemre also travelled and apparently must have visited Saqqara, for he – or a member of his entourage – had buried an ushabti with Puiemre's name near the enclosure wall of the Step Pyramid complex of the Old Kingdom ruler of Netjerikhet Djoser, the very same complex, which was a target of graffiti makers.[17] Most ushabti were placed in the tomb, but some were found in places of devotional importance, perhaps near shrines or other important sites, which were visited on occasion, perhaps of major religious feasts. It may well be that Puiemre was motivated to visit the Memphite necropolis on one of the local feasts connected to the deities Ptah or Sokar. It is not inconceivable that someone like Amenemhat might have also been an official in the entourage of men like Amunedjeh or Puiemre.

A writer in the desert

A graffiti maker was, in a way, a writer in the desert. The practice of graffiti was, of course, not limited to the desert, but attested there frequently. An educated Egyptian knew how to frame and interpret the desert as a part of his life-world. The desert was the 'Red Land', often hostile and hosting forces of chaos. However, it was an inevitable part of the Egyptian world for most of its recorded history.[18] A New Kingdom literate man who was schooled with the help of traditional instructions for pupils (see also Chapter 8, Inena)[19] would have seen the desert as a place of hardship, such as that suffered by the eponymous hero of the story of Sinuhe, whose parched mouth during a flight across the desert gave him the opportunity to 'taste death'.[20]

Literate professionals, however, still had a number of reasons to go beyond the edge of cultivation into the windswept world of sand and rocky outcrops. The desert roads of Egypt are lined with rock inscriptions and graffiti marking literate human presence in the landscape, which may be connected to travel, trade expeditions, quarrying, mining, local sacred spaces and sites,[21] and tomb building. Literature met the desert, when travelling literate personnel added quotations or paraphrases of literary texts to the rock inscriptions.[22]

A large necropolis, such as that of Memphis, was in continuous operation for several millennia. The tombs were re-used and recycled for centuries in varied ways, no less so in the era of the Eighteenth to the Nineteenth Dynasties. New tombs sprang up in unused cliffs[23] as well as over Early Dynastic subterranean complexes.[24] In the Ramesside period, something akin to a large building materials recycling business was in operation, although the idea of reusing previous building materials was not new.

Many (though not all) of these activities required the presence of someone literate, most of all when it came to organizing the building work. Although Memphis was a large necropolis with a number of building sites at any one time, as well as cult sites in and out of operation, its written record of the administration of the site is at present rather scarce and dispersed, compared to, for example, compact evidence of the Theban village of workmen at Deir el-Medina.[25] Nonetheless, some patchy records are available. Perhaps a century or so after Amenemhat, an administrator named Buqentuf was responsible for the construction of a tomb not far from the step mastaba (pyramid). Several papyri at present located in Cairo, New York and Vienna show a few work-journal entries by this scribe[26] and give an idea about what had to be done to start a tomb – the chosen place had to be adapted (flattened) so that the walls of the new edifice could be raised. The workmen, of course, had to be hired, fed and provided with tools. The accountant-cum-administrator had to organize all this. Similar procedures are to be expected among the other Memphite necropolis building sites throughout the New Kingdom. During the Eighteenth Dynasty, a large group of tombs appeared in Central Saqqara (the best known include those of Haremhab, Maya, Inuia, Meryneith, Paser and Ptahemwia[27]) and a number of scribes would have had a number of professional reasons to roam the desert.

Our protagonist Amenemhat's putative responsibility might have lain with tomb building or maintenance, but there were other professional reasons than overseeing a building site that warranted going to the monuments in the desert.

As the earlier case of Senenmut suggested, the Eighteenth Dynasty Egyptians had another, less tangible reason to interact in a systemic way with the monuments of their ancestors. There is scarcely a period of Egyptian cultural history which does *not* interact with the past, but Dynasty Eighteen was particularly prolific and creative in that respect.

Hatshepsut and Thutmose III excelled in producing both textual references and building projects, which demonstrated knowledge of history and a deliberate, if selective, use of the past (see also Chapter 2, Senenmut). Thutmose III's vizier Rekhmire rather famously remarked that his king knew what had happened, stock phrases comparing Thutmose and Hatshepsut favourably to their ancestors were repeated on stelae and in temple texts,[28] and both kings were inspired by very similar architectural elements (Deir el-Bahri again is exceptional), scenes and texts. There was rarely ever any mechanical copying, but certainly there were similar ideas, motives, maybe even parts of scenes,[29] such as those pertaining to the divine birth of a king[30] or to a ritual run in front of the goddess Hathor.[31]

How did the Egyptians get to know all this? One increasingly probable route of studying the old for the benefit of the new was the direct interaction with the monuments. One possible trace of the visiting students of the past is the graffiti left on the walls of the older monuments – i.e. the texts that annoyed Amenemhat so much. Was he, then, also an educated man with a mission, a head of craftsmen searching for ancient models? In any case, he encountered graffiti made by others. However, the mere fact that the graffiti existed did not annoy Amenemhat, it was more likely to have been some breach of a putative graffiti-making etiquette.

Graffiti etiquette

Making graffiti was not per se a criminal or socially subversive activity in ancient Egypt. Graffiti and rock inscriptions appeared in the Egyptian landscape and its man-made additions as traces of human presence. It does seem there was some sort of graffiti etiquette. For instance, when leaving graffiti in functioning temples, one often (but not always) limited oneself to out-of-sight locations.[32] When it comes to typical visitors' graffiti (recognizable by their incipit: 'The coming of the scribe NN was in order to see'),[33] a contemporary admirer of the temple of Hatshepsut in Deir el-Bahri (by handwriting, an Eighteenth Dynasty scribe) left his 'coming to see' note on an ostracon. It would have perhaps been inappropriate to write his comment on a clearly visible wall of a temple in full operation.

On the other hand, within tomb chapels and semi-abandoned cult buildings, as well as areas of landscape considered important (such as the cliffs of the Theban Mountain around the Valley of the Kings near the local sanctuaries of the goddesses Hathor and Meretseger) graffiti production thrived. A similar course of events may be assumed to have taken place in the pyramid complexes and temples of Old and Middle Kingdom rulers in the neighbourhood of Memphis. The graffiti was left in edifices located in an area that stretches from Abu Ghurob to Dahshur, with an extension in the area of Fayum, namely the site of Maidum. The visitors came mainly throughout the Eighteenth Dynasty. The Nineteenth Dynasty had a different graffiti system,[34] but since Amenemhat was most probably an Eighteenth Dynasty graffito maker, we will stay within the boundaries of this period.

Graffiti writing was an interesting business. It was taken seriously by many visitors and they adhered to a fixed structure of contents in the graffiti. For the Eighteenth Dynasty, this meant writing a short text in a rather fixed narrative structure also used in contemporary annalistic literature (structuring elements of the narrative are underlined): 'Coming[35] was done by the scribe NN to see a temple/tomb/pyramid of XY. He found it beautiful, like heaven/more beautiful than any other temple. Sun was rising in it. Let myrrh rain on its roof! And he said Let there be a thousand of bulls, fowl and all good and pure things for the ka of XY.'

Occasionally there were visitors with a less admirable style – for instance a graffiti maker in the solar temple complex of Userkaf at Abu Ghurob called his fellow visitor(s) 'f***ing bastard(s)'.[36] Along similar lines, only with less insolence, a visitor to tomb N 13.1 near modern Assiut commented on the sexual prowess of his colleagues.[37] However, this type of graffiti, which reminds us of many counterparts in different places and times of the world,[38] are a minority in the pyramid fields of Memphis.

The Eighteenth Dynasty graffiti writers came, on occasion, in smaller or larger groups. It is by no means clear which group might have been connected with a neighbouring building activity and which would have been sent to explore ancient architecture for study purposes. 'Staff graffiti' is likely – in Thebes, staff of the temple of Hatshepsut left graffiti in grotto 504 and other locations in Deir el-Bahri, close to the temple.[39] In addition, some graffiti-makers might just have come out of curiosity or because they were in the area for a local feast. A combination of all of these motivations should not be excluded.

Visitors wanted to be seen as literate, well-educated and capable, as was the ideal of their social group. The skills of a literate person – note that the texts show mostly men in the role – started with communication. To fulfil his obligations as a power holder and as a responsible man, a man of authority had to exhibit excellent communication skills, as Amenemhat would have read in biographical texts of dignitaries of his time (see Senenmut, Tjanuni and Paheri).[40]

Amenemhat was perhaps not a high echelon dignitary, but he would have known the elite requirements and expectations. To be calm, balanced, in control of one's own person, capable of making quick but well-considered decisions, and neither causing anger nor succumbing to it as the 'hot one'.[41] It would appear that Amenemhat's graffito goes somewhat against the grain of the training and behaviour of a competent bureaucrat or an educated executive. However, the Egyptian executive world was also competitive and asserting one's excellence was part of the self-presentation and self-fashioning of a scribe.[42]

The ancient man was no less sophisticated in formulating his position vis-à-vis the society than his later followers. It has been suggested that there was little dissent in Egypt and that identities were ingrained and seldom disputed.[43] However, more recently, a closer look has revealed that the Egyptians were quite apt at recognizing the difference between the ideals of a well-functioning community, pragmatics of bureaucracy and faults in both systems.[44] They did not routinely commit to writing all the registers of self-fashioning that are made of doubt and volte-faces, but preferred a re-assertion of shared values. However, this re-assertion could have taken place in different ways.

Competitive remarks and criticism were part of Egyptian rhetoric and argumentative power. Several generations after Amenemhat, a composition known as the Satirical letter (Papyrus Anastasi I, Papyrus BM 10247)[45] was written. It appears to be a letter from one scribe to another – and shows the haplessness of the addressee in various administrative, military and negotiation tasks. It was most likely not a composition aimed at an individual, such as an actual unfortunate scribe, but a work combining satire, education and entertainment. It could have been a jibe aimed by one administrative school at another,[46] or a playful reminder that a real professional knows the gist of things and is no name-dropper. A number of copies on ostraca survived, apart from the papyrus,[47] suggesting a well-known and much-copied text. Chapter 9 examines this work in detail, showing its complex interplay of written culture, professional identities and individual accomplishment.

Characterizations of other-than-scribal professions, such as those found in literary works including the *Satire of the Trades* (see also Chapter 9, Hori) also probably had a humorous effect.[48] However, a cultured person could not mock those who were less able, poorer or otherwise disadvantaged.[49] Mockery was thus not a regular tool to be used at all levels, but it was nonetheless firmly located in the arsenal of weapons in the cultural and community battlefield, especially when it came to a man asserting himself among his peers or actually defending the values deemed important for the entire society or for a social group. Ultimately, subversion and re-assertion were close to one another.[50]

In the irritated graffito by Amenemhat, however, not only competition and mockery, but also anger found their way into the text. Anger was against the values of an Egyptian elite[51] and demonstrated an inappropriate state of mind for a visitor to a sacred place.[52] Nonetheless – at least for Amenemhat – the state of the temple's walls warranted such a reaction.

Thus, Amenemhat comes across as a man with a nominal adherence to the values of the literati, as he defends the historical monument as well as the high expectations placed on writing; at the same time he is also veering towards critical and rude graffiti. Still, he was not the worst critic. A near contemporary of his in the pyramid complex of Senwosret III at Dahshur went one step further and obliterated the name of a graffiti-making predecessor.[53]

The scribe and the woman

Amenemhat the scribe also invites a further question – why was it a woman who was a foundation of negative parallels? It would be tempting to suggest that since the world of the scribes was a world of men, from which women were mostly excluded, they were, by extension, also derided as part of the illiterate world in keeping with the 'fear' of women as seducers and disruptive elements.[54] However, although there are some Egyptian texts that suggest exactly that, others suggest a more balanced reading. Examples comprise fiction as well as fact. If the *Tale of Two Brothers* displayed an unfaithful wife, the *Tale of the Doomed Prince* showcased one who was determined, reasonable and energetic. The *Instructions of Ani* demonstrated graphically that being a mother is a hard job (not to be pooh-poohed as a woman's lot, to be expected without a sign of gratitude). Letters show women as eager correspondents. The building job of the scribe Buqentuf mentioned above was supervised by a female member of the family, and so on.

Egyptian society did not separate people strictly according to gender; they shared both private and public spaces. Although there might have been many relative boundaries, few of them appear as absolutely impenetrable.[55] Still, in the administrative world, there seem to be few – if any – women in official positions. Likewise in the world of tomb builders, women were present but did not participate directly in the building process.[56] Thus, if Amenemhat was professionally connected to administration or a community of workmen and craftsmen, women were not a direct part of his 'office environment'. However, he might have seen female handwriting, which perhaps was not on a par with a routinely trained hand, and understandably so.[57] Hence the comparison, perhaps without further need of recourse to a presumed deep-seated scribal misogyny. His predecessors were ultimately 'not gifted by Thoth' – a far deeper criticism, which truly evicted these poor unfortunates from the circle of the chosen literati.[58]

Even if he were just an accountant in Memphis, his graffito carried a message of wider consequences for the world of intellectuals – that of desired standards of writing culture and knowledge, and of respect for an ancient place. Graffiti was not entirely free of social restraint as was on occasion suggested in Egyptology.[59] The standards were, at least for one Memphite scribe, to be enforced with a vigour that might have potentially compromised the writer's own status as a man of letters, who should have a calm and balanced character.

Unfortunately, as of now, Amenemhat's own application of writing standards is unknown. His text was rather badly preserved when first discovered in the 1920s by Battiscombe Gunn, and very little of it can be seen on the period photograph. Nonetheless, the British Egyptologist also had an opinion on Amenemhat's abilities as a calligrapher: 'large ugly writing. . .'.[60] Critical assessments have come full circle.

5

Tutankhamun

Two black and white photographs document the discovery of a palette in the tomb of Tutankhamun.[1] The photographer Henry Burton accompanied Howard Carter and his team of workmen and archaeologists, meticulously recording their discoveries. One of his photographs presents a view into the tomb's treasury chamber (Fig. 5.1). It shows a statue of the god Anubis seated atop a portable shrine, guarding the entrance to the room. A linen garment is draped around the jackal, leaving only its head and paws uncovered. A second photo focuses on the recumbent jackal (Fig. 5.2). In the moments that passed between the first and second photo being taken, the garment covering the jackal was removed, disclosing an ivory palette resting between Anubis's forelegs.[2] Adding to the wonder are the texts inscribed on the palette. They bear the name of Meritaten, the eldest daughter of Akhenaten and Nefertiti and (half)-sister to Tutankhamun.[3] Along with her palette, Carter found more than a dozen other pieces of writing-equipment buried with the boy king in his tomb.

Despite the abundance of writing equipment in Tutankhamun's tomb, Meritaten and her brother were never considered artists or scribes – neither in ancient nor in modern times. The princess's palette was best suited for drawing, like that of her sister Meketaten (the Meketaten palette, however, has four colours). With its six colours, one could paint figures on ostraca[4] or illuminate texts with colourful vignettes.[5] The palette's blue pigment is almost finished and almost all other colours show clear signs of usage, suggesting that it was put into use in ancient times, perhaps even by Meritaten herself. Similar signs of use appear on one of Tutankhamun's palettes. There, the black ink was slightly smeared outside of its well, recalling the state of many other ancient Egyptian palettes whose owners mixed their ink and dipped their pens without caring too much for the neatness of their equipment.[6] Despite the physical evidence for their literacy and artistry, the royal siblings never bore any titles or epithets, which refer to these skills.

Fig. 5.1 A view into the Treasury Room in Tutankhamun's tomb. © The Metropolitan Museum of Art, Egyptian Department Archives. Photograph by Harry Burton, TAA 55.

Meritaten and Tutankhamun's palettes thus draw the boundaries around scribes from outside the group. They point to a space in which the terms literate and scribe are in fact disjoined. They invite us to consider scribes along notions of inclusion and exclusion, not only of lower-ranking members of society, but

Fig. 5.2 The recumbent jackal with a palette between its forelegs. © The Metropolitan Museum of Art, Egyptian Department Archives. Photograph by Harry Burton, TAA 1004.

also of elite women and royalty.[7] The palettes of Meritaten and Tutankhamun paint the image of the scribe as that of a non-royal man, much like the hieroglyph 𓀀 (Gardiner A1), which accompanies the word *zẖ3.w*, 'scribe' (and any other male name or profession) in the ancient Egyptian script.[8] From the vantage point of royalty and women, scribe appears as a title and an office that belongs to the administration. Those who do not participate in the administration do not share it.

Meritaten and Tutankhamun's palettes, moreover, direct our attention to writing equipment and its significance. Palettes with a number of colours are often described as painters' palettes, and those with only two pigments, red and black, are labelled as scribal palettes. Such labelling immediately associates object with vocation or social group.[9] Yet, the palettes in the tomb of Tutankhamun suggest a case in which writing and its equipment are clearly not associated with scribes.

To study these palettes and the literacy of their owners, this chapter will first turn to Meritaten and to discussions on the literacy of elite women in Egypt. The evidence for this phenomenon is rather scarce and quite erratic, but

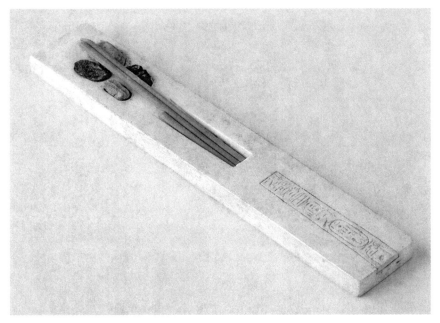

Fig. 5.3 Palette and brushes of Princess Meketaten. © The Metropolitan Museum of Art. Purchase Edward S. Harkness gift, 1926, 26.7.1295.

textual and visual evidence suggest that at least several elite women might have been literate. A similar state of affairs occurs with royal literacy, which is often taken for granted. This chapter will therefore discuss claims regarding Tutankhamun's literacy stressing the limitations of such arguments. Both discussions highlight ancient concepts of scribes, and even more so, they stress our own conceptualizations of literacy, scribes, and gender.

Meritaten's palette: Literacy among women of the elite

Two inscriptions adorn the rectangular palette found between the jackal's forelegs. The palette is made of costly ivory, and has wells for six colours: white, yellow, red, green, black and blue. Underneath the inkwells, the centre of the palette gradually declines into a cavity, in which reed pens could be stored. Below, running across the width, a single line of hieroglyphs identifies the owner of the palette as 'the King's Daughter of his Body, his beloved, Meritaten'. The other text, which is inscribed vertically, mentions Meritaten again and her titles, adding that she was born of 'the Great Royal Wife, Neferneferuaten Nefertiti' (Fig. 5.4).

The woman to whom this palette once belonged was Tutankhamun's (half)-sister, Meritaten, who once enjoyed an elevated status in the palace.[10] Meritaten

Fig. 5.4 Meritaten's palette. © The Metropolitan Museum of Art, Egyptian Department Archives. Photograph by Harry Burton, TAA 834, detail.

was probably born before her father even ascended the throne, while her grandfather was still celebrating his rejuvenation festivals on the west bank of the Nile at Thebes. Her image accompanies that of her parents in scenes from Karnak and she continued to appear with them in numerous occasions in the newly established capital, Amarna. There, she even received her own palace, situated at the north of the site, which was converted to bear her inscriptions.[11]

Towards the end of her father's reign, Meritaten assumed the queenly title, Great Royal Wife, and her name even became known to kings of foreign lands, such as Babylonia, who sent her gifts.[12] How and where she spent her later years are still much debated, as part of the on-going scholarly discussion on the events following Akhenaten's death.[13]

Was she buried as Maya, nurse of Tutankhamun,[14] or did she marry the mysterious pharaoh Smenkhkare? According to some, she herself reigned as pharaoh under the name Ankhetkheperure. However she spent her final days, the palette belongs to much earlier times, before she even bore the title Great Royal Wife.

Women of her status may have used similar palettes for drawing and writing. A small palette in the collection of the Metropolitan Museum of Art belonged to her sister, Meketaten, who predeceased Meritaten and their parents (see Fig. 5.3).[15] The palette is similarly made of ivory, but has only four pigments. In addition to red and black – the two colours to be found in every scribal palette – Meketaten's palette also has yellow in it. Arguably, the reed pens and the red and black ink hint at women's literacy, but they do so only tangentially. Even though the pens could be used to draw vignettes, drawing does not require any knowledge of texts.

Unfortunately, most evidence for women's literacy in ancient Egypt is riddled with similar doubts.[16] Women seem to have taken an active part in Egypt's economy, but one cannot assume literacy was necessary in such activities, whether men or women were involved in them. A few letters appear to be written and sent by women, and a letter from the Ramesside period requests that a certain woman prepare a letter and send it.[17] It is practically impossible, however, to prove that women penned the letters themselves, and it remains a plausible possibility that they dictated the letters to a literate person.

Literary references to women's literacy suffer from similar problems. Female voices in ancient Egyptian love poetry do not tell us anything about the gender of the person writing down the text, nor do biographical texts of women of later periods. The goddess Seshat,[18] who often appears writing along with Thoth in prayers and in temple scenes, might have served as a precedent and divine model for literate women, but even she could not be easily employed as evidence for literacy among women, and especially for the contexts in which they might have read or written.

A few women did bear the title *zḫȝ.yt* '(female)-scribe', but these examples are very rare. The most extensive dictionary of ancient Egyptian to this day, *the Wörterbuch der ägyptischen Sprache*, counts four examples for this word, to which one can add three more: Papyrus Boulaq from the Thirteenth Dynasty possibly mentions two women scribes, and a scarab bears another name of a female scribe.[19] Scholars have debated the proper translation of the term *zḫȝ.yt*, and it was suggested that the title should be read as referring to the duties of a cosmetician – a translation not entirely unaffected by some gender bias.[20]

Another piece of evidence arrives from tomb decoration. Occasionally tomb owners show themselves seated with pets and important objects beneath their chairs. Women frequently sit with a mirror and cosmetic equipment below theirs, but Betsy Bryan collected at least six tombs in which scribal equipment appears.[21] This would indeed suggest that these women were literate, or at least that they deemed literacy to be of great enough importance to be represented in their tomb. A few men also showed themselves in a similar manner, but they are often recognized in the scholarly literature as scribes. Here, another gender bias seems to show – women show writing equipment to indicate their literacy; men who represent a similar image indicate their profession. The conclusion here is not so much that women with scribal palettes need to be considered as scribes. Rather, the opposite – the palettes do not automatically represent a profession, and literacy needs to be seen as being separate from scribes.[22]

It thus follows that, despite considerable uncertainty, one could argue that literacy did exist among some elite women of ancient Egypt. Several modes of representation in which women might have taken greater part might remain outside the scope of the material that reached us from ancient Egypt. As such, these possible modes of representation neither disprove nor support any claim. For the most part, women hardly take part in most demonstrations of literacy, which are often tied to the administration. From this vantage point, scribes appear to be predominantly male, and, more importantly, tied to an administrative position.

Tutankhamun and royal literacy

The boy king, who became a household name in modern times, probably reigned for about a decade until his death at the age of eighteen after which his name was quickly omitted from history.[23] His tomb contained great riches jammed into three small spaces and an even smaller annex. Along with his elder sister's palette, the tomb contained other writing equipment such as a penholder made of gilded wood and inlaid with obsidian, carnelian, and glass. Other objects include a papyrus burnisher of ivory, gold and linen, a gilded scribal palette and a number of slate and glass slabs made to imitate the shape of a palette and its pens, often described as ritual palettes.

Even stronger than his sisters' palettes, Tutankhamun's writing equipment begs the question of his own literacy.[24] The pens and palettes seem to suggest that Tutankhamun was indeed skilled in reading and writing. Pen and palettes appear, however, in funerary texts of ancient Egypt in relation to the service the deceased will provide to the god Thoth. Writing equipment, therefore, may have been placed in the tomb for its symbolism, with no clear relation to its owner's literacy.

Kings were literate at least according to several of their officials. Men of the elite occasionally represented in their monuments letters addressed to them by the king. The earliest of these sources appears on a façade of an Old Kingdom tomb that belong to Sennedjemib Inti, a vizier of the Fifth Dynasty.[25] The tomb owner records a letter, which, according to the lines preceding the text, was written by the king 'with his two fingers'.[26] Similarly, Usersatet, a viceroy of Nubia in the Eighteenth Dynasty commissioned a stela and placed it at Semna in Nubia.[27] He opened the inscription with the words:

> A copy of the decree, which his Majesty himself made with his hands

In both texts, royal literacy appears in the paratext rather than in the texts itself. Other texts refer to royal literacy in the main part of the text. Haremhab, the protagonist of Chapter 6, portrayed Tutankhamun in one of his scribal statues as a literate king, who emulates Thoth in his writing. It is possible that Haremhab and other officials echo in their writing such notions of literacy that were held by their sovereigns. It is noteworthy, however, that such ideas appear predominantly in non-royal texts, and were not disseminated in most royal inscriptions.

An important exception to this rule is an earlier text commissioned by Neferhotep I, a king of the Thirteenth Dynasty.[28] In his stela, he describes how he entered the House of Writing in pursuit of knowledge:

> My heart wishes seeing the ancient writings of the first primeval time of Atum,
> Unfold for me up to the temple-inventory,
> Cause
> > that I may know the god in his form, the Ennead in their forms,
> > that I may offer god's offerings [to] them
> > that [I may offer] baked goods upon [the offering-tables]
> > that [I know god] in his forms
> > > so that I may fashion it like his first state . . .
> His Majesty proceeded to the house of scrolls

When his Majesty unrolled the texts with the officials,
Then his Majesty found texts of the mansion of Osiris-Khenty-Imentiyu, lord
  of Abydos.

As he wishes to create images of the god Osiris, Neferhotep I turns to the ancient texts housed in the library. The stela proceeds to praise the skills of Neferhotep I who 'found these texts himself, which no scribe who is by his majesty could ever find'. Ramesses II and IV commissioned inscriptions in which they boast of their knowledge of texts.[29] For the most part, however, these views on the relationship between royalty and literacy are unique to the Ramesside Period. For an Eighteenth Dynasty king like Tutankhamun, these epithets were hardly the norm.

The manner in which kings of the Eighteenth Dynasty viewed literacy may further be seen in a representation of Thutmose III writing on the *Ished* tree.[30] The scene depicts the king by the tree and the god Amun-Re writing the name of the king on the tree leaves. Also other kings of the Eighteenth Dynasty employed this scene in their representations, including Thutmose I, Thutmose IV, Amenhotep III and Tutankhamun himself. A few variants of this scene also entrust writing to the hands of other gods like Thoth and Seshat. The Ished tree is holy to the sun-god Re, and serves as symbol of long life and kinship. Writing one's name on its leaves symbolizes longevity and a long reign.

Another form of writing that abounds with royalty relates to the term *gn.wt*. This is often rendered as 'annals', but it may in fact cover a large range of different genres.[31] Haremhab indeed mentions that Tutankhamun writes texts of this genre according to the example of Thoth, and Thutmose III represents himself joining Thoth in their writing in a temple at Semna. More importantly, writing one's names and deeds in the *gn.wt* is comparable to writing on the Ished tree. It symbolizes the king's proper place in history. Thutmose III portrays a scene in Semna, in which Thoth is quoted as saying: 'I shall write your name as Thutmose and set the good annals with all life and dominion, as one who acts in million of Sed-Festivals.'[32] Other kings also refer to the *gn.wt* emphasizing their knowledge of their content. When Hatshepsut praises her achievements as those which 'never had the like occurred', she notes also that they are 'not in annals of the ancestors'. As we have seen with Senenmut (Chapter 2) her courtiers were again ready to emulate the concept.

Tutankhamun's references and those of his predecessors therefore point towards a specific understanding of literacy. Literacy as reading and writing skills might not have been common among all kings, but the very question assumes it to be quite narrowly defined. Pen, palette and letter writing, which are often mentioned in discussions on royal literacy, are all that is paramount to a non-royal scribe. It is, therefore, of little surprise to find they are mostly associated with kings by the officials. When sovereigns thematized their own literacy it was often in the religious and mythological context, as appropriate to kings. In addition to these forms of writing, one should also add stelae and monumental texts that many kings boast of erecting. The identity of the carver is often left unmentioned, when the king takes credit for the commissioning and erecting of the text. Thus, Tutankhamun and other kings may be considered literate, but their literacy would be quite separate from that shared among most ancient Egyptian scribes.

Concluding remarks

The writing equipment found in the tomb of Tutankhamun has allowed us to consider the relationship between women, kings, scribes and the literacy of the first two groups. The palettes raise quite a simple question: if Tutankhamun and his sister Meritaten were arguably writing and using palettes, could they be considered scribes? The answer is quite clearly negative, as the two never bore such titles. From their evidence it seems that scribes are closely tied to the administration, in which most women took no part, and in which the kings had a very specific and separate role.

The palettes point, therefore, to a certain incongruity between literacy and scribes. This point may seem trivial, but representations of writing and its equipment are nevertheless often read as depicting scribes. This evidence from the royal tomb here calls to extend the interpretation of palettes and pens; these were employed by a variety of people, from women and kings to scribes and men of the elite.

Tutankhamun's palettes and the preceding discussion finally raised an important point regarding literacy itself. Literacy covers a wide variety of different skills ranging from the ability to decipher a few signs, or sign one's name, to the ability to write an original text. These different activities don't quite co-exist, however, as a continuum on a spectrum, as each activity might be conceptualized differently in each culture. It requires inviting into the discussion the notion of multiple literacies, which takes into account not only the skill, but also its social context.[33] With this caveat in mind, scribes and kings are both to be proclaimed literate, but each group outlines its own kind of literacy.

6

Haremhab

A statue at the Metropolitan Museum of Art in New York presents us with a small detail of great curiosity (see Fig. 6.1).[1] The close to life size statue represents Haremhab – a military leader and future king – seated on the ground, wearing regalia of a late-Eighteenth Dynasty man of the elite. He wears a wig characteristic of military men of his day and elaborate garments that mark his high status. His right hand, now broken, was once held as if about to write on the long papyrus unrolled on his lap. On his shoulder, Haremhab depicts an archaic scribal palette that has a separate penholder attached to a palette and to a small sack containing the ink pellets.

With this detail Haremhab follows the footsteps of others before him in his own playful way. Earlier patrons of so-called scribal statues of the Eighteenth Dynasty sometimes depicted a three-dimensional image of the palette, with the bag and penholder falling over on the figure's back.[2] Haremhab replaces this image with two-dimensional renderings of the icon, placing the ancient Egyptian hieroglyph 𓏞 (Gardiner Y3) on his back and shoulder.

This change may denote more than mere decorative playfulness. The archaic form of the scribal palette, which the hieroglyph shows, had already fallen out of use towards the end of the Old Kingdom, centuries before Haremhab commissioned his statue.[3] Only the ancient Egyptian script preserved its old form which continued for millennia. Haremhab may have chosen the hieroglyph to indicate that he is very well aware that the object no longer exists outside the realm of a text. By shifting to a two-dimensional representation, Haremhab may have signalled his awareness of the sign's archaism and of the power of the script in maintaining tradition. The shift to script invites us, moreover, to read the sign as a hieroglyph, which could be rendered as *sš* or *zḫꜣ.w*: 'writings', 'to write' and 'scribe'.

To fully appreciate the whole range of meanings this sign carried for Haremhab, it is essential to place it in a wider context. Haremhab makes use of this sign throughout his career: from when he served as Generalissimo and

Fig. 6.1. Haremhab's statue. © The Metropolitan Museum of Art. Gift of Mr and Mrs
V. Everit Macy 1923, 23.10.1.

Royal Scribe until he ascended the throne as the last king of the Eighteenth Dynasty.[4] Unlike most kings, who arrive on the scene already in the full guise of a sovereign, Haremhab's pre-royal career is well known from a tomb he built for himself in the Memphite necropolis and from his statues and stelae. The hieroglyph 𓏞 appears on inscriptions from both sides of his personal watershed, providing a rich context to follow the meanings he ascribes to this sign. This chapter will focus on three of these occurrences: the hieroglyph of the scribal palette in his tomb, on the statue's shoulder and on one of Haremhab's royal inscriptions.

Together, these sources highlight the rich meaning Haremhab ascribed to writing and to the role of the scribe. It is a title he hails when positioning himself in relation to the king, and one that has great religious meaning, allowing him to compare to Thoth. Finally, he does not abandon it even when he becomes king. His references, however, to the actions and to those who carry them out are not without ambiguity. Haremhab's representations open up space to problematize the two terms – scribe and writing – in a new perspective, and to rethink our usage of them. Even if they fail to provide us with clear-cut answers, they at least provide an opportunity to acquaint ourselves with one of Egypt's unique characters.

•

𓏞 on the wall: Scribal titles in the tomb of Haremhab

After the swift succession of kings following the reign of Akhenaten, Egypt finally crowned Haremhab as its new king, and he immediately set out to restore order to the land.[5] He compiled decrees of law and refurbished neglected cult centres. Most importantly, he chose his next successors who brought a period of prosperity to Egypt. Haremhab himself was no son of a king, but rather a high official with a long and successful career in the military and in the administration.

Before ascending the throne, Haremhab had built himself a tomb in the New Kingdom necropolis in Saqqara, in the vicinity of the imposing monuments of Egypt's past: the Step Mastaba of Djoser (2670–2650 BC) and the Pyramid of Unas (2375–2345 BC). Though of a lesser scale, Haremhab's tomb did not lack much in grandeur. The tomb was buried under the sand until relatively recently, when a British-Dutch team to Saqqara hit upon it early on in their excavations.[6] The excavations revealed a massive structure, which was erected with a number of pylons, courtyards and chapels. The structure was built with mud brick, but cased and paved with limestone. The walls of the structure and its columns were decorated with finely carved reliefs portraying various scenes that relate to Haremhab's career in the military, to his service to the king, and his piety towards the gods.

With its grandiose architecture, the Memphite tomb of Haremhab was one of the most impressive monuments in the New Kingdom necropolis. A massive mud-brick pylon greeted visitors at the entrance to the tomb as they passed through a central limestone doorway. The bright stone was used extensively throughout the tomb to pave the rooms and courtyard and to case most of the walls. The First Pylon led visitors into a vast forecourt, which extended west towards the Second Pylon. Through this gateway, visitors entered a partially roofed courtyard, whose roof rested on twenty-four papyri form columns, which towered more than three metres high. Further to the west, two magazines flanked a room that housed statues representing Haremhab alone or seated with his wife.

On leaving the statue-room, the doorway opens to the Second Courtyard, whose roof lay lower and whose columns only reached to the height of two metres. A burial shaft in this area led to an underground complex of chambers, intended for Haremhab and his wife. Through this courtyard, three cult chapels were approached, whose floors was higher than that of the courtyards. The tomb most probably borrowed the architectural device of gradually diminishing spaces from ancient Egyptian temples, which comprised a gradual series of grandiose and then more intimate and secluded areas. Evoking this divine architecture, the tomb could conjure a sensation that visitors would recognize from visiting other sacred sanctuaries.

Work on the begun had not begin, with this plan in mind. At least four building phases are evident in the architecture of the structure. In its original plan, the tomb resembled the architecture of other tombs of the Memphite necropolis. The tomb of Ramose, for example, which lies to the north of Haremhab's tomb comprises two courtyards and three cult chapels, following a plan that resembles Haremhab's westernmost sections. As Haremhab advanced through the ranks, a statue room was created and another courtyard was added to the east, demarcated by the Second Pylon. Even after Haremhab ascended the throne and began constructing a royal tomb in the Valley of the Kings, his Memphite tomb was not deserted and a final forecourt and another pylon were added. Thus, Haremhab's rise from general and official to king left its trace on the developing architecture of the tomb, attesting to the gradual growth in power and status.

Along with the aggrandizement of the tomb, its walls and columns were progressively decorated with images and texts. Scenes in the First Courtyard depict Haremhab participating in a cultic activity and similar exhibitions of piety, in which Haremhab presents his adoration of Ptah, Sakhmet, and other gods, appear throughout the tomb.[7] Other scenes tell of Haremhab's service to the king, who reciprocates with gifts of gold, acknowledging Haremhab's accomplishments with Egypt's highest distinction of that time. His military achievements are portrayed in the Second Courtyard, depicting him surveying ranks of captives in the aftermath of successful military campaigns.

Haremhab's figure appears on almost every column, doorjamb and relief, and if not in image, then in name. When mentioned, Haremhab's name is preceded by titles and epithets, often three or four appearing together, out of a repertoire of about ninety different variants that appear in the tomb. Some refer to Haremhab's relationship to the king, like *smr wᶜ.tj*, 'Sole Companion (of the king)'; others relate to the general administration, like *ḥr.j-tp m tʒ r-ḏr=f*, 'Chief in the Entire Land' and to Haremhab's service to the gods, like *jm.j-r' pr n jmn-rᶜ*, 'Steward of the Domain of Amun-Re'.

Not all titles are made equal, and Haremhab's sacerdotal duties are hardly referred to in the tomb; in contrast, the title *jr.j-pᶜ.t*, Hereditary Prince, appears in almost every mention of Haremhab's name; it occasionally appears as his sole designation, especially when he is mentioned in titles of his subordinates. The following two most prominent titles—*jm.j-r' mšᶜ wr*, 'Generalissimo', and *zḫʒ.w nswt mʒᶜ mr(.y)=f*, 'True Royal Scribe, His Beloved' – refer to his scribal duties and to his service in the military. The two accompany Haremhab's image in focal points in the tomb: on walls that welcome the visitor as he enters, on columns, on doorjambs and surrounding Haremhab's statues in the tomb.

With these titles and especially the latter, Haremhab's tomb presents a puzzling disparity between text and image, which is common to most ancient Egyptian tombs.[8] Scribes and writing abound in the decoration of the tomb, which depicts them in the preparation of a banquet or in the aftermath of war. Despite the common textual reference to Haremhab as a scribe, none of the images depict him as writing. Instead, a few scenes depict a man standing behind him holding a scribal palette. The accompanying inscriptions describe him as Haremhab's military scribe. Haremhab seemingly delegated writing to his subordinate, albeit seeing himself as the scribe of the king.

We do not yet fully understand this disparity. After all, we still only partially understand the manner in which ancient Egyptian epithets and titles function.[9] Only rarely could we clearly say which titles were held permanently and which were held temporarily in different parts of the career. The material does not often allow us to easily translate such ancient Egyptian terms of hierarchy, when idioms and expressions do not map exactly to our language. These difficulties appear most prominent in the usage of scribal titles, which perhaps should be translated, as Quirke has suggested, as secretary, allowing it to denote the true range of the term, which extends from the office secretary to the secretary of state.

In addition, we could ask how central writing was to the work of the scribe. The sign itself is clearly an equipment of literacy – archaic as it may be – and very often tomb decoration ascribe scribal titles to men who are writing lists or forming accounts.[10] However, the realistic feel of these scenes of everyday life – the manner in which they easily lend themselves to be interpreted as true to life depictions of events and customs – often hinders the appreciation of their complexity.[11] Like other scenes in the tomb, they are highly selective in their iconography and are ideologically motivated. Among other functions, these images are invested in depicting an administration organized and in full control of the economic system.[12] What the true nature of the Eighteenth Dynasty administration was still merits further investigation. Similarly, it calls into question the nature of literacy required to be a scribe, and which of the wide range of literate activities was central to it.

A stela in Haremhab's tomb points at one way to go about it. The stela, which once stood in the First Courtyard of the tomb is now in the British Museum (BM EA 551).[13] In the lunette at the top, Haremhab raises his hands in adoration to three gods who stand before him: Rahorakhety, Thoth and Maat. Each of the three gods receives a hymn in the text below in the order of their appearance. Haremhab is mentioned with his titles at the beginning of each hymn and in the lunette, and all but one hymn neglect to mention his scribal titles. It is in the hymn to Thoth, that Haremhab refers to his role as a scribe, saying:

> The hereditary prince Haremhab, he says:
> I adore you, since your beauty is in my eyes and your rays shine upon my
> breast.
> I present truth to your majesty daily.
> Adoration to you, Thoth, Lord of Hermopolis, who brought himself into being
> who was not born, unique god, leader of the Netherworld,
> who gives instructions to Westerners who are in the following of Re
> who distinguishes the tongue of every foreign country
> may you cause the Royal Scribe Haremhab to stand firmly by the side of the
> sovereign as you were at the side of the lord of the universe
> as you fostered him when he came forth from the womb

The hymn is remarkable and rich with intriguing phrases. The interest in the languages of the world appears, for example, earlier in the Amarna period, but the distribution of this phraseology is otherwise quite limited. More to the point, however, Haremhab asks the god Thoth to place him before the king like Thoth stands before the Lord-of-All. The mention here of his role as scribe is of note, since Thoth is considered the divine scribe. Haremhab thereby positions his own activities as comparable to divine and cosmological events. It would be missing the point to describe these scribal activities as inherently inferior or insignificant. Rather, it suggests reading Haremhab's understanding of the title scribe as a relational attribute, placing one in affinity with his sovereign. Another idea of writing appears on the statue of Haremhab at the Metropolitan Museum of Art.

𓏞 on the shoulder: Haremhab's scribal statues

The writing statue of Haremhab was probably not the first he commissioned in this form. A similar statue was found at the end of the nineteenth century at Karnak, showing Haremhab seated with his legs crossed and unrolling a papyrus across his knees.[14] The statue is badly damaged, missing its head and torso, as well as parts of its base and papyrus. Though fragmentary, the text on the scroll clearly sings praise to Tutankhamun and mentions a title, Overseer of Works, which was possibly held by Haremhab earlier in his career.

The term, scribal statues – statues that represent their owners seated on the ground with a papyrus – with which these statues came to be known in the Egyptological world is often misleading.[15] More often than not, Egyptological discussions of these statues reveal our own biases regarding writing and literacy in the ancient as well as in the modern world. First, the term was often taken to include all crossed-legged statues, whether holding a papyrus or not. Complicating the matter even further, the modern discussion often conflates the literate with the scribe. Until the middle of the Eighteenth Dynasty, a large number of statues show their owners reading rather than writing. The two textual activities are very distinct and bear divergent connotations in ancient Egypt. Moreover, since the ancient Egyptian *zḫꜣ.w* often appears as a title, describing the statues as scribal often runs the risk of placing them in a strictly professional sphere. Interestingly, Haremhab's hieroglyph on the statue's shoulder does not quite resolve this ambiguity, as it could be read as both the verb 'to write,' as well as the nouns 'writer' and 'scribe.'

By Haremhab's time, the icon of the cross-legged man with a scroll had already been circulating for over a millennium. The first statue known to employ this form depicts Kawab, the eldest son of Khufu (*c.* 2589–2566 BC), the Fourth Dynasty king who built the Great Pyramid at Giza.[16] This form was further emulated by Egypt's prominent figures in later periods. Mentuhotep, a vizier, who served under Senwosret I (*c.* 1971–1926 BC), commissioned at least four scribal statues.[17] Centuries later, highly influential officials in the court of Amenhotep III commissioned similar statues.[18] Adopting this statuary motif, Haremhab associates himself with this elite group of great officials.

Throughout their history, the main features of these statues remain unchanged, but subtle developments in the form of the statue indicate significant changes in its interpretation during the New Kingdom.[19] As mentioned earlier, from its first examples, patrons of such statues represent themselves either reading or writing. No clear distinctions can be drawn between the two gestures during the Old and Middle Kingdoms. With the New Kingdom, statue owners like Haremhab began to favour writing over reading. From the reign of Amenhotep III onwards, every six out of seven statues appear as writing. The increasing attention to writing and to the writer corresponds to similar developments in textual practices of that time. Colophons – the concluding lines of a manuscript bearing information regarding its production – mostly refer in the Middle Kingdom to the completion of the text and to the accuracy of its copy. In contrast, New Kingdom manuscripts often focus on the copyist of the text himself (q.v. Inena). Colophons and statues thus indicate a growing awareness to the importance of literacy and to the prominence of the act of writing.

Both of Haremhab's statues articulate an unprecedented claim regarding authorship. Similar statues inscribed with hymns often showed their owners reading-reciting them. Others wrote laws and regulations. In contrast, Haremhab shows himself as the writer of the hymns inscribed on his papyrus. The text on his statue that is now at the Metropolitan Museum of Art in New York begins with the lines:

> Adoring Thoth, son of Re, the moon, beautiful of processions, great of appearances, who enlightens the gods by the nobleman, the mayor, fan-bearer on the king's right, the commander-in-chief and royal scribe Haremhab, true of voice.

The title of the papyrus, 'Adoring Thoth', adequately describes the hymn that follows it. The title furthermore corresponds with the image of the statue, which represents Haremhab writing a hymn to Thoth. The image of Haremhab adoring through text provides a new reflection on the nature of texts and on the act of their production. Haremhab's statue may suggest that writing itself is a performative act that is equally as powerful as reciting a hymn.

𓏞 on the stela: Haremhab's writing laws

Finally, when Haremhab ascended the throne, he did not abandon the sign of the scribal palette. As he sought to establish order in the land and dispel crime and injustice, he evoked its image in a decree of laws that prescribe severe punishment for acts of corruption and exploitation of power.[20] In the prologue to the edict, Haremhab alludes to the importance of scribes and of the act of writing itself.

The text is known from two copies, one found at the temple of Amun at Karnak, and the other is said to be from Abydos.[21] The latter is badly broken, comprising only fragmentary lines of text. The former, which is still in situ suffered great damage, leaving not even one line complete. When it was complete it probably measured three metres wide at the base and reached a height of five metres. It must have been a text of monumental scale intended to leave an immense impression on its viewer.

Haremhab's decree sets out to prevent corruption and abuse of power. The text defines certain acts as illegal and prescribes severe punishments to each. The laws include, for example, penalties against men who interfere with the delivery of dues to the Pharaoh or of divine offerings. Other laws prevent officials and military men from abusing their power and authority by extorting men of lower ranks. The punishment often involves cutting the nose of the criminal and sending him to Tjaru, a fortress on the eastern border of Egypt. The final part of the stela proceeds to reorganize the judicial system and setting courts (*knb.t*). Those who serve on these tribunals are also warned about taking bribes or even associating themselves with men of power who might influence their verdicts.

The hieroglyph of the scribal palette appears in the first lines of the text, which comprise its introduction. The text reads like a *Königsnovelle*, a common narrative genre in ancient Egyptian royal inscriptions, which describes the king as the protagonist of the ensuing decision-making process or as the recipient of divine inspiration. The decree portrays Haremhab as he is contemplating what would be beneficial for Egypt. It is here that Haremhab incorporates an interesting reference to writing:

> . . . his Majesty.
> Then he took the palette and the document
> Then he made in writing,
> > like everything that his Majesty said.

The passage is seemingly redundant in the flow of the text, as the decree of the king is assumed to be the main point of interest. Moreover, the writing down of decrees is rather uncharacteristic of royal inscriptions. Here, however, Haremhab refers not only to the act of writing, but also to the writing equipment itself – the scribal palette. Haremhab, thus, does not merely write about 'writing'. He visualizes in the text the practice of writing itself.

This writing is placed within the context of the law. The prevalence of written laws in Egypt is still very much debated.[22] Yet, establishing laws already appears a textual activity in the Middle Kingdom, when owners of scribal statues often inscribed the papyrus on the statue's lap with texts that interpret writing as giving law. Similarly, Haremhab emphasizes this important relationship between the two in his decree of laws, as he says with regards to the *knb.t* courts: 'Before them I gave regulations and laws in their daybooks.' The stela thus adds the realm of the law as another context in which writing and scribes are of importance.

Concluding remarks

The hieroglyph of the scribe accompanies the career of Haremhab from military and civil life to the throne. Haremhab offers a very expansive interpretation of the roles of the scribe and that, which pertain to writing – it is an office, but also of a matter of piety; it places one in relation to the king, but also relates one to justice and law.

Despite the richness of material, the case of Haremhab remains ambiguous. When his scribal title and paraphernalia appear in the tomb, its cotext of epithets and titles seems to anchor it within the administrative realm. Its occurrences, nevertheless, call into question the true nature and scope of responsibilities given to a Royal Scribe like Haremhab. When it is featured on his statue's shoulder, its translations range from a profession or a title to the action itself, neither of which are easily distinguishable.

Having ascended the throne, Haremhab acquired a position of great power. Like his sovereign, the vizier Paramessu commissioned scribal statues for himself and placed them in Karnak before he himself ascended the throne as Ramesses I, the first king of the Ramesside Period. It is thus of little surprise that the period which began with these two kings, Haremhab and Ramesses I, boasted of a very rich scribal culture.

7

Dedia

In the preceding chapters, we saw dignitaries carving their place in history, including a historiographer memorializing his sovereign and a king codifying law in written word. In this chapter, we return to explore the nexus between scribes and artists through one specific literate artist, entrusted with the particular task of reshaping the memory of events that happened in the past.

The reign of Menmaatre Seti I was an era when New Kingdom Egypt was finding some of its roots again. That was, in any case, the king's proposed ambition. Like his predecessors Tutankhamun, Haremhab and Ramesses I, Seti was interested in returning an established order of things in the wake of a disquieting time.[1] This was the reign of Amenhotep IV, Akhenaten, who became, the 'enemy from Akhetaten' (modern Amarna), and disappeared from king-lists, monuments and – as was intended, but not entirely achieved – from memory. An entire era was to be misremembered and reinterpreted, but not integrated into the official cultural memory.[2]

The effort to erase the memory of this period and its rulers quickly became tangible. Following Amarna's demise, royal names were removed, monuments dismantled, statues destroyed. In part, this *damnatio* resembles the actions carried out by Akhenaten and his followers, in their attack primarily directed against Theban gods, such as Amun and Mut, erasing their names and mutilating their figures.

Along with destruction, restoration was also needed. Reversing the effect of Akhenaten's attacks, names of gods once removed were to be firmly re-established. Indeed, in many ways they had never left, and even in Amarna, workmen and artists still venerated deities that were ruling their world and assuring their afterlife.[3] Nevertheless, resuming worship throughout the land required tremendous efforts, or so the royal inscriptions tell us. Among Akhenaten's successors, Seti I was conspicuously productive in the restoration effort, giving it consistent publicity,[4] which encompassed visual and written culture.

At the forefront of these projects were workmen and artists tasked with rebuilding the kingdom's traditional identity. Artists and craftsmen wielded the tools that carved, sculpted, drew and painted the walls of devotional and funerary monuments. They each had practical training in a number of different skills, from planning a statue in a block of stone, to composing a relief scene, to cutting the stone, to polishing it; applying polychromy was highly complex. Select artists also had to know hieroglyphs, as opposed to an administrator or accountant scribe, who operated with hieratic script. Their skills were critical to restoring the damaged monuments and to rewriting the hacked-out gods' names.

A story of one of Seti's memory makers, Dedia, the chief draughtsman of Amun, is at the centre of this chapter. Dedia lived through times of change and probably served Haremhab,[5] Ramesses I and Seti I in a prominent position of Overseer of Works and Superintendent of Craftsmen, i.e. he stood at the helm of a team of 'monuments men' in Thebes. The 'monuments men' in question titled themselves craftsmen and draughtsmen, but probably also scribes for short,[6] and as a social group they were rather diverse. Our protagonist Dedia was most likely a literate man as well as one proud of his heritage and ability as a craftsman, and aware of his unique role in the shaping of Egyptian cultural identity.

Artists in ancient Egypt

Much has been written about artists in ancient Egypt, and more still awaits to be written. In the following few paragraphs, we hope to highlight some of the aspects of the lives and works of ancient Egyptians like Dedia.

Texts as well as complex scenes had to be composed and arranged in the correct order on the walls or statue surfaces, colours chosen and also applied following defined guidelines. The use of colours alone was like a complex code. Not only did one colour stand for a complex of meanings, such as green for revival and youth, freshness, papyrus plant; red for life, blood, warmth, significance, but also chaos, and so on, but select colours were also grouped. It is more precise to speak of *deshret*, an Egyptian term often translated as 'red', as of a group of warm colours 'focalized in red'.[7] The terminology used for colours had a limited vocabulary (in fact, four colour groups centred around white, black, red and blue/green), whilst the practical application was immense – on occasion delivering a very naturalistic portrait (e.g. of birds or plants), but often conveying an ideal description of a category of beings, plants or objects – plus, one aim did not exclude the other. The New Kingdom colour palette was among the richest[8] in the history of Egyptian art (before classical antiquity) and the painter or sculptor applying the polychromy required a range of technical knowledge, actual painting skills, as well as an understanding of the symbolic coding on a large scale. From practical skills to planning, the craftsman and artist were among the most complex jobs in ancient Egypt. In addition, each commission – royal, non-royal, temple or tomb – must have had its requirements which were directed in theory by the king and practically by overseers of royal works, the vizier and other dignitaries who were entrusted with the building of the façade of kingship, either directly in the area of monumental edifices (like Senenmut, q.v.), or via composition, selection and pertinent use of texts that were applied on the walls (Tjanuni, q.v., and a dignitary turned King, Haremhab, q.v.).

Often, the artists were in much closer contact with these executive echelons of the Egyptian state[9] than one might at a first glance expect to be the case for artists, let alone artisans or craftsmen; some of the Egyptian master craftsmen and painters thus resembled somewhat the state-sponsored efforts of Le Vau and Le Nôtre, who were in the inner circle of Louis XIV and his 'image makers'. A number of masters of the art are known by name, although the concept of an artist's signature or indeed individual authorship in a modern interpretation was not applied in Egypt. Nonetheless, a sense of pride in one's artistic achievements – and, more clearly – a sense of importance of one's works stands out in biographical texts of the artists, especially top ranking echelons. The texts often encapsulate the role of the literate artist as a memory maker in very specific terms.

From a Middle Kingdom sculptor Irtisen to the Ramesside sculptor Userhat, artists asserted technical skill as well as privileged knowledge of human and divine appearances. The Middle Kingdom stela of Irtisen[10] suggests strongly that knowledge of hieroglyphs as well as practical knowledge of how to draw different human figures and capture different themes (from distinguished dignitaries to prisoners of war) were key to the craft (and a playful rendering of Irtisen's palette with brushes of a draughtsman perhaps underlined the message[11]). The craft itself gave access to the elite standing and to memory making: 'I know the secrets of hieroglyphs [. . .] for I was an artisan excellent in his art, who advanced to the top by means of what he had learned.'[12] Closer to Dedia's time, the well-known Amarna period sculptor (*sꜥnḫ*) Bak[13] has claimed that he was taught in the new art style by the king (i.e. Amenhotep IV/Akhenaten) himself. Dedia's near contemporary sculptor Userhat 'saw Re in his transformations, and Atum in his manifestations'.[14]

However, artists and craftsmen, from head sculptors to chisellers and apprentices, possessed a wide range of skills. A broad professional range of artists and artisans was employed by the royal workshops, the temples and also by private patrons. They also probably formed diverse professional groups or communities. The well-known community of royal workmen linked to the Theban site of Deir el-Medina is just one example, and not necessarily a universally applicable model of such professional group.[15] There were also other workmen in service of wealthy non-royal tomb builders or of Theban or Memphite temples and elsewhere. What all these professional groups shared, however, were craft skills – work with stone, plaster and pigments – and probably, although to an unknown degree, literacy skills.

History and memory writing

Writing, drawing and chiselling were essential skills in the two-sided remodelling of memory of Egypt under Seti I as had to be both erased and recreated written memories. Names of Akhenaten came down, while those of the gods (and consequently also mortals with names containing divine appellations) he had suppressed went back up, not just on the walls of temples and tombs, both royal and non-royal, but, in the memory of the literate elite, and consequently, the cultural memory of Egypt.[16]

To understand the scale of this effort, we first need to realize where Akhenaten's teams of memory erasers went. Akhenaten's workmen, tasked with the destruction of divine names, went to the divine temples of Thebes, memorial temples in Western Thebes (including both Mentuhotep and Hatshepsut at Deir el-Bahri). Their work exceeded the obvious temple walls; they also visited royal tombs, non-royal burial places (probably including Senenmut, q.v.) and stelae, even partially abandoned temples of sovereigns who had been deceased for several centuries, such as Senwosret III at Dahshur, or Mentuhotep II at Deir el-Bahari. Amun was under attack almost constantly throughout Egypt, as were other deities (his consort Mut, the Memphite patron Ptah, ruler of the netherworld Osiris) but much less frequently. The erasures within Theban precincts were often among the most thorough, perhaps because this was Amun's stronghold – and the royal eye was probably most watchful close to his residence.[17] It was a widespread, if not necessarily consistent, attempt to change a state's ideology, including its past.

In the three decades that followed the end of Akhenaten's reign, Tutankhamun and his successors,[18] Ay and Haremhab, restored a large number of vandalized texts and figures. Each sovereign added his own element to the restoration effort and publicized it accordingly in his inscriptions. Tutankhamun used a classical theme of abandoned shrines[19] and gods that consequently have abandoned Egypt; Haremhab took over his rhetoric and expanded it.

Haremhab might have also taken over work already started under his predecessors, whose memory *he* then started to alter.[20] Haremhab also ordered the stone blocks in Amarna to be re-used,[21] and thus compounded the re-establishment of the previous cultural framework with an attack against the offending presence of the 'enemy from Akhetaten'.

It was Seti I, 'however, who is perhaps best known as a restorer of vandalized reliefs because he frequently marked these repairs with a *smȝwy-mnw* formula', i.e. literally saying that he renewed the monuments,[22] something other post-Amarna rulers did not do so explicitly. Seti I also located his restoration inscriptions in prominent locations – gateways, façades and so on. It is somewhat unlikely that the number of restorations under Seti I would actually correspond to the conspicuous character of his restoration inscriptions. He may well have usurped the restoration efforts of his predecessors and relabelled the works to suit his own commemoration enterprise.[23] Also, whatever the actual extent of damage, Seti was keen to leave a large restoration imprint, since the restoration effort was not only to mark the return of Amun but was also aimed at enhancing the memory of Seti and his dynasty.[24] In part, the reworkings linked Seti to great kings of the past, in Speos Artemidos, in Karnak or in Western Thebes, as shown above, or on the monuments in Nubia. One king whose monuments were often restored with much care was Thutmose III,[25] another was Amenhophis III.

To reverse Akhenaten's undertaking and make the new royal enterprise successful, men like Dedia were crucial. In the context of reviving the national memory, Dedia was a man interested in his own past; this proved very helpful in restoring him to memory and history. But only just – despite a formidable number of monuments connected with his name (including his deliberate personal commemoration), his stelae and a statue were quite overlooked, i.e. including within Egyptology. He may be seen as a prime example of history that is extant, but passes unseen. An early study of his monuments was only carried out in the 1970s.[26] Fortunately, since then he has become part of Egyptological studies[27] on a more regular basis, although he has not captured as much attention as the Amarna 17 age artists such as Thutmose or Bak.

The memory maker

The chief draughtsman of Amun, Dedia left several commemorative monuments[28] set originally in different locations. An eye-catching monument is the two-sided Stela Louvre C 50. It shows Dedia and his family, both in visual and written representation, venerating a number of deities including the Abydene triad of Osiris, Isis and Horus, and the kings of the Eighteenth Dynasty, Thutmose III and Amenhotep I, and Queen Ahmose Nefertari. The provenance of this stela is unknown, but the formulae addressed to Abydene gods as well as the Abydos triad suggests that it might have been Abydos itself. The presence of Amenhotep I and Ahmose Nefertari, however, would point towards a Theban connection. Whether this signified a Theban location intended for the stela, Theban production[29] or simply a Theban residence and professional scope of Dedia's family, is a moot point.

The stela contains an offering formula securing a good and well-provided afterlife for Dedia. The text part also comprises an historical section, which shows the genealogy of a family of draughtsmen reaching back seven generations. Dedia was the son of Hatia, also a chief draughtsman. He offers to his father and to his forefathers Turi, Simut, Ptahhotep, Atuwa and Patabaal. Turi was the father of Hatia, and son of Simut, who was the son of Ptahhotep, son of Atuwa, who was the son of Patabaal. All men were titled as head draughtsmen of Amun. Their wives, titled 'Ladies of the House', i.e. heads of the household,[30] were included in the memorial. Interestingly, as shown above, a number of men and women had non-Egyptian names, identified as of Semitic and possibly also Hurrian origin.[31]

The family history as represented here thus stretches back to the mid-Eighteenth Dynasty, possibly to the reign of Thutmose III.[32] Given the foreign names, perhaps Dedia was a scion of Asiatic immigrants who came to Egypt or were brought there as prisoners of war during the reign of Thutmose III. Given the extensive campaigning of this king, it is a plausible option. It would also explain the veneration of Thutmose III by Dedia, especially if, eventually, the coming to Egypt was perceived as a positive element ushering in a proud chapter in the family history: a privileged draughtsmen of Amun.

However, it would be inappropriate to classify the family as foreigners in Dedia's time, because the entire family, at least as presented on the monuments of Dedia, adhered to the Egyptian cultural canon. The written message communicated by the stela was that of firm roots in the sphere of *sš.w ḳdw.t*, 'draughtsmen' and in the service of Theban Amun.

Stela BM 706[33] is another monument of Dedia, this time with a known provenance from the temple of Mentuhotep Nebhepetre from Deir el-Bahri. The provenance of the stela is of considerable interest. Locating statues and using other commemorative strategies in the memorial temples of past kings was a practice well attested for the New Kingdom. Statues and stelae in New Kingdom temples frequently used to commemorate important people, who thus participated in the sacred space of the temple and its prestige and connectivity to the divine sphere;[34] however, the memorial temples of past kings might have been more accessible to certain social groups.

Possibly some of the visitors' graffiti (as discussed in Chapter 6, Amenemhat) might have been part of a strategy of re-appropriation of and participation in the functions of the sacred space of a royal mortuary establishment. Dedia thus located his own monuments both in a divine temple of a major deity of his time (see above stela C 50), and in the memorial precinct of an important ruler of the past. It was apparently an effective strategy for one's own commemoration and hence survival.

Appropriately, the stela BM 706 (as well as the probable Abydene C 50) was inscribed with a Call to the Living, addressed both to priestly personnel and to scribes 'skilled in writing' – the scribes were specifically mentioned on the Deir el-Bahri stela. A person skilled in writing might read not only administrative texts but also tomb and temple hieroglyphic texts. Some Calls also identify that the audience was supposed to be knowledgeable in 'god's words' – another specification of hieroglyphic texts.

The 'scribes skilled in writing' appear again as visitors in the visitors' graffiti in the west of Thebes, including the Deir el-Bahri area of complex of temples. The implication probably was that these were literate men with capabilities exceeding the standard training of an office apprentice. Were they meant to include highly qualified literate draughtsmen? Were they an intended audience of Dedia? If so, was Dedia a literate man himself, knowledgeable in both hieroglyphs and hieratic? It would appear probable.

There is no doubt about the relatively high social status Dedia and his family achieved, quite in line with other artists of the New Kingdom, such as Thutmose (of Memphis fame[35]), Nebamun and Ipuky (who shared a magnificently decorated tomb TT 181 in Thebes) or indeed some top Deir el-Medina artists. Thutmose of Memphis – possibly like Dedia – enjoyed a 'double social status, that of a dignitary and a royal artist'.[36] The sculptor Userhat, mentioned above, specified that 'the Lord of the Two Lands knew me, and I was greatly esteemed in his heart'.[37]

The very fact that Dedia was allowed to locate a monument in a major temple precinct was a favour allowed by the temple personnel and – quite probably – sanctioned by the king himself. The Temple of Nebhepetre Mentuhotep, however, was a temple of the past that Dedia may also have visited out of curiosity – after all, he was an artist, and we are repeatedly coming across hints about the important role the material study of the past played in the training and education of Egyptian craftsmen and artists.

The privilege of locating one's monument in an important temple was to be compounded by another monument. Dedia had placed another statue of his in the temple of Amun at Karnak. Statue Cairo CGC 42122 (JE 36957) was originally located in the Karnak temple precinct.[38] It is the epitome of self-presentation from Amun's chief painter. The offering formulae asks the king (Mentuhotep) Nebhepetra and Thutmose II, Amenhotep I, and Queen (Ahmose) Nefertari for the offering favours, alongside other Theban deities. Also, cartouches of Djeserkare (Amenhotep I) and Menkheperre (Thutmose III) – two great builders in the Karnak precinct – adorn the statue. Devotional aspects are combined with local knowledge in this text; both aspects are expressed in ties to locally venerated divine patrons, all of them also significant figures of Egyptian history, who were recognized as such by Egyptian annalists.[39]

An extended call to the living on the statue is addressed to priests and scribes and then again in particular to 'every scribe adept in his post, who shall read out (my) name on this statue' (note the monumental statue inscription was again in hieroglyphic script).[40] The address of the Call thus summarizes important elements of the expected commemorative outcome and stresses the importance of a specific literacy in the process. We suspect that scribes here might again include literati and qualified artists capable of reading a hieroglyphic inscription on the statue and reading it out to their audience.

The text continues with biographical information that includes a list of temples, where Dedia was professionally active: Akh-menu, Men-isut, Akh-isut, Djeser-akhet, Djeser-Djeseru, Henket-ankh.[41] The temple of Akh-menu of Thutmose III is located in the Karnak complex of Amun. The other named temples – Men-isut, originally in Dra Abu el-Naga was of Ahmose Nefertari, Akh-isut was the temple of Nebhepetre Mentuhotep, Djeser-akhet of Thutmose III, Djeder-Djeseru of course of Hatshepsut, and Henket-ankh finally of Thutmose III again (in the West Theban area)[42] – are located on the West Bank and all appear to share a commemorative mission accorded to the memorial temples or 'temples of millions of years', as they were also known.

These temples combined the cult of the king, and his divine and earthly ancestors – and Djeser-Djeseru, the memorial temple of Hatshepsut (q.v. Senenmut) provides a prime example.[43] The tradition was further to be developed in the massive Ramesside memorial temple complexes of Seti I himself (at Qurna), and Ramesses II (also known as the Ramesseum) and Ramesses III (Medinet Habu). Dedia was closely connected to the cult places of deceased kings, hence his veneration of the most respected among them. Note that the names on the temple list matches the kings on Dedia's monuments.

Tomb and statues, whether placed in a temple or in one's tomb,[44] were an important way to preserve the social memory of an elite individual and his family.[45] Some monuments bore biographical texts; others were limited to epithets and strings of titles. The written message containing one's name, titles and even brief characteristics mediated by select epithets, expanded far beyond the monumental record. This type of written message also adorned objects of everyday use.

Palette Louvre N 2274 is another witness to Dedia's work. It is a painter's palette with nine cavities for the cakes of paint and four narrow brushes in the brush holder, and bears his name and titles. Palettes such as this were status symbols. A possible near contemporary of Dedia, chief draughtsman Thutmose (owner of the tomb Bubasteion I.19)[46] is depicted holding his palette as a symbol of his office on a number of occasions within his tomb.

The text on the palette gives Dedia's name and title including the professional affiliation to Amun of Ipet-sut and of the west of Thebes, indicating once again the reach of his professional activities. The list unsurprisingly covers two major areas of interest of Seti I: the east and west bank in Thebes, where the king applied his restoration policies. Seti restored or purported to have restored a number of reliefs and texts in Karnak,[47] including obelisks of Hatshepsut, stelae of Thutmose III (e.g. CG 34011), pylons and other monuments of Dynasty Eighteen; his efforts continued in Luxor where they included the colonnade and the solar court of Amenhotep III,[48] and the Opet festival reliefs which included the work of Tutankhamun and Haremhab, i.e. reliefs that post-date Amarna. Seti, however completed the decoration schemes of the Opet festival colonnade.[49] This was more a finalization of previous kings' work than a restoration. Seti's attested traces at the West bank included the temples of Amenhotep III, and Thutmose III (stela CG 34015).[50]

Dedia's effort was the Pharaoh's wider campaign to rebuild the national memory, in which he himself was to take a prominent place. As someone responsible for the restoration and reworking of the Eastern and Western Theban temple monuments, Dedia would have been in frequent contact with monuments of the past, thus gaining a steady incentive for his own historical awareness.[51]

Workmen in Dedia's service

Dedia almost certainly had a number of men at his command. Many of these might have been stonemasons, some of them draughtsmen, others painters – in short, artists with qualifications close to his own. We tend to assume there would have been many well-qualified workmen in the Egyptian capitals of the New Kingdom, because of the well-built edifices, decorated temples, palaces and tomb walls, of which we know only a few have survived.

Who were these people? What social position did they occupy and where did they live? The royal tomb builders' settlement is the best-attested location and is known as the village of Deir el-Medina. Dedia, a painter from Amun, might have been entirely unconnected to the village proper, but when trying to understand the life and profession of men like himself and his workers, the village is an indispensable model.

In the study of the Egyptian everyday life, the village known as Deir el-Medina is a household name. Almost every treatise on the New Kingdom or on the life of ancient Egyptians, includes some reference to it. Deir el-Medina is, in many respects, unique. It is wedged into the West Theban cliffs, and its inhabitants were privileged workmen building the Valley of the Kings and Queens. The state was their main employer and, despite the fact that it was described as a 'village' in Egyptology, it operated more like a guarded compound inhabited by a specialist workforce.

The village was clearly set apart from other settlements, despite the logistical demands its seclusion placed on the transport of water (there was no well), wood (for fires) and victuals. It was walled and supervised. Although it is not likely that the villagers would have been entirely isolated – they communicated with their relatives and had property outside the village – there was probably a degree of control over them and their families' movements.[52] This control could have served both as the workmen's security and state control – they had knowledge of a state secret – the location of the royal tomb. One of the first architects of the Valley of the Kings, Ineni, stressed in his biography that he responsibly discharged his task of designing and building the tomb of his king,

Thutmose I, suggesting that keeping the location secret from the public was quite important.

The work on the tomb was complex – first the heavy stonemasons' drudgery of cutting and tunnelling in bedrock, then the finer jobs of carving and smoothing the walls and architectural elements, and finally the decoration of tomb walls and ceilings. The teams followed one after the other or perhaps one and the same person might have had more than one specialization. They prepared their own plaster and lamps.[53] Ostraca from the Valley[54] denote heavy toil with hammers and chisels eating the rock wall, as well as scaffolding used inside the unfinished tombs to make and decorate the exquisite walls. Polychrome relief or paint was used, depending on the quality of the bedrock and possibly also other individual decisions.

The workmen's life is – despite many exceptions – often assumed to be a representative example of the Egyptian life of the New Kingdom. But royal workmen – in this case also builders of the royal tomb – were a privileged community living in exceptional circumstances. They were a community of highly valued workmen with many special skills ordinary villagers working in the fields would have no chance of having. One such skill might have been literacy, but here Deir el-Medina gives a more complex picture than expected.[55]

The village was founded probably in the early Eighteenth Dynasty and its community then seems to have corresponded more to the image of painters and stonemasons; no extensive written corpus seems to have survived, although various Eighteenth Dynasty ostraca have survived from other locations in Western Thebes. It would appear that the royal tomb builders were specialists in their own world. They had, however, their non-royal counterparts – people who built exclusively decorated non-royal tombs in Western Thebes. These workmen, although their work was more complex even than that of their royal counterparts, are elusive. Workers from outside Deir el-Medina appeared at first in random finds, such as texts from Deir el-Bahri preserved on ostraca and documenting the building progress, tasks and deliveries of material at the tomb of Senenmut. However, literary texts found in the area suggest these workers had wider interests and qualifications – they were undoubtedly readers. They read classics of Egyptian literature of their time, such as the story of Sinuhe and the instructions (or wisdom) texts. Traces of their training tools survive on apprentice boards from the Eighteenth Dynasty.[56] An example from Dra Abu el-Naga shows training in drawing as well as writing skills. Here we focus on the draughtsman, but the connection between an artist's training and a degree of literacy on this board is unmistakable (see also Chapter 8, Inena).

The Dra Abu el-Naga board has drawings of two royal statues, drawn en face and several columns of the didactic text *Kemyt* (q.v. Inena). The editor of the artefact, José Galán, pointed out that one of the statue drawings was done with a confident hand, whereas the other corresponds to an apprentice's copy made with less confident and less graceful brushstrokes. Both the copied drawing and the copied text underline the connection of the piece with training.

These workmen – for instance builders of the tombs of Senenmut[57] – also liked to title themselves 'scribes' instead of their full title outline scribes, i.e. draughtsmen, perhaps with the aim of suggesting their training in writing and reading skills. Another hint of a professional artist and an educated man of letters in one person of Dynasty Eighteen is given in the story of Paheri (q.v.). He too embodies the confluence of a scribe and an artist.

It would appear, then, that the elusive non-royal workforce offered a more nuanced and complex picture of an at least partially literate community, whereas the Dynasty Eighteen Deir el-Medina appears comparably mute. But the picture was set to change significantly at the end of Dynasty Eighteen. Under the Amarna kings, the village was probably abandoned. The new settlement(s) of workers in Akhetaten do not appear to have been direct heirs to Deir el-Medina. Some workmen might have left not for Amarna, but for Memphis, another capital city, the necropolis of which lived through a boom in the Amarna period.

The Memphite necropolis boasts a beautifully decorated tomb of Thutmose, as mentioned above, a *zẖ3.w ḳdw.t*, outline scribe (draughtsman), whose family members, were also defined as outline scribes. The tomb decoration is very fine and invites questions if it was also a family work. The high quality of the artwork inspired some thoughts that the man might have been the artist of Akhenaten, who is supposed to be the maker of the bust of Nefertiti. There is indeed a studio of a sculptor in Akhetaten (supposedly Thutmose) but the identification of the two is somewhat precarious.[58] Undoubtedly, what remains is the exceptional quality of the art and social status of the Memphite Thutmose and his family. He might have been a man closer in position and ambition to Dedia than to an ordinary (but still comparably privileged) workman at Akhetaten or Deir el-Medina.

When Deir el-Medina was re-established by Akhetaten's successors, it was a different community, in terms of its relationship with writing. If the Dynasty

Eighteen left ostraca other than places Western Thebes, and graffiti in select tombs, the decoration of which seemed an applicable model; if the main ostraca and graffiti makers were temple personnel and most likely non-royal workers; if many Deir el-Medina ostraca from that time sported special signs used by royal workmen probably lacking full training in literacy, then in Dynasty Nineteen the number of ostraca and graffiti that can be traced back to the Deir el-Medina community simply seems to explode. Thousands of graffiti and tens of thousands of inscribed fragments of limestone and shards of pottery were produced by the Ramesside community of workmen.[59]

The privileged group in Deir el-Medina was probably the tip of the iceberg when it came to qualified artisans – outline scribes (draughtsmen) – who worked in temples and also for the non-royal tomb builders. Dedia's men were probably to be found among members of the larger communities outside of Deir el-Medina.

Is an outline scribe also a scribe?

Dedia himself was literally an outline scribe (draughtsman). People, who in modern terminology may be termed as draughtsmen and painters, used the title. Mostly, these were highly qualified artisans, or indeed artists. Despite a difference in understanding of what constitutes being an artist in antiquity and in modernity, the skills, specialist training and creativity of the Egyptian painter are not adequately expressed by calling him merely on artisan, let alone craftsman (for whom the Egyptian also has a different term).[60]

A *zḫ3.w ḳdw.t* (outline scribe) might have been a man of standing and authority, as was Dedia, or a member of a crew of artists who built non-royal or royal tombs. The social standing of an elite director of painters and a crew member might have been very different.[61] Yet, in both cases, though at different levels, their work consisted of the preparation and execution of complex multi-coloured decorative schemes; their training was not only in the actual making of a painting, but also consisted of learning the schemes, figures and combinations with texts. A training in Middle Egyptian classical works might have helped considerably;[62] such a craftsman was ready to line up with scribes, as opposed to workmen whose jobs were derided in the *Satire of Trades*.[63] It is even likely that some *zḫ3.w ḳdw.t* referred to themselves as *zḫ3.w*, 'scribes', either as an abbreviation, or to enhance their literacy and their cultural competence.

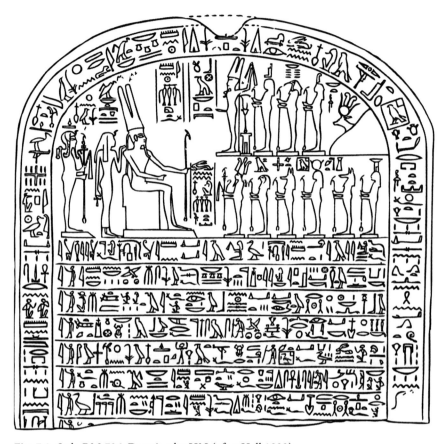

Fig. 7.1 Stela BM 706. Drawing by HN (after Hall 1922).

A man like Dedia, who uses *zḫ3.w ḳd.wt*, might be assumed to be literate, but this might have been due both to his high status, inherited within the family, or because of his profession itself. Artists of his rank might have gained access to court, even to the King's person, which shows the range of privileges.[64] His contemporary Userhat included specific references to a direct access to the royal person and privileges he was accorded as a 'humble man', who, for his capability, was selected by the king to be his director of works, pleased the king with his results and was allowed to work on the images of the gods.[65] We will never get a definitive answer to the question of percentage and the level of literacy among tomb and temple artists, although a few guesses are perhaps allowed even outside of the peculiar and privileged community of Deir el-Medina.[66] First, the background of makers (e.g. of the tomb of Senenmut) gives a few hints that at least some of the workmen there might have been literate (q.v.

Senenmut). Second, Dedia himself repeatedly refers to the ability of a scribe apt in his profession – he aimed his Calls to the Living at religious personnel as well as at scribes capable of reading the texts aloud. Whilst this might have been connected to the wish that as many visitors as possible are aware of the memory and deeds of Dedia, the call might also have been referring to the not-so-common ability to read a hieroglyphic text. After all, the monuments men had a very specific command of literacy, which differed from that of an administrator.

8

Inena

On one of the papyri from Deir el-Medina, there is a long composition of love poems. A scribe claims to have written them down: 'the beginning of sweet verses discovered in the document box and written by the Scribe of the Tomb Nakhtsobek . . .[1] A certain Nakhtsobek, who claimed to have worked in the royal necropolis, says he had copied (from a document box), perhaps even authored the texts. In any case, the name Nakhtsobek is written erasing someone else's name. He might have claimed the role of the copyist only, but even that was important enough to falsify.

What was the role of a copyist of a text? Was it allowed, or, actually, important to sign one's work, be it a copied, compiled or composed text? How were the literate men of ancient Egypt schooled, after all? How did they meet the texts that formed the basis of their cultural competence? Some of these questions may be long overdue after we have met so many literati and scribes. This chapter offers some evidence; the Ramesside compilers and copyists will be our guides.

The copyist

The Ramesside papyri carry remarkable works of literature, alongside treatises on ethics and satire.[2] Papyrus D'Orbiney[3] hosts the *Tale of Two Brothers*,[4] a story replete with religious references, and including an initial plotline, that strongly resembles that of Potiphar's wife and Joseph. The text concludes with a statement: 'It has come to a good end for the ka of the scribe of the Treasury Kageb, of the Treasury of the Pharaoh, *Iph*, for the scribe Hori and the scribe Meremipet, done by the scribe Inena, master of this manuscript.[5] Who(ever) will talk against this writing, Thoth will fight him'.[6] It almost looks like a proud signature line with a dedication, yet there is a more complicated story behind it. Among papyri and ostraca, there are others that end in a rather personal-looking line that runs approximately as follows: 'So it ends, from start to finish, as found in writing,[7] written by the scribe NN.'

Like some of his contemporaries, Inena appended his name at the end of the texts he was writing, compiling or copying on a papyrus roll, which may have been in his possession or written by him on behalf of or for someone else. His formal autograph exceeds the role of a signature line; in a manuscript, it resembles the modern imprint and copyright page in books and it is called a colophon.[8] The colophon usually denotes the end of a manuscript or its part;[9] it is not typical of monumental inscriptions, but for manuscripts only, 'less bound by place and time, and operating within the horizons of a mortal human lifespan'.[10]

It is often situated at the end of texts, which Egyptology defines as literary – i.e. texts that were neither accounts, administrative memoranda, religious texts nor specific tomb texts, but which described and embodied a cultural tradition of Egypt. The literary texts functioned, were copied and read as part of education, as part of training in Egyptian cultural values, but they were also read to be enjoyed.[11] In addition, funerary texts – whether coffin texts in the Middle Kingdom, the Book of the Dead in the New Kingdom, or later ritual texts also occasionally had a colophon.[12] The Book of the Dead had colophons at the end of specific chapters as well as at the end of the papyrus.[13]

Literary and religious texts had colophons from the Middle Kingdom onwards. Its usual Egyptian rendering, found often on papyrus rolls and occasionally on other writing surfaces, such as ostraca,[14] was '(being) from its beginning to its end as it has been found written',[15] occasionally expanded by 'it (= the book) comes well' or indeed 'in peace', followed by the name of the copyist. Consequently, the way Inena chose to conclude his manuscript was entirely proper.[16] Authorial names (or putative authors' names, as we shall see) could also appear at the beginning of the manuscript, introduced by a characteristic formula *ir n*, 'made by', but the colophon at the end of the manuscript made a different kind of attribution – attribution to the writing hand that had assured the existence and transmission of the text.[17] The colophon often also stated that the manuscript stood under the protection of Thoth and that its maker was an accomplished writer.

Inena wrote his credit line at the end of more than one papyrus – we find it at a copy of the *Satire of Trades* (a.k.a. *Instructions of Khety*) in papyrus Anastasi VII, and in papyrus Sallier II; moreover, his name is connected directly and indirectly to several other papyri[18] pigeonholed as the *Late Egyptian Miscellanies*. These texts appear on ostraca and in two large groups of papyri. There is a Memphite group including Papyri Sallier and Anastasi as well as d'Orbiney (see also Table 8.1 and Prologue) and the Chester Beatty group from Deir el-Medina.

Table 8.1 Table Papyri with the Late Egyptian Miscellanies of suspected Memphite origin

Papyrus	Contents	Select editions
P. Bologna 1094	account note, provision for a royal jubilee, instruction for a scribe, praise to Amon-Re, horse care, provisions, agricultural problems, unteachable pupil, instructions on organising a jubilee, problem with conscripts, taxation, letters of ladies, various letters with well-wishing formulae, various letters, letters with short instructions	Gardiner 1937, Caminos 1954: 3–36.
P. Anastasi II	eulogy on Royal Residence, eulogies on Ramesses II and Merenptah, eulogies of kings, prayers to gods, eulogy on the scribal profession	Gardiner 1937: xiii–xiv and 12–20, Caminos 1954: 35–65, Select Papyri in the Hieratic Character from the Collection of the British Museum: lxiii–lxxiii, Bellion 1987: 9, Lichtheim, 1974, 111–112, Bresciani 1999: 324–326, Pernigotti 2005: 64–74.
P. Anastasi III	epithets of a scribe, description of a Royal Residence, advice for a scribe, a scribe congratulates his teacher, hymn to Thoth, bad is the life of soldiers, and of officials, how to collect taxes, eulogy on Merenptah, on the verso a part of an accounts book, a letter, official's journal, list of persons	Select Papyri in the Hieratic Character from the Collection of the British Museum: pls lxxiv–lxxxi, Gardiner 1937, xiv and 20–34, Caminos 1954: 69–112, Bellion 1987: 10, Bresciani 1999: 326–328, Pernigotti 2005: 75–86.
P. Anastasi III A	a duplicate of Anastasi IV, 15,11–16,7 (LEM 117),	Caminos 1954: 117–122, with further references.
P. Anastasi IV	letter phrases, fragmentary texts on fishing and fowling, bad life of soldier, prayer to Amon Hana 'that he may grant you a good old age, followed by a description of ideal Egyptian life + phrases defined by Quack as 'social rivalry' eulogy of an official including well-wishing formulas for his afterlife, royal decree, critics of an errant scribe, a bad post, preparing for a royal arrival, verso: list of scribes, exercise on dating documents (?), letter on a decoration of a royal palace,	Select Papyri in the Hieratic Character from the Collection of the British Museum: pls 82–98; Gardiner 1937: xiv–xv and 34–56; Caminos 1954: 125–221, Bellion 1987: 11–12, Bresciani: 1999, 328–330, Pernigotti 2005: 87–102.

(Continued)

Table 8.1 *Continued*

Papyrus	Contents	Select editions
P. Anastasi V	wishes, congratulations, orders for the Medjay; admonition for a Medjay official, admonitions for scribes, ('I have been a bad student too'), prayer to Thoth, scribal life is better, soldier's life is bad, congratulations, 'be a good student'	Select papyri in the Hieratic Character from the Collection of the British Museum II: 99–121, Gardiner 1937: xvi and 56–72, Caminos, 1954, 225–275, Bellion 1987: 234–253, Lichtheim 1974: 113, Bresciani 1999: 331–332. Pernigotti 2005: 87–102.
P. Anastasi VI	royal protocol of Sethi II, lamenting letter, a letter reporting on Bedouin immigration and a report	Select papyri in the Hieratic Character from the Collection of the British Museum II, pls. 122–127, Gardiner 1937: xvi–xvii and 72–78; Caminos 1954: 279–300, Bellion 1987, Pernigotti 2005: 103–122.
P. Sallier I	letters, series of (fictitious?) letters, life of scribes, bad life of soldiers, scribes' work is better than anyone else's, eulogy on Merenptah, admonition to a frivolous student, report	Select papyri in the Hieratic Character from the Collection of the British Museum, I, pls. 1–9, Budge 1923: 53–62, Gardiner 1937: 79–88 Caminos 1954, 303–329, Bellion 1987: 234–253, Lichtheim 1974: 114, Bresciani 1999, 332–333, Pernigotti 2005: 123–130.
P. Sallier IV verso	wonders of Memphis, letter praising Thoth, jottings, letter on quality of grain, threshing, notes, diary of work on threshing floors, list of commodities, colophon, titulary of Ramesses II, date + titulary of Ram. II, titles of a royal scribe,	Gardiner 1937, Caminos 1954: 333–371
P. Koller	equipment of soldiers, idle scribe /parallel To Anast. IV, 2,4-3,2 + Anast. V., 5,1), Nubian tribute, preparation for Pharaoh's arrival	Gardiner 1937, Caminos 1954: 431–446, Ragazzoli 2014, with further references.
P. Turin A	instructions, idle scribe, scribe who in punishment is temporarily an agriculturist. Protest against conscription of some persons,	Gardiner 1937, Caminos 1954: 447–464
P. Leyden 348, verso	fragmentary letter, titulary of Ramesses II, long report letter, organisation of workpeople, a list of professions	Gardiner 1937, Caminos 1954: 487–502
P. Rainer 53	duplicate Anastasi III, 1,11 ff., eulogy of Piramesse	Gardiner 1937, Caminos 1954: 505–506, Krall 1894.

The latter group is mostly known under its modern name, the Chester Beatty Papyri,[19] and originally formed part of a family library of the administrators of Deir el-Medina. Collections of texts from the Chester Beatty Papyri include, alongside administrative and other literary texts, literary selections or didactic excerpts. The archaeological context in which the papyri were found is not easy to reconstruct. However, during the excavations of the Institut français d'archéologie orientale in 1928,[20] a group of papyri was found which might belong to the same group as the Chester Beatty collection. A few texts in both the Chester Beatty group and the 1928 IFAO find were copies by or for Kenherkhepeshef, a Nineteenth Dynasty Scribe of the Tomb (q.v. Djehutimose). Therefore, the Chester Beatty collection might be considered a Deir el-Medina find.

The name *Miscellanies* derives from the rich composition of literary and administrative texts a single papyrus could have included. Their purpose and social setting has been much debated. Were they student texts, exercises for relatively advanced students, as A. Erman and A.H. Gardiner mostly considered them? Or perhaps rather scholarly texts – a reference text collection of sorts, compiled by and for advanced scribes, who were coming to the end of their training or perhaps even in the early stages of their professional career?[21] The latter option is more likely as many of the texts name dignitaries to whom the new scribe ('compiler' of the miscellany) reported, and the texts show more knowledge than simpler training texts found on other writing boards or ostraca.

The name of Inena thus appears on several occasions within a large group of Ramesside papyri, probably from Memphis – naturally it need not always be the same scribe being mentioned across the manuscripts, but it seems likely it is the same writing on a number of them.

Inena's artefacts are papyrus rolls of average size, neatly inscribed with texts in hieratic. On occasion, they show verse points, dots over the text spaced at intervals dividing units of meaning, suggesting that the writer checked his finished texts carefully. The papyri are mostly the work of an experienced hand, but they also have signs or words in the margins as if Inena was training someone else.

P. Anastasi III mentioned an Inena son of Ptahemwia (Anastasi III, vs. 4,11)[22] and another Inena, without affiliation (Anastasi III, vs. 5A,3). Both of them obtained 100 units of an unknown commodity. However, nothing seems to indicate what they did to receive this.

P. Anastasi IV is quite clear – it is an instruction in writing, prepared perhaps by a scribe of the Treasury Kageb for his apprentice,[23] scribe Inena, who dutifully copied model letters, didactic texts warning against idleness, an exhortation to serve the god Amun, model compliments to a high official, and reports. There is also a text expressing a longing for Memphis which contains an ancient Egyptian characteristic of a depressive mood suffered by someone far away from his beloved city ('I crave sleep all the time, but my heart is not in my body, evil has seized all my limbs . . .'[24]). It further includes supplications to Amun, and also text in which dutiful student praises his teacher. Finally, there are complaints and commands . . . in short an entire array of documents an administrator in the capital might have used, accompanied by cultural texts reinforcing the status and importance of the literate (because writing is the way to achieve good social standing and a teacher is to be praised for enabling it) and the administrators, who are shown as competent organisers who have many demands placed on them.

In P. Anastasi VI, there are numerous reports from Inena to his superior Kageb, concerning, for example, a resettling of a Bedouin tribe, supervising activities of other officials and so on. These memoranda and reports might have been copied from or modelled on actual office files. In either case, they form what looks like a good office handbook.

Inena also produced copies of the Instructions of Amenemhat I, Khety and a hymn to the Nile in P. Sallier II, a copy of another Middle Kingdom Nile hymn in P. Anastasi VII and, as we have seen, the text of the *Tale of Two Brothers* in P. d'Orbiney. Another *Miscellany* papyrus, P. Koller from the Koller collection, now in Berlin, is also ascribed to him.[25]

Inena left a rather rich collection of texts that attested to his knowledge and training. The dates on papyri helped to reconstruct parts of the puzzle of his life. He lived in the reign of Seti II. Since this reign probably did not exceed six years and Inena was an advanced apprentice copying long texts by year 1 (the date of P. Anastasi IV), we may assume that he was born during the reign of Ramesses II, studied his scribal profession under Merenptah and finalized his schooling under Seti II.[26] He was assigned to the scribe of the Treasury Kageb, whilst titling himself first an apprentice and then a scribe (in Anastasi VI). Once, perhaps whilst training his hand on a list of names, he wrote down his own alongside the title the 'scribe of the treasury'. This might have been his ultimate aspiration, but the texts in which we meet Inena suggest a developing career of someone with both administrative training and a flair for selecting literary texts.[27] Before we address the issues of copying and/or authoring texts, we would need to see more of the Ramesside training process, but first, we look at whether the colophons, were exceptional and how permissive the Egyptian culture was about asserting one's individuality.

Leaving one's name

The manuscripts of Inena are, on the face of it, personalized among a number of seemingly anonymous texts and artworks of ancient Egypt. The modern concepts of individual and independent authorship, did not apply to this ancient culture. To place the Egyptian version of a 'signature' in context, we must digress into a rather wide field. The way to personalize one's contribution were many and disparate. Directly signing one's work as a painter, sculptor and also a writer – or copyist of a decorative Book of the Dead manuscript – was not the norm.

Nonetheless, there were many ways to link a particular work to a particular person. As we have seen elsewhere in this book, elite artists were proud of what they did and on occasion their name appeared in or on the monuments they took part in decorating, either directly (as did Paheri in Elkab, q.v.), or indirectly on their own inscriptions, stelae or statues. For example, on the monuments of Dedia, q.v., Samut, owner of TT 111, was the head draughtsman who noted that he worked in Karnak and in the Ramesseum under Ramesses II (pertinently his family members included scribes of the temple of Amun, and of the House of Life, an institution we will see more of shortly).[28]

The literate had another advantage in the form of rock-inscriptions or graffiti – staff graffiti of workmen and priests adorned their places of work.[29] Eventually, some non-textual marks might have also played a similar role, comprising signs of illiterate or semi-literate workmen, perhaps including pottery marks.[30] Non-textual signs of Egyptian workmen were not only their personal marks, but were used as such in the administrative process.[31]

The range of practices mentioned in the previous paragraphs might have left the reader confused. Surely, a statue in a temple like that of a famous sculptor who had worked there or who might at least have taken part in similar temple works, is different from a potter's mark? Indeed it is; the social and cultural settings differ in many ways, but there is a sociocultural acceptance of the fact that a manufacturer or maker has a name and a professional identity. Leaving one's imprint in the form of a name or sign was without doubt a concept deeply embedded in the Egyptian mind-set.

All of the above elements are connected by the idea that leaving one's name and a positive memory of one's achievements was a decisive constituent of an Egyptian's identity. These colophons could be anonymous – i.e. marking that the work had come correctly and completely to an end – or have a name, which appears with increasing frequency in the New Kingdom, particularly in the Ramesside age. Were the colophons a mark that a work was, chiefly, complete?[32] Or was it also indeed a statement of the copyist, his personal mark? For some writers and copyists it clearly became the latter.

In our quest to become acquainted with an Egyptian writer, author or copyist such as Inena who left his name, we first met the artefacts created by his (as they seem to be mostly male) hand – the papyrus rolls and other writing materials. This chapter will also introduce the practicalities of training to write – how was a scribe taught? What steps did one have to take before a pen touched a papyrus? What was the day-to-day writing routine of someone like Inena?

Mastering the art of working with texts was the result of a long process of schooling. Inena – as well as his nameless coevals – had to undergo years of training before he set pen to a papyrus roll. All the great scribes, administrators, dignitaries and literati, who fill in the pages of this book, started with scribal training as students. Some of them, like Dedia or Paheri, or Senenmut perhaps, also knew how to draw and understand hieroglyphs; others like Inena trained mainly in elegant hieratic writing and entered the world of texts inherited from previous generations copying endlessly on papyri, ostraca and writing boards (q.v. Prologue).

Inena lived in the Ramesside period, after a great New Kingdom watershed of the Amarna period (the reign of Akhenaten), which was understood as a time of change in the antiquity as it is in modern Egyptology. He no longer trained just or prevalently with classical texts in Middle Egyptian, like *Kemit* (see below) or the *Satire of Trades*, or *Sinuhe*. At that time, Middle Egyptian was mostly used in religious texts and select literary classics. Inena also trained his hand on Late Egyptian texts written closer to his own everyday language. We will therefore follow the training of a scribe like him, visiting Ramesside teachers and students, and also institutions that were concerned with making and preserving texts.

Beginnings of an administrator and of a literato

The Ramesside material – including some texts Inena copied – allows us to gather more than glimpses of the educational process. A reconstructed curriculum of a Ramesside administrator, who might have become a literato, probably started relatively early with regular schooling. The word 'schooling' or school in Egypt is used with a caveat – we use it as an umbrella term for the training of future literate Egyptians. It does not denote a school in any modern sense, and, as will be shown further, was perhaps closer to the idea of an apprenticeship. Similarly, terms like 'teacher' or 'student' are interachangeable with 'mentor' and 'apprentice'.

As men were expected to look for a job and start a settled professional life after the age of twenty, it is quite likely that a boy of around ten if not earlier would already have been attending regular classes.[33] The classical scribal miscellany would have been introduced at a later stage of the curriculum, as it already treated the student as a young man who needed to be warned against drinking and womanizing, i.e. someone most likely to be in advanced puberty or post-puberty.[34]

What was the key to the world of Egyptian literacy? Not hieroglyphs – an epitome of ancient Egyptian script for classical antiquity and modern Europe alike – but the hieratic script. The method of teaching might have included copying rather than writing to dictation.

Some texts were identified as probable training texts and one of them stands out – the *Kemit*. But its role is far from clear. The text was named already in antiquity as *Kemit,* or the 'Sum, Compilation' or perhaps 'Fulfilment',[35] and the title suggests a sum of knowledge. The text itself is written in a type of script that straddles the hieroglyphs/hieratic divide, and comes as a step in writing system development close to the cursive hieroglyphs used in funerary papyri and in tombs.[36]

Most of the surviving *Kemit* texts are written in columns, which limit the ligatures between cursive signs,[37] providing Egyptological arguments for a didactic use of the text. Some copies indicate a didactic process: signs were first outlined in red and then redrawn in black by a less experienced hand. Alternatively, a text was written by a master, and the apprentice copied it next to the model lines. A drawing board from Dra Abu el-Naga[38] (see Chapter 9, Dedia) shows two apprentice copies of an opening passage of *Kemit* next to the master lines. The apprentice's text is written in slightly hesitant lines and there are occasional smudges.

Our ideas on the role of *Kemit* remain speculative, but its role as a training text would be quite logical as the text is composed of seemingly unrelated sets of phrases, including letter greetings and phrases applicable to biographical inscriptions as well as instruction texts. 'A servant to his master, *Iph'* opens the composition that soon turns to the matters related to someone named Au, who is absent from his household, but is required to return. As he (or the narrator showing to Au the advantages of such behaviour) does so, he 'found his father on a festive day and his mother on her way to the sycamore, I am loved by my father, praised by my mother, beloved by my siblings and I have never made my father sad or my mother angry.' After this generic praise, good character and then finally scribedom are appraised. The text also – suitably – ends in a standard colophon. 'It has come well to a good end'.[39]

The didactic interpretation, however, becomes more problematic, when we note that – although there is a Middle Kingdom attestation – most of the extant copies come from the Eighteenth and Nineteenth Dynasties. By that time many elements, primarily letter formulae (the so-called Memphite formula, using the reference to 'your servant' or 'your scribe', as a parallel to 'yours truly' perhaps) used at the beginning, were obsolete.[40] Also, the phrases of *Kemit*, whilst practical and acting as the building blocks for longer texts, are hardly high literature.

Could the provenance help to unravel *Kemit*'s secrets? Copies of *Kemit* were found throughout Egypt from Thebes to Memphis and to the oases. However, most copies come from the site of the New Kingdom settlement at Deir el-Medina (Western Thebes) which stands out due to its exceptional treasure of ostraca with excerpts from literary texts. The main locations were the so-called Kom Sud[41] and also – but with fewer examples – the Great Pit.[42] Kom Sud is a treasure trove for literary and possibly didactic texts.[43]

It has been suggested that the simpler lines and closeness to the hieroglyphic script (the writing system with which most Egyptologists start their training in Egyptian) were an ideal starting point and *Kemit* was perceived as suitable for beginners. This assessment was perhaps somewhat influenced by the Egyptological practice, which also took for granted that schooling starts with Middle Egyptian. However, the language of Ramesside Egypt was Late Egyptian – Middle Egyptian was used for monuments.

In addition, many literate Egyptians never used hieroglyphs on a regular basis, whilst craftsmen and artists did so frequently, hence the prevalence of *Kemit* in Deir el-Medina may not only be due to the fact that they have been preserved but also to specific requirements of the craftsmen and artists' training. The columnar format and archaizing writing, as well as a command of Middle Egyptian, would all make sense to someone who was destined to work in the necropolis art.[44] To sum up, the role of *Kemit* in training might have been much more important for draughtsmen than for administrators. Interestingly, the question of how a draughtsman and/or painters perceived their craft or art, often arises when looking at the corpus of preserved Deir el-Medina texts. *Kemit*, which praised the scribal profession, and another Middle Egyptian classical text, the *Satire of Trades* were widely copied in Deir el-Medina. The craftsmen-painters indeed disassociated themselves from toiling craftsmen, potters or carpenters and builders, even though the dividing lines must have been very uncertain in the actual process of carving, plastering and painting a tomb.[45]

Future administrators like Inena perhaps started with hieratic which they had to copy laboriously until they reached a 'writing fluency'. In the Ramesside era, they probably also specifically trained to write in Late Egyptian, their current language, as opposed to Middle Egyptian, the language of formal and religious texts, and which was used in *Kemit*.

The schooling process took some years to complete and our knowledge of it still has gaps.[46] The army of scribes had its rank and file, but someone like Inena perhaps had a more specific schooling and a wider training, which gave him access to model administrative documents as well as literary texts and which might have opened up wider possibilities to him, including, perhaps, those closer to the Deir el-Medina scribes (q.v. Djehutimose), some of whom collected personal libraries and who created written compositions of their own.

We will probably never know much about the 'pen-pushers' of ancient Egypt. Many scribes we meet throughout this book were, in fact, exceptional personalities whose ability went beyond registering, accounting, running work-logs and collecting taxes paid in grain. The ordinary scribes are seen in the fields checking on grain and measuring fields, then seated in rows in an office,[47] or counting army recruits and so on. They were perhaps not always given texts to copy or asked to compose a 'Late Egyptian Miscellany', they were not collecting a personal library (q.v. Djehutimose), and they might have been ignorant of the finesses of classic literary Middle Egyptian. Yet all began their life with texts as students or apprentices and some must also have accepted the role of teacher or mentor.

Teachers and students

Among the *Late Egyptian Miscellanies*, a conspicuous group tried to produce a characterization of an ideal teacher as well as that of an ideal student. The model of a dignified teacher surrounded by dutiful pupils also had an exalted parallel in the king, 'teaching' his dignitaries, such as the vizier, about their duties.[48] Inena had teachers in the Treasury to whom he also dedicated his manuscripts (as we saw at the beginning of this chapter).

Several papyri among *Late Egyptian Miscellanies* detailed the characterstics of an ideal teacher and an ideal student, with P. Lansing[49] and P. Anastasi VI being especially prominent. P. Lansing[50] included a section where a master scribe informed his apprentice being on the material advantages of being literate and capable of taking up managerial work as opposed to manual labour. 'Be a scribe, as your body is tender and your limbs weak; you will not burn out as a lamp because of your bodily weakness – there is no firm bone in you, you are slim and willowy, easily tired … it would be good for you if you studied writing, … you won't be like an ox'.[51] The scribal social body was – in the *Satire of Trades* tradition – a cultivated, supple, well-dressed figure of authority, but here the image is offered with a twist – a warning against one's bodily limits.[52]

Upbringing, training, schooling, in short successful socialization and education, played a dominant role in Egyptian instructions, also known as wisdom texts, teachings or, in an earlier tradition, admonitions. The need to train, become skilful, conquer one's bad habits, cultivate manners, courtesy and ultimately ethical and responsible behaviour – all these aspects featured in the instruction or wisdom texts dated, or purported to be dated, to the Old and Middle Kingdom. Only one earlier text – the *Satire of the Trades* or *Instruction of Khety* – is as focused on the writing skills and the need to become literate. However, in the *Late Egyptian Miscellanies*, many New Kingdom have explained good manners or personal ethics. Many Late Egyptian compositions from the New Kingdom aim at just that – become a scribe! As the characteristics of the jobs a scribe does[53] are administrative and managerial, the instructions show that a literate person, i.e. a scribe, is capable of taking responsibility and organizing the work of others, whilst his tasks (the texts are aimed at men and written, or purportedly written, by men) give him control and protection from ordinary toil. That is the preserve of those who were not patient, hard-working or skilful enough. However, the privileges of the literate status must be emphasized, and contrasted heavily with the disadvantages of other jobs.[54] Also, at least within the universe of the *Miscellanies*, the scribal 'class' does not reproduce automatically – at least one text suggests that the family of the student who needed instructing were farmers.[55] Images projected by the instructions are those of a meritocracy of skilled and characterful literati.

The images were rather idealistic, but not necessarily completely untrue – offices were often but by no means always inherited and the administration was open to newcomers who worked their way up because of their ability (q.v. stories of Deir el-Medina scribes in *Djehutimose*). In that respect, the instruction texts were offering a reflection of an ideal practice which had some grounding in real life.

This was set against the danger of neglect and half-hearted effort. The fictional student of P. Lansing (and his contemporaries in other *Late Egyptian Miscellanies* papyri) was warned in strong terms because he was allegedly neglectful of his studies and preferred doubtful pleasures. However, P. Anastasi IV and P. Lansing also presented dutiful students who followed instruction as they knew that their teachers had their best interests at heart. 'I was brought up as a boy beside you, you smote upon my back, and your teaching entered into my ear. I was like a pawing horse-team . . . saying "I will be one who is useful to his master even as a slave is useful to his master". I will build for you a new villa . . .'[56]

Formal praise of teachers was a special chapter of the relationship; day-to-day routines were perhaps captured better in model letters and reports, such as those Inena wrote for his superior, the scribe Kageb.

Institutions and practices for text preservation and text production

An interesting portion of the textual production was closely related to education and training. Text copies and excerpts were named students' copies and the entire collection of *Late Egyptian Miscellanies* was seen as a 'school text'. As already mentioned, this was an over-interpretation.[57] Schooling, even training compilations for personal use, obviously did not cover the entire text production. Inena trained in administrative texts, and could have been a copyist on someone else's behalf, but he may also have copied longer literary texts for his own use or for his own interest. Inena's papyri form a library – perhaps a real library of his and/or his colleagues. The Egyptological ideas of Egyptian private libraries[58] are based mainly on a New Kingdom papyri group, namely manuscripts from Ramesside Memphis and Deir el-Medina.

Besides these, we assume an existence of libraries and archives in ancient Egypt, but these seem to be a complex territory, where practices of private libraries-cum-archives, such as the Chester Beatty collection or the Anastasi papyri, seem to be rather clearer than ideas on institutional archives and libraries. Still, there were also institutions connected with texts and text re/production and storage. Some, but not all, were connected to the practice of training.

One of these was defined as an *ꜥ.t n sbꜣ* – a house of instruction – and there is evidence for these in Memphis and Thebes. In the area of the Ramesseum temple, such an institution was probably physically present,[59] although its character in terms of an actual building may be a moot point.[60] In the Memphite area, at least one group of the visitors' graffiti makers was also from an *ꜥ.t n sbꜣ*.

Another, perhaps related, institution was *pr ꜥnḫ*[61]– a House of Life – often attached to temples or palaces. This appeared to be a complex institution related, but not exclusively dedicated, to the educational process of specialist scribes in the service of temples. Its main task, however, might have been the preservation of manuscripts, perhaps ranging from official royal documents to the *Vorlagen* of ritual texts. The institution also produced and re-produced texts that were needed in funerary and ritual use, as well as other sorts of knowledge including medical manuscripts. Although a House of Life was not an ancient Egyptian equivalent of a 'university', it stored, reproduced and developed knowledge.

Another storage place for manuscripts[62] appears to have been a *pr mḏꜣ.t* – literally a House of the Book – possibly a place storing ritual and historical texts. On occasion, the House of the Book as well as the House of Life were locations of sensational finds by kings or wise men, who had located an important manuscript in their book collection. Royal and elite interest in religious as well as historical texts that needed to be rediscovered is attested throughout Egyptian history, with the most notable examples being King Neferhotep of the Thirteenth dynasty, Thutmose III of the Eighteenth Dynasty and Ramesses II of the Nineteenth Dynasty. However, the kings claimed to have been interested in previous royalty, i.e. royal annals or in the ultimate traditional structure of a proper conduct of rituals and ceremonies.[63]

A private library or archive must have had a very different purpose, such as the storage of private legal deeds or copies of literary and professional texts.[64] Where the ostraca and papyri were stored is another matter – a private office at home does not seem to have been the norm, but a papyrus collection was often stored in a family tomb (as suggested in P. BM EA 10326).

Finally, a very special kind of library consisted of select tomb texts, which were part of the ritual for securing a good afterlife. Although the 'tomb as library' was specifically conceptualized in the first millennium,[65] large tombs in the New Kingdom were a library of sorts, offering a selection of pyramid texts, coffin texts and the new versions of funerary texts grouped in the Book of Coming Forth by Day (Book of the Dead) on their walls. It is highly likely that some of the visits to the tomb chapels were motivated by a curiosity to look at new arrangements of these texts.

Private or public, in a House of Life, or in a tomb, text collections show work with texts that went beyond schooling and training. People wrote, read and possibly re-read the texts in their possession, adding to their knowledge by the use of literary classics as well as everyday documents.

Working with texts

People working with texts – another large group of Egyptians hiding behind the cipher 'scribe' – were no exception if they marked their work with their name. This might have been unnecessary or superfluous, but one's own compositions as well as – in Inena's case – personalized compilations or copies, were certainly a legitimate exhibition of one's literate and cultivated character.

'Personalized' texts have another aspect that has just been hinted at – any individual writing or even copying a text does so with a number of other texts in mind. We all carry a virtual 'archive' of texts in our memory, and so did the Egyptians. This does, in part, overlap with texts we own or have read directly, but also contains texts or excerpts we have accessed via references, quotations and so on. An entire textual experience influences how we write our own texts. Various relations between texts – quotations, references etc. – can be subsumed under the name of intertextuality '. . . the ancient Egyptians respond anachronically to the post-structuralist concept of "intertextuality", which supposes that a text is never the original creation of its author, but that it forms a part of a dynamic universe of texts to which it is related.'[66]

The New Kingdom texts offer a range of intertextual events. *Late Egyptian Miscellanies* were generally toying with principles, ideas and references to the *Satire of Trades* on a large scale. P. Chester Beatty IV praised the wise and their books[67] as these texts were a monument which survived the generations, unlike tomb chapels and offering tributes. The long satirical letter in P. Anastasi I (see Chapter 9) referred to a desirable knowledge of ancient texts, which ought to have been a real knowledge, not superficial haphazard quotes without a deeper understanding.

References to literary texts were, however, not limited to genres with a possible didactic relation. They appear in biographical texts as well as in letters. One literate draughtsman in Deir el-Medina inserted references to major literary classics into his real or fictitious letter – a Deir el-Medina workman, Menna, wrote to his son, Merysekhmet (both were as real people), concerning Merysekhmet's rather wayward behaviour, especially the seduction of married women, which is also found in other period documents.[68] The letter is preserved – so far – in one full copy only on ostracon OIC 12074 + O. IFAO 2188 (KRI VI, 215–7).[69] Menna points out that his son is wayward and unsettled, and then complains of his own misfortune using probably the words of the Eloquent Peasant, which Menna quotes,[70] and the Shipwrecked Sailor, which is referred to.

There was some debate as to whether we are dealing with a real letter or with a literary text, possibly a variation on instruction texts, shaped as a letter – very much like the didactic letter on P. Anastasi I. On the one hand, Menna is much less explicit than P. Anastasi I; he hints,[71] of a shared literary legacy of which both he and his son were aware. On the other hand, Menna's letter applies a rich literary style, as if his author had a very good training in both Ramesside model letters and period literature. This sets his letter apart from most of ordinary Deir el-Medina correspondence, which tends to be concise.[72] Consequently, there is no final answer as to Menna's text genre.[73]

In any case, as a literate workman in Deir el-Medina he was no exception, nor was he so as an author of an original text – the scribe Amennakht of Deir el-Medina composed an instruction text, and some of the love poems might also have been written in the community of workmen. We have seen one scribe, Nakhtsobek, usurping someone else's love songs manuscript in P. Chester Beatty

Fig. 8.1a & b. Baboon of Thoth from P. Lansing/Thoth as ibis-headed man from P. Lansing, P. BM EA 9994,7. Drawing by HN.

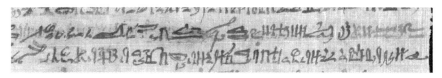

Fig. 8.2. Detail from P. Chester Beatty I: Nakhtsobek's interpolation. © The Chester Beatty Library, Dublin.

I. Adaptations of literary texts also appeared in different spheres – they also appeared in biographies, as in the biographical text of Samut Kyky.[74]

Similarly, Inena, who copied a large collection of works, maybe possessed some papyrus rolls himself and experimented, like his Deir el-Medina colleagues, with his own take on different literary genres. Was he not an author like Amennakht or Menna in Der el-Medina? There is no direct proof of authorship except, perhaps, for his letters, but Inena was in any case part of a long line of copyists-cum-authors or text editors; men who not only preserved texts inherited from the past, but also adapted them and wrote their own cultural texts enshrining the values of their world.

Eventually, Inena's story gives another meaning to the word scribe, namely that of a writer, or indeed an author, as well as copyist of other authors' writings. The New Kingdom Egyptians were aware of the existence of individual authorship and praised select great writers of the past, yet the copyist was also an important figure in the world of writing. Both author and copyist were aware of their role[75] and commemorated this by including their name in the manuscript. As the example of Nakhtsobek in Chester Beatty I shows, having your name made timeless in this fashion mattered so much that it was worth a falsification of memory.

9

Hori

'Accomplished Brother,' writes Hori, a scribe in his Majesty's stables to a fellow scribe by the name of Amenemope, 'Your letter reached me in an hour of rest . . . I was gladdened, rejoiced.'[1] When he opened the letter and began reading it, Hori admits, his excitement quickly turned to dismay:

> I found it to be neither praise nor scorn.
> Your phrases mix this with that.
> All your words are capsized . . .[2]
> Your speech is neither sweet nor bitter.

At first, Hori seems to be primarily enraged at the lack of refinement in Amenemope's letter. A few lines further into the text reveal the real point of contention. Amenemope's letter was full of contempt, alleging that Hori is no scribe, and that he holds the scribal palette with no authority. In response, Hori writes the letter before us with its own share of disdain, pointing out his colleague's error and lack of skill. Hori intends to edify Amenemope, whom he addresses and quotes throughout the text, and to teach him what it really means to be a scribe, as he explains in his text. His letter thus reads as part of a private correspondence between two contesting scribes, each seeking to prove their superiority.

Hori's letter, however, is hardly a private matter. Brimming with ironic turns of phrase and rich with detailed descriptions of territories far and wide, it become extremely popular. The letter, in fact, was one of the most commonly copied texts of the Ramesside Period, known from at least eighty different sources of varying lengths.[3] The longest variant of the text, P. Anastasi I (pBM EA 10247) was written with a fine literary hand on a long scroll of papyrus, on which corrections were noted.[4] The letter thus appears to be a work of fiction, in which the contentious exchange between the two scribes is the main literary device around which the text is constructed. It might have even been required that students of writing and scribal skills acquaint themselves with the text.[5]

Hori's words thus carry great weight when he reproaches Amenemope for his incompetence as a scribe. Hans-Werner Fischer-Elfert suggests, therefore, that the text was written as a critique of the overall educational system and the kind of knowledge it disseminated among the scribal elite. In our context, it is interesting how irony and contempt in P. Anastasi I create a fictional battle between scribes that provide its readers with an outline of what constitutes a scribe.[6] A scribe, according to P. Anastasi I is a man of letters and numbers. When Hori chastises Amenemope for his contorted speech, he highlights eloquence as an important aspect of the scribal profession. When he criticizes his adversary for failing to solve practical mathematical problems, he presents arithmetic as being important to anyone who would like to call himself scribe.

Hori's letter calls to mind many contemporaneous texts, written in the Ramesside Period, an era perfectly described as *le temps du scribe*.[7] Scribes of this period wrote texts for and about scribes, which were as engaged with the profession of scribes and their culture as the text of papyrus Anastasi I. Nevertheless, none of them sets the bar quite so high as Hori with regard to the style and quality of writing.

Hori's letter also differs from other texts in its treatment of the relationship between military and scribes. Most scribal texts scoff at military life and sneer at the horrible fate that awaits the soldiers.[8] In contrast, Hori is more than happy to prove that he is both scribe and soldier, and he dedicates almost half of the text to the figure of the *mhr*, 'intelligence and reconnaissance officer'. The image of a soldier-scribe recalls the activities of Tjanuni and Haremhab (see Chapters 3 and 6), but it is unprecedented in Egypt's literary history. Altogether, Hori's vision of a scribe stands out in the cultural landscape of its time.

A much copied letter

When P. Anastasi I was first published, its intricacy and true nature were not immediately recognized.[9] The British Museum acquired the 8.25-metre-long manuscript in 1839 from Giovanni Anastasi, the Swedish-Norwegian Consul in Egypt at that time. Anastasi lived a remarkable life, having been born to a Greek merchant from Damascus, who supplied Napoleon's armies in Egypt.[10] As the French left Egypt, his father went bankrupt, and the son took it upon himself to rebuild his father's business. Among his many endeavours, Giovanni Anastasi carried a large trade in antiquities, many of which – most probably including P. Anastasi I – came from Saqqara.[11] Three years later, the manuscript was published as a 'continuous series of statements made apparently by a royal scribe in command of the troops'.[12]

The translation of the text was greatly advanced in the next fifty years, but it was only towards to the end of the nineteenth century that the text was recognized for what it was. First, P. Anastasi I was described as a biographical memoir written by a scribe's pupil for his master, and then as an authentic narrative of a voyage in Syria retold to the scribe who undertook it by his pupil.[13] Others viewed the text as an imaginative picture of the dangers awaiting travellers to Syria, intended to deter the colleague to whom the text was addressed from embarking on a journey there.[14] Perhaps the most far-reaching interpretation of them all was the suggestion that the text speaks of none other than the biblical Moses, whose name, it was suggested, is implied in the term *mhr*.[15] This series of partial renderings of the text is especially interesting, as it highlights two of its most prominent aspects: its deceptively realistic feel and its conversational nature, in which only one side is heard.

These two aspects of P. Anastasi I – its realistic feel and its conversational manner – are tied to the ancient Egyptian epistolary formula employed in the text. The text begins by identifying the writer and the addressee, followed by a series of greetings, as was customary in letter writing in ancient Egypt. The parts that follow are differentiated through epistolary idioms such as *ky dd* and *ḥnꜥ dd*, which introduce a new subject in letters from the New Kingdom.[16] The use of the epistolary genre outside its original context is not surprising. A few authors of the Ramesside Period experimented with this genre in the literary sphere, producing such literary works as *Menna's Lament* and *The Report of Wenamun*.[17] For years, the latter was understood to be a truthful report written by an historic figure by the name of Wenamun, but now the report is understood to be a work of fiction.[18] It was Erman who recognized that the text of P. Anastasi I belongs to literary texts adopting the form of a letter, suggesting that the text only presents itself as a response to a contemptuous and pretentious communication.[19]

In the century following Erman's ground-breaking work, the translation of the text was further improved, especially with the discovery of more variants of the text. When Alan H. Gardiner published his hieroglyphic transcription of Hori's letter and its translation in 1911, he collated P. Anastasi I with another papyrus and eight other ostraca on which variants of different lengths were preserved. Since then, many more variants have been discovered, the majority at Deir el-Medina. Fischer-Elfert, who published a thorough study of the text, counted three more papyri and almost seventy other ostraca, which indicate a much wider circulation of the text than might have been expected from an exchange between two military scribes.[20] Gardiner postulated that the text was greatly favoured thanks to the Egyptians' love of repartee and irony. To him, however, the literary achievement was not quite so grand:

> If it must be confessed that the quality of the wit is poor, and that the satirical vein is intolerably insistent, still, that a Ramesside author should so well have understood to use language in a way not immediately suggested by its plain face-value is an achievement to be respected.[21]

Hori's ironic tone of voice indeed abounds in the text. He frequently praises Amenemope with hyperbolic epithets – 'the one who lights a torch in the darkness before the troops and makes light for them'[22] – only to chastise his adversary by disclosing Amenemope's flaws and failures.

A different tone appears at the beginning of the text. It opens with a long series of epithets, such as 'a scribe of chosen heart, who gives counsel, at whose speech one rejoices, craftsman of the sacred writing, to whom there is nothing unknown'.[23] The praise extends for more than a whole column, and it is dedicated to Hori, rather than to the imagined addressee of the text. Amenemope's share of acclaim is much shorter, running to a mere three lines. Only then does the text turn to the first and second person, indicating that the main part of the letter has started. After bestowing greetings on his fellow scribe, Hori turns to the task of proving Amenemope's inferiority.

Skill and record

To Hori, Amenemope's letter is like vinegar mixed with wine.[24] The whole letter is disjoined and unconnected and fails to produce a clear message. Amenemope begins his without the proper greetings one would expect to find in a letter. The letter Hori produces is therefore not only a letter of reproach but even more so a letter of demonstration. It begins, for example, with greetings before turning to scorn. He similarly says: 'My words will be sweet and pleasant in speech'.[25] In his letter he might be demonstrating in another way in his conscious choice of language. Throughout the manuscript, the text makes use of different registers: some of the more classical language and others belonging to the non-literary form.[26] These are employed according to the subject matter: the literary is used for adulation and congratulation, the non-literary for the geographical sections of the text. Adding to this, he makes use of foreign words and phrases, demonstrating a detailed knowledge of languages and their proper usage, one from which Amenemope and the reader should learn.

Amenemope's failure to produce a clear message, according to Hori, arises from his decision to ask others for their help in writing the letter. The results prove the proverb 'too many cooks spoil the broth':

> They sit plotting, the six scribes, and you hurry to join them, the seventh. You give each two sections and complete a letter of fourteen. When one praises, two vilify, and another is about to examine them according to the rules. The fifth tells them: 'do not hurry, be patient about it, in making (it) perfect.' The sixth hurries to measure the canal, quadrupling it in cubits so that it would be dug. The seventh stands by the receiving of corn-rations for military men, but your lists are too confused, and cannot be set apart . . .'[27]

The cabal of scribes ends up producing a second-rate letter, inadequate for one who considers himself a scribe. To compose a truly well-written letter, a scribe needs to rely on his own talent, which Hori claims to be doing 'from beginning to end, full of utterances of my lips, which I alone created by myself, no other with me'.[28] His words might evoke a wisdom text of the Middle Kingdom, written by Khakhepereseoneb, who opens his text by wanting to compose an original text: 'If only I had unknown utterances and extraordinary verses in a new language that does not pass away, free from repetition, without a verse of worn-out speech spoken by the ancestor'.[29] Khakhepereseoneb ended up writing a text that resembles many others. Hori, on the other hand, wrote an original text which is truly unique.

Practically, the only quotations in the text belong to excerpts from Amenemope's missive, which Hori often quotes verbatim only to criticize his adversary: 'You say: "feeble-armed (and) powerless." You undervalue me as scribe and say: "he knows nothing."'[30] Amenemope's critique quoted here focuses on two themes: knowledge and strength. Hori then dismantles this in the following lines. Hori does not try to disprove Amenemope's claim regarding his lack of strength, rather, he exposes his misconceptions regarding body and power by taking his claim quite literally. He recalls a number of characters whose malformed bodies perhaps lacked strength but who were not devoid of either power or ability: 'I know of many people without strength, feeble-armed, [even] lame who are not forceful, [but] who are might in their homes with food and provisions. They do not say: Would I have'.[31] He then mentions a number of characters who exemplify this rule: Ray, who had not moved since the day he was born, or old Amenwahsu, who spent his life in the workshops near the armoury. His characterization of the different characters might seem ludicrous, especially when he describes Paheripedjet, who is smaller than a cat and bigger than a monkey. The light tone might in fact be a trap: laughter shows ignorance of the principles which the *Instructions of Amenemope* summarizes so adequately: 'Do not laugh at a blind man, nor mock a dwarf, nor cause hardship for the lame . . . man is mud and straw, the god is his builder.'[32] In one stroke, Hori dismantles Amenemope's attack regarding knowledge and strength.

Amenemope, on the other hand, cannot even adequately put a quote to proper use. Hori notes that Amenemope quoted a passage from *The Teachings of Hordjedef*, the son of the Fourth Dynasty king, Khufu, to whom a Middle Kingdom wisdom text was ascribed.[33] Amenemope, unfortunately, does it poorly, without understanding the context from which it came, or whether its meaning was good or bad. The irony in Hori's following statement then does not fall on deaf ears, when he says: 'You are a wise scribe at the front of his colleagues. The teachings of all papyri are engraved on your heart. It is wise, your tongue, and your words are broad'.[34]

Documents play an interesting role in the discussion whether one is a scribe or not. Amenemope claims to have checked the records and found no evidence to support the fact that Hori is a scribe. Hori sends him to observe the records in the Office of the Texts, and there, to look into the box of name lists. As he looks in his report, he will find Hori's name on the list as a soldier of the great stable of Ramesses II and find evidence for his command over the stable, with a bread ration. For both men, authority is given to texts and records. If a name is missing from a list, it casts doubts on someone's professional standing. If his name appears there, then it is clear evidence. Very little is actually known about archives, but this image implies a central registry of employees. Being a scribe is not just about the skill and experience of the individual; it also has to do with external evidence. In this instance, the document defines the man.

Three and four mathematical problems

Writing takes a prominent role in the first sections of the text, as Hori berates Amenemope for the poor quality of the letter he sent. As the letter moves on, it becomes clear that there is more to being a scribe than writing. Hori then shifts to discussing Amenemope's mathematical skills.[35] The premise for this attack is an occasion in which Amenemope was called to the task of calculating rations from a field, and abandoned it so Hori had to do it for him. Hori then introduces three different cases that relate to material quantities, rations and manpower, each presented with specific numbers and details. He then adds a fourth task, in which he fails. Together they paint a picture of the scribe beyond the realm of texts.

The first question belongs to the territory of construction. A ramp needs to be built, and Amenemope is required to estimate the number of bricks needed for the task. Its measurements are given at length: 730 cubits, 55 cubits wide, consisting of 120 compartments, full of reeds and beams. At its head, the height is 60 cubits with a batter of 15 cubits and whose base is 5 cubits. Hori magnifies the dramatic sense of the task and describes a consultation of scribes, all struggling to find an answer for the overseer of the workforce. They turn to Amenemope and say: 'Don't let it be said of you there is something you don't know'.[36]

In the second question, Amenemope is asked about the transportation of an obelisk, and Hori once again sets an elaborate scene. This time, Amenemope stands at the palace gates. A dispatch from the crown prince with a message: an obelisk was made, engraved with His Majesty's name, and it is waiting in the quarry for workmen to bring it from there. Its measurements are 110 cubits in length; its pedestal 10 (square) cubits, the block at its base makes 7 cubits in every direction; its pyramidion – 1 cubit in height; its plain – 2 fingers. Amenemope is entrusted with the task of calculating how many men are required to transport the obelisk from the quarry.

After a ramp and an obelisk, Hori discusses the erecting of a colossus, and introduces another factor: limited time. Amenemope is told to empty a storeroom of sand to make room for a colossus statue and the base upon which it would stand. Again, specific measurements are given, 30 cubits on the ground and 20 cubits broad, as well as other details. The task must be accomplished within six hours, and Amenemope is expected to assess how much manpower would be needed to perform the task in time.

After three mathematical problems, Hori returns to the question of rations and presents a case in which Amenemope fails. Amenemope, he recalls, was sent at the head of troops to subdue a rebellion in Djahi (Syro-Palestine). The forces consist of different troops (archers, Meshwesh, etc.) amounting to 5,000 men in all, not counting their leaders. A delivery of bread, sheep, goats and wine arrives, but the tally of people is too great for Amenemope and there are not enough rations for them. Amenemope is called upon to act quickly and divide the rations, but he fails to do so, causing turmoil in the camp. The troops begin to threaten him that if he won't provide them with food, they will complain to the king, who will send word to kill him.

The cases present an interesting array of tasks which a scribe would encounter. The most common task relates to manpower and providing proper provisions. The specificity of the amounts and measurements are intriguing and call to mind the mathematical texts of ancient Egypt. Along with its humour and irony, the text therefore emphasizes the importance of arithmetic. The last example shows the implications of being incapable of doing proper calculations: turmoil in camp and failure to conduct an important mission.

More than arithmetic, then, this section of the papyrus places the scribe in context, and shows the importance of his role. Without him, a ramp can't be built, as his calculations permit a qualified assessment of the required number of bricks and a colossus can't be erected, for without his calculations, the task could not be accomplished in time. While calculating numbers might be understood to be a task of an accountant, according to Hori, the scribe appears more to be an administrator who has a great deal of responsibility. But without a solid grounding of knowledge he cannot fulfil them successfully.

Courage and knowledge

After surveying mathematical thinking and writing eloquence, Hori turns to the third section of the text, which for the most part is engaged with foreign locations, mainly in Syria-Palestine. Gaza, Raphia, Qadesh, Bet-Shan, Byblos, Tyre and many other cities fill the next columns of the text, making a seemingly endless list of foreign toponyms, the roads that lead to them, and their properties.

What prompts it is the self-praise of Amenemope, which Hori quotes at the beginning of the section.[37] Amenemope, according to Hori, praises himself not only as a scribe, but also as a *mhr*, a West-Semitic word that has cognates with words that relate to 'swiftness' and 'to be fast'.[38] The word appears in Egyptian in syllabic orthography, which points to its foreign origin. As *mhr*, Amenemope would have been trained as a scribe, and would be able to give reports on his journeys. As Hori's immediate reaction notes, however, to serve as *mhr*, he is in need of military knowledge about riding a chariot, reining horses, pulling a bow and later on using a quiver and a knife. He is close to an equivalent of a *maryannu*, another foreign word that entered Egyptian meaning a 'chariot warrior'.[39] Otherwise, he might be described as 'intelligence and reconnaissance officer', as his knowledge ranges from geography and the handling of horses to communication skills and dealing with strangers. Hori calls upon Amenemope to prove himself as a *mhr*, mockingly asking Amenemope to teach him and his imagined audience what that constitutes:

> Your letter is rich with jabs, laden with big words. See, they award you with wanting. Load, load for yourself as you wish. 'I am a scribe and a *mhr*,' You also said. If there is truth in what you said, come outside, and be proven, a horse shall be harnessed for you, fast as a panther, whose ear is red, which is like a gush of air, when it goes forth. Loosen the reins and take the bow, so that we could see what your hand does, you having explained the nature of the *mhr*.[40]

As a soldier-scribe, Amenemope would be expected to be able to deal with hardship with courage and self-composure. In his letter, Hori does not expect much of his addressee, and he repeatedly portrays scenarios that would leave Amenemope completely at a loss. Once, Amenemope sleeps at night only to wake up and find that thieves had stolen his horse and his clothes, and his servant had taken the rest. There, Hori mockingly says, 'You are indeed an equipped *mhr*.' Another time, Amenemope is imagined to be stranded in the mountains, no army or helper in sight. His chariot completely falls apart, and the skies open, leaving him to pray for a bush to appear or perhaps even an enemy. Most remarkable is a scene, in which Amenemope is imagined to reach Joppa, coming upon a local beautiful girl in the surrounding vineyards. After a sexual encounter, he is required to pay *mohar*, bride-price for her, and ends up losing his shirt again.

These incidents occur against the backdrop of landscapes in Syria and Palestine. Throughout his letter, Hori introduces mockery through questions that ask Amenemope about cities and locations, of which the hapless protagonist clearly knows very little. In his long survey Hori mentions Syrian coastal cities like Tyre and Byblos, the land of Takhsi and the past-Jordanian region, Canaanite cities like Meggido and Bet Sepher, or Qiryat Anavim, Joppa, Gaza and the Horus way that leads back to Egypt. Phrasing his question ironically, Hori often asks: 'What is [Geographical Name] like? Didn't you enter [Geographical Name]?' as if Amenemope should have visited them: 'I shall mention to you another "hidden" town, whose name is Byblos.'[41] The irony of 'hidden' is especially poignant here as Byblos has held trade routes with Egypt since its earliest days. Hori continues: 'What is its goddess like? . . . did you not enter it? Teach me about Beirut, Sidon, Sarepta. The stream of the River Litani – is where?' The knowledge that the text presents comprises more than toponyms and their relative location. It is detailed local knowledge, of local gods and the direction in which rivers flow, the distance from one location to another, and the nature of the surroundings and the people there. Syro-Palestine appears in P. Anastasi as an exotic and dangerous location, which a *mhr* needs to know well in order to survive.

It seems, however, that the skills that Hori notes as being important are well beyond the knowledge of cultural geography and stamina to withstand the hardships. They also involve an ability to interact with the people within a camp. Otherwise, it is hard to understand one of the final sections that mention a visit to the armoury. Hori explains that had Amenemope visited the armoury, the whole ordeal he experienced with the chariot could have been averted. The relations within the camp are high on the list of a successful military scribe.

It is probably in this section that Hori's comic skills reach their peak. Clearly referring to Amenemope expected failures, he recalls his claim to fame again and again. Hori finally says: 'May you become the name for every Maher who passes the beloved land [Egypt]. May your name become like Qadardi, the ruler of Assiru, when the bear [?] found him inside the *bkj* tree.'[42] We might miss the exact point of the story of Qadardi, but the comparison of Amenemope to a 'hero' found hiding in a tree is hardly lost upon us.

Scribal literature

The content and style of Hori's letter place it within the literary and scribal culture of its time. The Ramesside Period, to which the text dates, saw a flurry of texts celebrating the scribal profession. Such texts are often grouped together as *Late Egyptian Miscellanies*,[43] which as their name suggests is a collection of texts of varying character and genres. These manuscripts have much in common with Hori's letter, and yet differ from it in its scope and depiction of the scribe.

Among the various genres included in the *Late Egyptian Miscellanies*, letters play a prominent role. A few of those texts may be described as model letters, as the content does not seem to have any relevance to the copyist, the addressee or the adjacent sections in the text. Other letters are dedicated by fathers to their sons or by masters to their students reproaching them for leaving the scribal profession. While doing so, they often enumerate the benefits of the scribe's life, especially when compared to other professions. Soldiers were a common target in the literary and scribal world of the New Kingdom. Their miserable existence and terrible fate were described with great detail:

> A soldier is taken as a child, *nbj*-height, and shut up in barracks, [which is] made in troops, with a commander in charge of them. He is imprisoned, he does not leave until he becomes a soldier . . . He wakes up in order to receive beatings, until he bursts with open wounds . . .[44]

Hori's letter presents a decisively different approach to the view of the military presented by scribes. Hori cannot accept Amenemope's allegation that he is neither scribe nor soldier: he claims the honour of being both. Moreover, while the *mhr* and scribe could be differentiated in the text, with separate sections dedicated to each, the text does not hold them to be mutually exclusive. On the contrary, soldier/*mhr* and scribe appear to be equally important both being worthy of respect. It might very well relate to the fact that the two figures of the text, Amenemope and Hori, describe themselves as soldiers and scribes. It still remains to be seen how such a text received so much popularity in the village of Deir el-Medina, whose men were, for most of its history, as far removed from the military life as possible.

Concluding remarks

The satirical letter of Hori appears as a sophisticated literary work that ridicules the claims of a self-proclaimed excellent soldier-scribe. Combining different registers, a multiplicity of Semitic words and pointed phrases, it projects very specific expectations from a scribe that extend far beyond laying down the written word. A scribe, according to the text, must be independent and self-reliant. He must be confident of his style and skilled in practical mathematics. As a soldier-scribe, he must be courageous and have extensive knowledge of his chariot and the foreign territories in which it might run.

The scribe of P. Anastasi I does not exist alone. He is self-reliant in his writing, but he relies on others when performing his tasks, and he has to communicate efficiently with them. Other professions appear in other texts of the New Kingdom date, but often only as background for the scribe and his good fortune. P. Anastasi I depicts a different social world in which the scribe's tasks have implications, and an inability to perform them has consequences. In this world, the other professions appear as his partners rather than the backdrop to his activities.

Finally, through its phraseology and text making, Hori raises questions that relate to the relationship between text and speech in interesting ways, especially between time in the text and time in the real world. We learn that the text is not really the beginning of a narrative but relates to a timeline that extends towards the past, when the letter of Amenemope was composed and sent to Hori. Towards the end of the letter, Hori reproaches Amenemope for not answering the questions he has raised. This remark opens another path to understanding the text – not only as a humorous critic of the state of affairs, but also as a self-aware, slightly self-ridiculing text, in which Hori's is clearly eloquent but perhaps worthy of as much ridicule as his addressee.

10

Djehutimose Tjaroy

One day in Thebes, the scribe of the community of royal workmen Djehutimose Tjaroy was handed a letter by a messenger. He must have opened it with a sense of foreboding – what will his superior demand? This is what the letter said:

> The commander of the Pharaoh's, *lph*, army to the scribe Tjaroy of the necropolis:
> Concerning the said matters you had reported, i.e. the report on the comments by the two rangers, namely [contents of] what they said. Do take joint action with Nodjmet and with Paishuben. Let them [= the Medjay] be brought to my house, verify the statements, and if indeed it is their statements, put them into two sacks and let them be thrown into the river at night, so that nobody knows. Well, regarding the Pharaoh, *lph*, is he in control of this land at all?

We may imagine the proceedings that followed – capturing the two men, harsh interrogation and a secret night-time killing without a trial. Was this a job for a scribe? Egyptology knows the letter as P. Berlin P 10487 and it has inspired much speculation.

Djehutimose Tjaroy, to give him the full name under which he appears in his correspondence and other documents, lived in the second millennium in Thebes, the religious capital and administrative centre of Upper Egypt in the New Kingdom. Parts of his life story are well known,[1] mainly for two reasons – one was his connection to the exceptional community of royal workmen located in Deir el-Medina, the other was his service to the chief participants in the Theban political scene at that time – the priesthood of Amun and high officials of the state.

Three P. Berlin 10487, 10488 and 10489 were addressed from general Piankh to Tjaroy, to the overseer Paishuben and to the lady Nodjmet. All three letters demand that the three addressees join forces to act on behalf of the general, investigate the two Medjay, verify their (loose) talk and kill them. Piankh's orders are quite unequivocal. Their bodies were to be disposed of in secret, suggesting that the entire case was of special importance. The Tjaroy letter, which opened this chapter, P. Berlin P 10487, is also known as letter A of the three.[2] It is a letter format papyrus roll 17 × 21.5 centimetres in length and probably came from Thebes, although – like with many papyri – its exact provenance is unknown.

Its modern reader is thrown into a convoluted criminal story with two victims, a tough superior who seems to disdain even the power of the Pharaoh and a scribe caught in turbulent times. To unravel the threads of the mystery, we follow the scribe who started his career in the village of Deir el-Medina, as well as his victims and collaborators.

Victims or traitors?

Who were these men and what was their crime, if a crime there was? 'Medjay' is commonly translated as – 'policemen' – in the New Kingdom context. Detective stories by modern authors set in ancient Egypt occasionally portray them as a police force of sorts, giving them, on occasion, the role of the doggedly dutiful but not very insightful Inspector Lestrade.

The role of the Medjay is, however, outlined rather less sharply in historical evidence. The name was given to a group of inhabitants of the desert areas of Nubia and/or Eastern Desert, who occasionally came to Egyptian settlements, e.g. fortresses in Nubia, in the Middle Kingdom. They were given sundry jobs as guardians or sentries, until their originally ethnic name changed into a profession.[3] The situation may be more complex according to some more recent observations;[4] Medjay in the New Kingdom might have been state employees in different roles and their corps might still include foreigners, or people of desert area origin. However, given the fact that the Egyptian understanding of 'foreigner' was rather flexible, identifying foreigners and Egyptians among the Medjay in Deir el-Medina may be far from straightforward. In any case, many of them had Egyptian names – Amenkhau, Mentumose, Pentuer, Nesamun among others.[5] Their roles in Deir el-Medina were probably broader than the more recent concept of a 'policeman',[6] but included messengers, as well as security personnel.[7] If indeed the roots of the Medjay included, as seems probable, people who were accustomed to moving on the fringes of uninhabited land, knew desert roads and had other specific training and tasks, then a term such as 'ranger', which has a number of military, as well as militia and security connotations, and may be redefined in each historical period, might perhaps give a broader understanding of their role.[8]

Now two of these people, who appear most likely to be connected to maintaining security and/or delivering goods and information in Western

Thebes, had to be investigated and killed in secret. This happened in turbulent times that allowed for such 'shortcut justice'.[9]

Times of change

The end of the Twentieth Dynasty changed the city of Thebes. The local power holder was the priesthood of Amun; the king mostly resided in the northern city of Piramesse. However, royal tombs continued to be built in the Theban valley,[10] known today as the 'Valley of the Kings', and the kings continued to add to the large Theban temple foundations.

Thebes had lived through several difficult moments during the reign of the last Ramessides – kings of the Twentieth Dynasty. There was a power struggle centred around the figure of Amenhotep, High Priest of Amun, in the reign of Ramesses XI. The High Priest Amenhotep seems to have been deposed and replaced. One high priest might have been suppressed, but the Amun priesthood remained centre stage at Thebes.

There were also repeated tomb robberies very close to the West Theban communities – royal tombs in the Asasif and Dra Abu el-Naga area were attacked, and several papyri documented the trials of alleged robbers. The royal workmen themselves had experienced delays in payment of their wages and supplies in the reign of Ramesses III and they were also afraid that their community might have been endangered by marauders or Libyan tribesmen operating in the Western Desert. Already in the reign of Ramesses VI the chief Medjay Mentumose had been killed by intruders.[11] Nonetheless, the workmen continued to build royal tombs in the Valley, or at least to take care of the necropolis. P. Turin 2018 registers salaries for the crew in years 8 and 10, probably of Ramesses XI.[12] There were two scribes, two foremen, two deputies and fourteen workmen, two doorkeepers, a guard and a dozen outside workers supervised by two more scribes. It was a far cry from the standard Ramesside number of forty to sixty workmen, let alone the 100 reached in the reign of Ramesses IV (as shown on P. Turin 1891, recto).[13] The crew started work on the tomb of Ramesses XI (KV 4 in the Valley of the Kings), but neither the cutting nor its decoration were ever finished and it was never used for an actual royal burial. Still, at least for several years of that reign, the tomb building community must have been active.

At one point during the reign of Ramesses XI the situation in Thebes became increasingly chaotic and a Nubian viceroy, Panehsy, had to intervene – possibly on behalf of the king, who was in Piramesse. One of the issues was local security. The situation was definitely to deteriorate towards the end of the Twentieth Dynasty, and Černý, noticing that already P. Turin 2018 (in the year 10 or later) had no water carriers on the salary list of the crew, suggested that the workmen might have repaired beyond the walls of Medinet Habu,[14] where they founded or became part of another West Theban community. The water carriers were essential for a community living without direct access to a water source such as Deir el-Medina, but their services could be perhaps dispensed of at Medinet Habu. Alternatively, the scribes, i.e. the family of Djehutimose, might have moved into the Medinet Habu precinct, as a later house of scribe Butehamun seems to indicate, and the workmen resettled to other parts of Western Thebes.[15]

Panehsy probably aimed to re-establish local control and he also organised local supplies; in year twelve of Ramesses XI we see the scribe Djehutimose in charge of tax collection for Panehsy in the region north of Thebes.[16] It would also appear that the specialist status and privileges of the community began to be eroded[17] as not only the scribes of the tomb, but also workmen could have been tasked by the state officials to undertake chores outside their usual remit.

The Turin Taxation Papyrus betrays the complexity of land revenue collection: the so-called *khato*-lands of the king 'produced state revenues, although at this date they are frequently found under temple management'.[18] On top of that, part of the revenues was due directly from individual cultivators or estate managers. Equally interestingly, the revenues were used in part directly to fund state projects, including the necropolis workforce (Djehutimose Tjaroy's primary responsibility, after all), but they were also used for other temple endowments,[19] taking part of the finances from the state redistribution process.

In this complex financial as well as administrative set up, Panehsy probably exceeded his brief in one way or another and became a liability. The man who was in charge of suppressing his excesses was a dignitary named Piankh, best known under his military title of a general. Piankh might have built his local connections in Thebes (possibly already strong) by marrying a lady Nodjmet (known as Nodjmet A, because several important women of that time – and possibly from the same family – had the same name).

Piankh pushed Panehsy out of Thebes and it appears he chased him into Nubia. Here the local Theban connections came into play for backing and supplies. He needed various commodities, mostly grain to feed his troops, but also cloth – not only, as would seem obvious, to clothe the men, but also to wrap the bodies of war casualties. The scribe Tjaroy was in charge of several contingents of supplies – it seems that he had to travel on behalf of the general to collect grain and other commodities including cloth. He must have travelled north of Thebes first, and then back to Thebes.[20]

Collecting taxes in grain, should one listen to instruction texts carefully, was a typical responsibility of a scribe, i.e. a literate man in a position of responsibility. Deir el-Medina administrators, nonetheless, were not typical taxing masters, as they were usually in command of a community of workmen with state supplies; it was just another sign of changing times that Tjaroy had to tackle this responsibility.

The first time we encounter Tjaroy as grain collector he was already under the administration of Panehsy;[21] at that time it would appear that his mission was to collect grain to provide for the community of workmen. A.H. Gardiner, an early editor of the text, suspected Tjaroy of 'doctoring' his accounts, as some sacks of grain seemed to be incorrectly deducted from the collected amount. A more recent assessment modified Gardiner's accusation and 'the reputation of *ḏḥwty-ms* as an honest and reasonably careful scribe is entitled to restoration' as S. Vinson suggests. Djehutimose indeed made a few minor mistakes in his accounting – after all he had to collect grain from several resources, pay for transport and then redistribute the rest in the Theban area.[22]

In any case, grain was only one among several commodities for which Tjaroy was responsible. One letter suggests that Tjaroy,[23] anxious to reach Thebes to provide cloth and other supplies for Piankh, who was about to depart for Nubia, missed the rendezvous with his commander. His men noticed that 'he nearly died'[24] when they were late. The lady Nodjmet, however, was organizing the train for her relative's army and sent Tjaroy to follow the commander in Nubia.

Thus Tjaroy's travels also took him far south of Thebes – consequently, he travelled north and south of Thebes. We also know he made a stop in Elephantine and then continued to follow the army of Piankh further south. However, did he make just one trip south, or repeated trips?

He was not a happy adventurous traveller,[25] but he had to fulfil his duty. Piankh needed him to organize his army's supplies at Elephantine, and then to follow (repeatedly perhaps) the army into Nubia. Collecting supplies and overseeing their transport was, however, not the only aspect of Tjaroy's new job. Other tasks, some of them perhaps more sinister, awaited him in Thebes.

The usual work of the Deir el-Medina community seemed to cease gradually. Yet the workmen – and their scribes, in particular Tjaroy's son, Butehamun – were still active in the Valley of the Kings. The graffiti in the Theban mountains are one of the best resources for this final period in the life of the community.[26] Tjaroy, Butehamun, as well as their successors, alongside workmen, appear in graffiti on the mountain paths, in Deir el-Bahri, and in the Valley of the Kings. The location and relative distribution of the graffitti – alongside other period texts – strongly suggests that the community of workmen as well as their scribes had a new, possibly top-secret task: the removal and reburial of the New Kingdom sovereigns in cachettes.[27]

Suspicions

Speculation may abound as the Berlin papyri suggest that the two Medjay were either in possession of information they should not have had, or they betrayed their expected discretion. K. Gabler suggested[28] that being trustworthy and discreet were perhaps two of the hallmarks of a responsible and successful Medjay. The necropolis crew had to assure Piankh they were ready to serve him, perhaps even in difficult circumstances. Were these Medjay loose talkers who overstepped the mark? Was betrayal of trust the two men's main crime? Or did Piankh need to cover the activities in the necropolis such as reprocessing of the wealth of gold from the royal tombs? With possibly a large part of the former Deir el-Medina crew involved in locating and possibly emptying the royal tombs and subsequent reburials that were carried out across a longer period of time,[29] it is difficult to imagine large-scale and long-term secrecy. But perhaps it was not impossible to achieve if the crew and security personnel engaged were taciturn and dedicated to their job. The ethics of the operation and the double standard that a generation ago saw tomb robberies judged and punished (as shown in trial documents, for instance, P. Abbot), may be one thing, the *Realpolitik* of Piankh and his successors, high priests of Amun in Thebes, quite another.

That the Valley of the Kings irrevocably changed at the end of the New Kingdom, and that the Deir el-Medina crew was moved to Medinet Habu or other parts of Thebes and given different tasks is a fact. That the scribes Djehutimose and Butehamun had close ties to the new administration in Thebes is also a fact – they had to serve Panehsy and they had to serve Piankh. Further narrative details remain in large part in the realm of speculation as just shown. Whatever the crime, if there was a crime, the responsibility of the scribe Tjaroy, originally an administrator in charge of a community in Western Thebes, gained a new dimension. Ultimately, were the letters also to encourage Tjaroy to tackle a task he'd rather not have, giving him an unwanted license to kill? It was certainly very different from the job description of his predecessors.

A line of scribes

The name of the village of workmen, the ever-present Deir el-Medina, has appeared several times throughout the volume and in this chapter, its history will conclude as we follow the story of one of its last scribes.

To be a scribe of the community of the royal builders was a highly prestigious assignment, entrusted to a line of men not always related by blood but by training, duties and status.[30] Some of their life stories were quite well publicized within Egyptology. Several scribes left both professional and personal material ranging from handwritten documents[31] to personal libraries.

Each of these biographies demonstrates a different aspect of activities and the professional scope of an administrator responsible for an exceptional workgroup tasked with the making of and care for the royal necropolis. The scribes were not the only literate men in their community, as its draughtsmen and foremen are attested as literate – although their literacy might have had, as we have seen in the case of Dedia, a different emphasis.[32] However, the scribes were the administrative link of the community to its superiors, and as state officials they enjoyed the status of authority. They were an interface for the community as well as an important authority inside it. They had to write down logs and journals, check rations and, together with the foremen, oversee the logistics and workflow of the tomb building as well as communication with state officials, such as the vizier.[33] Within the community, they also recorded local and personal business, although this was not done in their capacity as state officials, even if their status might have given them the role of official witnesses to important legal deeds.[34]

Back in the times of Ramesses II, there lived one of the best-documented Deir el-Medina administrators, the scribe Ramose. Ramose came from administration of the West Theban memorial temples and was called to Deir el-Medina from a post of a 'treasury chief' in the temple of Thutmose IV. Ramose must have been recognized as a capable and effective officer by one of the most powerful men in the Ramesside state administration, the vizier Paser.[35] Paser must have helped to get Ramose the Deir el-Medina position, however, Ramose was no resented protégé of the vizier but developed and maintained cordial relationships with fellow foremen and other crew members. His wife Mutemwia was in priestly service of the cults of the goddesses Hathor and Taweret; the couple were evidently popular as they appear on other people's commemorative monuments, such as in a tomb decoration of the sculptor Qen, workmen Penbuy and Kasa, and others.[36] Ramose was also one of the most affluent, if not the richest, men in the village; he left several tomb chapels and many objects were found that are associated with his name.

'However, the records do betray the dichotomy of an affluent man, effective and content in the workplace, but forever in turmoil at home over the inability to produce an heir and eventual successor'.[37] Ramose and his wife dedicated ex votos to the goddess Hathor[38] and prayed to the god Min and the goddesses Taweret and Qudshu – a goddess worshipped in Syro-Palestine and in Ramesside Egypt – for fertility,[39] but ultimately there was no heir. Ramose assured a continuation of the line of scribes by adopting another trained scribe found outside the community, a man called Kenherkhepeshef.

If there is considerable attention in Egyptology dedicated to Ramose, then his adoptive son has gained an ever-wider reputation, no doubt because he is seen as a very gratifying figure for any narrative – the complete opposite of his adoptive father Ramose.[40] Kenherkhepeshef[41] was indubitably a capable administrator and a man of culture, as he owned a number of manuscripts bearing many interesting literary as well as scientific and administrative texts that later became part of the Chester Beatty collection of papyri.[42] He also had an interest in history as shown by his compilations of several king-lists.[43] However, several aspects of his personality were exactly the opposite of his father's, starting with Kenherkhepeshef's excessively cursive handwriting and ending with his character. He was not a favourite companion or a much-cherished superior, but comes across as somewhat of a bully.[44] For instance, as a village administrator, Kenherkhepeshef was in close contact with the foremen of the crew and the workmen at least once suspected him of covering up for a foreman, namely Paneb, a foreman of ill repute, who was accused of molesting the wives of his workers and of committing fraud.[45]

Kenherkhepeshef, too, had no surviving issue, and the scribal position went to other families in the village. Kenherkhepeshef married late and his wife, Naunakhte, was a young widow; as a woman of some means after being widowed for a second time, left her property to those of her children she deemed worthy of their inheritance. The scribe who wrote her will and related documents was named Amennakht.

Among the generations of scribes after Kenherkhepeshef, several figures are of particular interest, among them Naunakhte's probable 'notary' Amennakht.[46] He was a draughtsman, an administrator and an author who was active throughout a large portion of the reign of Ramesses III, living through the challenging strikes at the end of his reign.[47] Another figure of importance was his son Harshire, who was in charge – at first as a junior scribe – alongside, and then as a successor to, his father.

The scribe Amennakht is a well-known figure in Egyptology due to his authorship of an instruction text and other literary works,[48] his career development from a draughtsman to a scribe, and his two sons who had two closely interrelated careers. The above mentioned Harshire was a draughtsman first and a scribe – administrator of the crew – second;[49] another son, Amenhotep, became a head draughtsman.[50]

Amennakht was no doubt well-schooled and put his training to a use far exceeding the tasks of an administrator. He was an artist and a literato, who experimented with several different genres.[51] His literary production spanning an instruction text, as well as a royal eulogy and a hymn, gives a hint as to the formation of the Ramesside literary production, which was considerable in numbers, as well as in range of genres.[52] He contributed to the formation of the Ramesside literary 'archive'[53] and it is also likely that he was himself in possession of works that gave him the conceptual and intellectual impulse – he probably owned a private library and it might have been the same as the growing collection that once belonged to Kenherkhepeshef, i.e. the future Chester Beatty papyri,[54] or a collection of a similar sort. He bequeathed his collection of manuscripts to his son Harshire, who in turn bequeathed it to his descendants. The 'history and career of the draftsman made scribe, Harshire . . . has been the focus of extensive study by a number of scholars'.[55] The draughtsman and scribe Harshire was active from the reign of Ramesses IV to Ramesses IX.

Toward the end of Dynasty Twenty, possibly from early on in the reign of Ramesses XI,[56] the tomb crew had two senior scribes ($z\underline{h}3.w \ n \ p3 \ \underline{h}r$), responsible for the right and for the left side respectively. Harshire had a son Khaemhedjet.[57] Khaemhedjet was active throughout the reign of Ramesses X and Ramesses XI; he might have been working until the early years of the latter monarch and was responsible for the left side of the tomb and its crew. Probably already during the reign of Ramesses X, if not earlier, Khaemhedjet had trained his son Djehutimose to succeed him, which eventually happened in the reign of Ramesses XI.[58]

'Our' Djehutimose, also known as Tjaroy, inherited the office and perhaps also the family library[59] and accordingly trained his son Butehamun as a responsible administrator and literato, who was expected, ideally, to bequeath the same training to the next generation, as Tjaroy formulated his stance in a letter: 'Don't let the young who are at school to let their hands go off writing' he later wrote to Butehamun, paraphrasing popular exhortations.[60] Whether Butehamun was ever officially promoted to be a senior scribe alongside his father (succeeding his father's colleague Nesamenope), or whether he was a junior, deputizing for his father and eventually succeeding him, is a moot point.[61] The long line of the scribes of the necropolis, who viewed themselves as specialists as well as generalists,[62] as competent organizers as well as wise men, ended in the changing times that deeply affected the lives Djehutimose Tjaroy and his family.

Letters, business and private life

Personal and business particulars of the lives of Djehutimose and his son Buhetamun are known in some considerable detail thanks to a large collection of letters known as the Late Ramesside Letters. This group of letters on papyri has been distributed among several major museum collections and published in collections by the Egyptologists Jaroslav Černý, Edward F. Wente and Jac J. Janssen.[63]

The letters are dated mostly to the long reign of Ramesses XI and their protagonists are generally either located in the Upper Egyptian Thebes or closely connected with the Theban region because of their tasks in the administration and government of Egypt or because of their position in the priesthood of Amun.

The names of Djehutimose and Butehamun often appear throughout the letter corpus. There is an entire group of letters that the two scribes exchanged directly. In addition, they received letters from their superiors as well as from other Theban officials and inhabitants. The letters consequently have varied content. Ancient Egyptian letters generally have very rich content, combining both personal and professional aspects.

Greetings, good wishes and appropriate formulae used to open and close a letter text were formalized to a large extent,[64] especially in correspondence with superiors, but the language of Late Egyptian letters could also be very personal and expressive.[65] Both men and women corresponded and people were not shy about writing to their superiors and peers as well as to their inferiors. There were also missives that might have included a business account, personal notes and greetings all in one.[66] The letters of Djehutimose and Butehamun often covered several aspects. Butehamun wrote thus:

> The [. . .] Shedemdua, Hemeshire, and her little daughter are well; no harm has come to them. Don't worry about them. You are the one whom they tell Amun of the Throne(s) of the Two Lands, Amun united with Eternity [. . .] to bring you back,

alive, prospering, and healthy, that they may fill their embrace with you. When the Medjay Hadnakhte reaches you, you shall despatch him very quickly.[67]

These letters are far from a simple family exchange, despite being correspondence between father and son. Djehutimose was a very busy administrator and his duties took him, due to a peculiar character of obligations of the community in Western Thebes far from his original Theban work location, where his son perhaps either started to work alongside him, or deputized for him in his absence. Be that as it may, instructions flew from the older scribe to the younger. Matters of business were followed by matters of family economy, for instance agricultural works, probably on family fields. Also, family members had to be provided for and, when Djehutimose travelled, Butehamun had to step in. Thus, a more personal picture of the two scribes emerged from the letters, which were corroborated by other sources of both written and material culture.[68]

Djehutimose was first married to a woman named Baketamun, and Butehamun was the offspring from this marriage.[69] As we have seen, Djehutimose came from a long line of scribes at the community of workmen settled at Deir el-Medina,[70] and his son continued in the family tradition and also in the dynasty of scribes.[71] Butehamun married Ikhtay and had a son, Ankhefenamun, who was also to become a scribe.

Both father and son experienced widowhood. There are no references to either of their wives by the end of their surviving correspondence (Late Ramesside Letters). There is also the letter of Butehamun to his deceased wife Ikhtay's coffin (O. Louvre Inv. 698), full of his grief.[72] Nonetheless, the ladies mentioned most often in the corpus of letters were Shedemdua and Hemetshere, although 'who [they] were is never said'.[73] It would seem likely they were new partners. Apart from turbulence in their personal lives, both father and son also held their offices at a time, when the life and work of their West Theban community was to change forever.

A tough superior, a brusque correspondence, an all-purpose scribe?

Now it is time to return to our story. The small group of missives, literally three letters, addressed by Piankh to his Theban backers that we have seen in the introduction to this chapter, reveal a peculiar situation. All three letters are very brief, and two are almost without any paraphernalia normally associated with letters, such as greeting formulae – they might be termed brief communications.[74] These are addressed to Tjaroy and another Theban agent of Piankh, Paishuben. The third letter, more polite and effusive in formal formulae, is addressed to Nodjmet. Formal or not, however, the three missives share disquieting information.

Compared to the demanding, but regular tasks of Djehutimose Tjaroy's predecessors in the role of a scribe, even compared to his own tax collecting duties, conducting secret investigations and meting out secret punishments is a new aspect of the role of a scribe of the tomb. Consequently, Tjaroy had many requests to oblige in his career. He was not a courtier like Senenmut, yet he had to cope with the requirements the high echelons of the state administration; he saw a material change in his duties and in the very existence of the community he was charged with.

Summing up previous glimpses at his biography, we assume he spent some time in the village working in the role of local administrator, and he made sure that his son, Butehamun, inherited the role as was usual. The turmoil in Thebes then caused the workmen to cease or limit their standard activity, consider leaving the village and become involved, willingly or not, in local struggles. The scribes had to make sure that Theban men and supplies were available to the authorities that demanded them, and perhaps they had to assume a new role in the care of royal tombs – namely in their use as a coffer of the new Theban power-holders. Not even the community of workmen seemed to avoid conscription to Piankh's forces – for instance, Tjaroy was in charge of army supplies. He became a taxing master in order to feed his crew; he organized his crew of the tomb subject to the requirements of the service – to supervise the tombs and possibly to start the removal of royal burials. He and his colleague Nesamenope and later his son Butehamun might have been the men who organized the move of the royal necropolis administration, if not the entire community, from Deir el-Medina to Medinet Habu. He put himself, as well as his workmen, in whatever service abroad Piankh required. He was one of Piankh's contacts in Thebes for a secret mission that disposed of unwanted personnel who betrayed their superior's trust … His new roles made him relevant to the country's new administration, however, documents also give the impression that he could have hardly resisted such a radical reformulation of the position of the scribe of the tomb.

Tjaroy's letters, official and personal, show a man who had to become an all-purpose manager, from administrator to secret judge. They also provide a glimpse of the human being between the lines.

Glimpses of a personality

The fragments of Tjaroy's biography emerge from a number of documents. But as soon as we compose a relatively neat narrative, the gaps in its weave start to appear as many details remain unresolved. For instance, the precise chronology of the letters of Tjaroy and Butehamun (which tend to be used as a mainstay of interpretations of their lives) can still be disputed. We also know he had extended family and friends. The names of ladies Hemetsheri and Shedemdua appear in the letters, alongside their children. But who exactly were they? Partners with small children? Relatives? Perhaps we may not venture beyond saying that there was a circle of people close to Tjaroy and dependent on him in one way or other. The clear connections are few – his son Butehamun being relatively unproblematic.[75]

Nonetheless, the personal story of Djehutimose Tjaroy emerges at least in glimpses. He had to adjust his expectations in times he found challenging and perhaps tedious. He had to fulfil his duty and failing his superiors caused him distress. His superiors, however, also failed him in the traditional Egyptian picture of an orderly society the administrators and men of letters sought to maintain. There was danger in Thebes and Tjaroy did not enjoy it. He had to accept unasked for responsibilities, such as to change from a man in charge of men working in the necropolis to a taxing master in charge of civil and military supplies. Finally, as a reliable person in the eyes of his master, he was given what looks like an undercover mission using enhanced interrogation techniques and certainly a secret killing. Tjaroy, however, does not seem to have been made for these roles.

Yet, he must have been reliable, otherwise the general would not have entrusted him repeatedly with these vital missions. Tjaroy fulfilled them but he also missed his family when he travelled, he fell ill and his thoughts were centred around his home, Thebes, although it too had changed. He might have understood well the melancholy of *Praise of the Cities*—a literary genre dedicated to the qualities of major cities,[76] mostly Thebes and Memphis—when he was far away. His letters were written using standardized phrases, the chosen phraseology of Tjaroy's letters contained his sensibilities and anxieties.

Djehutimose Tjaroy was a man who was aware of his responsibilities – that was the image every New Kingdom official needed to project; but the Ramesside sensibilities were also centred round a trust in divine presence and intervention.[77] Tjaroy was – at least in letters – also a man of a new sensibility – entrusting his precarious existence into the hands of gods. Tjaroy's histories not only provide pieces in the puzzle of the end of the New Kingdom, they also provide a record of the overhaul of administrative roles in Thebes, Finally, they also have the attraction – one which is perhaps deceptive – of personal contact.

Epilogue

In the context of more recent studies on cognitive anthropology, it has been noted that

> '... culture seems too often to be conceptualized as a phenomenon somehow separated from people, constituting some kind of public style or pattern to which individuals conform. Humans actively model the worlds they live in, and it is these models that are the basis of culture ...'[1]

Historians, especially after the cultural turn, are often prone to the same fallacy, namely they miss the specificity of different human communities or indeed an individual's agency. We hope that this book has at least attempted to avoid these pitfalls, when addressing Egyptian scribes.

Scribe in ancient Egypt appears to be a code name to cover extensive, sometimes almost elusive, elements using a single word. We have set out to explore in this book the many and multifaceted aspects of the term through the eyes of those who considered themselves scribes in New Kingdom Egypt. In these few final pages, we wish to highlight some shared links as well as differences among the many different scribes who appeared in this book.

Literacy seemingly appears as the foremost feature that these men share. It was arguably crucial in their work, with whatever script or text they were required to engage. Through their literacy, scribes participated in power, and according to ancient apologists of the *métier*, they *were* the authority. And indeed, New Kingdom scribal representations make continued recourse to authority as an immanent element in the scribe's role.[2] To what extent, however, do authority, literacy and scribehood truly converge?

The lives of our New Kingdom protagonists suggest otherwise. They were altogether exceptional personalities in the Egypt of their time: men of authority, whether they came from the royal family or served in the court. Others were heads of artists or temple administration. Not all, however, chose to represent themselves as scribes: Senenmut boasted of his eloquence and knowledge, but he saw no need to speak of himself as a scribe. Similarly, Tutankhamun was buried with a number of pieces of writing equipment, but nowhere is he given the name scribe. It thus follows that even though literacy and scribehood do at times converge, their sociology is markedly different.

What we hope to have shown is not only that the boundaries of literacy and scribehood were not identical, but also that those of individual scribehood were fuzzy and allowed for accepting different roles – and different self-presentations[3] – even in one's lifetime. A scribe in the New Kingdom, might have been an administrator – like Djehutimose – or an artist – like Dedia – or indeed both, like Paheri.

The image that arises from the preceeding discussions is that of a lively and continuous negotiation of what it means to be a scribe and who is allowed to be called one. Throughout the chapters a few argumentative lines seemed more conspicuous than others. The relationship between scribes and draughtsmen, or outline scribes – as the term in Egyptian literally translates – seems to be clearly contentious, especially questioning whether strict lines separate the two. Another seems to lie between scribes and military men and specifically concerns the men with a double loyalty, military scribes. Others draw the demarcation lines around a scribe according to quality, character and skill.

This constant negotiation of the notion of a scribe and his role in society employs variety of media and contexts. Some figures, like Inena and the author whose voice was impersonated by Hori in P. Anastasi I, chose to articulate their ideas within the written medium. Others we meet in their tombs, where the context uses both text and image to decorate the tomb walls. Haremhab, in addition, commissioned a statue and placed it in a temple, where it would be met by priests, visitors and gods. Thus, art and text both take part in the lively discussion as to what constitutes a scribe. Also seemingly informal texts, such as graffiti, became an arena for opinions as to who is a deserving scribe and who is a mere scribbler. We may suggest that among the literates of ancient Egypt, scribes, armed with cultural competence that went beyond literacy, discussed their own position and promoted it with vigour. In the Egyptian administration, itself a flexible 'complex adaptive system',[4] scribes were omnipresent and important, but did not control it. Consequently, they battled for the boundaries of the 'scribe' within themselves and against others, but also for a good scribe to represent knowledge, literacy and authority.

Glossary

The glossary contains short descriptions or definitions of select Egyptian and Egyptological terminology.

Amun Ancient Egyptian deity, in the New Kingdom a patron deity of Thebes, the king and all Egypt; chief deity of the Egyptian pantheon in the New Kingdom, the name means 'the Hidden One'. Depicted usually in human form, or in animal manifestation, a ram.

Archive (1) a place of document storage, institutional or private; (2) a virtual archive, texts read and used in a community; shared knowledge.

Chester Beatty papyri A large collection of papyri located in Dublin, London and Cairo. These papyri contain a wide selection of texts from literary excerpts, love songs, to historical texts, a dream book and accounts and administrative memoranda. They were probably found in the area of Deir el-Medina and belonged to one or more families of scribes and draughtsmen from that community.

Deir el-Bahri An archaeological site on the west bank of the Nile opposite Karnak; in antiquity an important cultic site, place of veneration of Hathor. Several royal memorial temples were located in Deir el-Bahri, including Middle Kingdom sovereign Mentuhotep Nebhepetre and New Kingdom sovereign Hatshepsut.

Deir el-Medina A settlement of craftsmen and artists in Western Thebes. It was founded in the early Eighteenth Dynasty and existed almost until the end of the Twentieth Dynasty with a short break during the Amarna Period. Amenhotep I might have been considered its traditional founder; the earliest royal name attested so far is Thutmose I. The village grew throughout the New Kingdom and reached its peak in the late Nineteenth/early Twentieth Dynasty. Its inhabitants built the tombs in the Valley of the Kings and the Valley of the Queens. The village grew gradually. The crew of craftsmen could have included just over twenty or up to over 120 people. Its members were chosen from capable artists from inside and outside the settlement. The administration was run by foremen and scribes and directed by high state officials, including the vizier. It was abandoned at the end of the Twentieth Dynasty, when the valleys in the Theban cliffs ceased to be used as a main dynastic burial place.

Foreman (Deir el-Medina) Chief craftsman in the community of the makers of royal tombs. For most of its working life, there were two foremen in the crew at Deir el-Medina. Foremen were responsible for their workmen and acted as an authority over them. They were also part of the local administration and judiciary.

Graffiti In ancient Egypt texts or figural scenes are usually added to man-made surfaces (including perhaps man-altered natural surfaces, such as quarries and mines as well). They may be incised/scratched, pecked, carved or drawn or painted.

Ink This was made of organic pigments: black ink of soot and red ink of natural ochre/ red coloured minerals. The solvents were also organic including egg white and gum Arabic. The ink was produced in firm lumps of pigment and had to be diluted on the palette rather like Chinese inks.

Instruction texts Also known as wisdom literature. Ancient Egyptian literary texts with a didactic character. The texts usually contain both general considerations on ethics and practical information on etiquette, for example. In the Middle and New Kingdom, a significant component is an exhortation to a diligent study of writing; literacy is much praised, for example, in the *Instruction of Khety*, of *Ani*, and in several texts within the corpus of *Late Egyptian Miscellanies*.

Late Ramesside Letters A corpus of letters dated to the late Twentieth Dynasty, exchanged mostly among Theban dignitaries and administrators.

Late Egyptian Miscellanies Collections of papyri with mixed contents, hence *Miscellanies*. *Miscellanies* were identified both in the Memphite context and in the Theban context (the group of Chester Beatty papyri). They have been considered as part of the training of scribes, however, it appears more likely that these texts were a collection written by more advanced scribes, perhaps as a future reference textbook, letter-writer and collection of literary excerpts.

Literati A general term applied to intelligentsia, people with education and cultural competence, often also with artistic, literary interests.

Maat An ancient Egyptian concept of world order, justice and truth; also an eponymous deity – the personification of truth and order. The gods, king and also ordinary human beings were all expected to contribute to the maintenance of *maat,* which governed natural laws as well as ethics.

Medinet Habu A toponym and an archaeological location in Western Thebes, a site with a number of important buildings, including several temples of New Kingdom date, e.g. the memorial temple of Ramesses III. After the village of Deir el-Medina had been abandoned, the community moved to a more secure location in the Medinet Habu area, possibly within the temple precinct of Medinet Habu. Later a Coptic city of Djeme thrived close by.

Medjay A group of inhabitants, possibly originally of specific ethnic origin, but increasingly connected with a social role of an inhabitant of the desert fringe, scout, ranger; in Western Thebes probably also employed as a security force in the area of the necropolis including Deir el-Medina and the Valley of the Kings.

Memorial/mortuary/funerary temple Names applied to large temple foundations located mainly in Abydos, Western Memphis and Western Thebes. They were connected with the cult of deceased kings as well as royal ancestors and deities closely related to the afterlife and to the royal ideology.

Memphis Mennefer, Graecized form Memphis, the ancient capital of Egypt, located almost at the border of Lower and Upper Egypt. Its origins reach back in the Archaic Period (The White Walls) and to the Old Kingdom pyramid towns, i.e settlements attached to the pyramid complexes and housing their staff (one of which, Mennefer

Pepi, probably gave the latter city its name). Memphis remained one of the most important cities of Egypt even when the kings were not permanently resident there. New Kingdom Memphis was the seat of one of the two viziers, and also a part time royal residence.

Ostracon, pl. ostraca A piece of limestone either picked up or produced (chipped off) purposefully; also a potsherd. Ostraca can range from large pieces of over a foot tall to several inch-long chips of stone or pottery.

Papyrus The 'paper' of ancient Egypt. It is a plant-based writing material produced from different species of *Cyperus papyrus*. Its stems were cut lengthwise and the resulting strips layered and beaten to form a sheet. Individual sheets were glued to form differently-sized rolls. Papyrus was only relatively expensive, but its use might have been limited simply because the commodity was less accessible. However, papyri surviving to modern days are likely to be only a tiny fraction of the papyrus production on ancient Egypt, as papyri were often re-used, recycled in cartonnage and eventually used as organic fuel.

Pigments Colours were produced using natural materials, usually ground minerals. They were mixed and diluted to obtain suitable inks to write and paint on papyrus, and paints to use on polychrome statues and reliefs.

Piramesse A Ramesside capital city located in the Eastern Delta. Built under Ramesses II and inhabited till the end of the New Kingdom, when the capital was moved to Tanis, along with a number of monuments.

Ramesside or Ramessid Concerning Dynasties Nineteen and Twenty, who used the royal name of Ramesses frequently.

Rock inscriptions and drawings Texts and figures located on natural rock surfaces found in the Nile Valley and in the desert, especially along desert roads and at other spots frequented by humans. The rock art dates far back in prehistory. Rock inscriptions may be closely related to graffiti in terms of contents.

Rush brush/pen Egyptian pens resembled hard brushes and were made from rush, cut and chewed at the end. Reed pens with a nib-like tip came to use in the Graeco-Roman period. Still later, the Roman stylus was used.

Sinuhe Hero of the *Tale of Sinuhe*, a Middle Kingdom story that adapted the autobiographical genre to a (probably) fictional narrative of a life of an ideal Egyptian dignitary who survives and thrives in exile to be invited to return in his old age – and re-affirms the true allegiance to his culture and country.

Thebes The New Kingdom capital, royal residence and the city of god Amun. Egyptian name Waset, or Niwt ('The City'). Located in the area of modern Luxor.

Thoth God of writing, literacy and wisdom, patron of literati and scribes; depicted as an ibis, a baboon, or a human with a head of an ibis.

TT An abbreviation for 'Theban tomb', i.e. one of tombs in the non-royal cemeteries of Western Thebes. Most tombs in the area are known under a code consisting of TT + number. Royal tombs are abbreviated KV for Valley of the Kings, and QV for Valley of the Queens.

Valley of the Kings, Valley of the Queens Royal burial grounds of New Kingdom
sovereigns, located on the west bank of ancient Thebes, today's Luxor. The tombs are
cut into the cliffs of wadis and decorated with a complex programme of religious
texts and scenes concerning the netherworld.

Vizier The most important government official, the king's chief minister, responsible for
the running of the country, for the judiciary, royal court, an Egyptian equivalent of
the Prime Minister. There were two viziers, at least from the reign of Thutmose III
onwards, if not earlier. The seat of the northern vizier was Memphis, the southern
resided in Thebes, where he was also responsible for the royal building projects
including the royal tombs.

Chronology

Dates used follow E. Hornung, D. Warburton, and R. Krauss, *Ancient Egyptian Chronology*, Leiden 2006. Most dates preceding the seventh century BC are considered approximate.

Chronology of Egypt: a general outline

Archaic/Early Dynastic	*c.* 2900–2545 BC
Old Kingdom	*c.* 2543–2120 BC
First Intermediate	*c.* 2118–1980 BC
Middle Kingdom	*c.* 1980–1760 BC
Second Intermediate	*c.* 1759–1539 BC
New Kingdom	*c.* 1539–1077 BC
Third Intermediate	*c.* 1076–723 BC
Late Period	*c.* 722–332 BC
Graeco-Roman	332 BC–395 AD
Byzantine	395–642
Arab conquest	642
Fatimid	909–1171
Ayyubid	1171–1249
Abbasid	1261–1517
Ottoman	1517–1914
Dynasty of Muhammad Ali	1805–1882
Modern	from 1882–

Kings of the New Kingdom: *c.* 1539–1077, all dates BC

Dynasty Eighteen *c.* 1539–1212

Ahmose	*c.* 1539–1515
Amenhotep I	*c.* 1514–1494
Thutmose I	*c.* 1493–1483
Thutmose II	*c.* 1482–1480
Thutmose III and Hatshepsut	*c.* 1479–1458
Thutmose III	*c.* 1458–1425

Amenhotep II	*c.* 1425–1400
Thutmose IV	*c.* 1400–1390
Amenhotep III	*c.* 1390–1353
Amenhotep IV/Akhenaten	*c.* 1353–1336
Smenkhkare /?Akhkheprure Nefernefruaten	*c.* 1336–1334
Nefernefruaten Aknhkheprure	*c.* 1334– ?
Tutankhaton/amon	? –1324
Ay	*c.* 1323–1320
Horemheb	*c.* 1319–1292

Dynasty Nineteen *c.* 1292–1191

Ramesses I	*c.* 1292–1291
Seti I	*c.* 1290–1279
Ramesses II	*c.* 1279–1213
Merenptah	*c..* 1213–1203
Seti II	*c.* 1202–1198
Amenmesse	*c.* 1202–1200
Siptah	*c.* 1197–1193
Twosret	*c.* 1192–1191

Dynasty Twenty *c.* 1190–1077

Sethnakhte	*c.* 1190–1188
Ramesses III	*c.* 1187–1157
Ramesses IV	*c.* 1156–1150
Ramesses V	*c.* 1149–1146
Ramesses VI	*c.* 1145–1139
Ramesses VII	*c.* 1138–1131
Ramesses VIII	*c.* 1130
Ramesses IX	*c.* 1129–1111
Ramesses X	*c.* 1110–1107
Ramesses XI	*c.* 1106–1077

Notes

Introduction: Exploring the Social Figure of the Scribes

1 Wb 3, 475.6–476.15.
2 The suggestion, therefore, of translating *zẖ3.w* as 'secretary' is not without merit, as it evokes the wide variety of meanings, ranging from the office secretary to secretary of state; see for example Quirke 2004b: 15–17.
3 Baines's articles from the late sixties and the seventies were republished with updates in Baines 2007; Eyre, who wrote one of those articles with Baines, also published in 2013 a study of the use of documents in ancient Egypt, see Eyre 2013.
4 Street 1984 and 1993; for similar discussions in studies of the ancient world, see for example Thomas 2009.
5 Ragazzoli 2010; Ragazzoli 2011.
6 Pinarello 2015. Rather than scribes, which to him is located in colonial and orientalistic discourses, he speaks of *writing performers*, who take part in a broad array of practices in which media are marked for communication. Archaeology can hardly substantiate, according to his approach, the categorization of certain performers as scribes and their equipment as scribal. His investigation verges on treating categorization and grouping as modern phenomena, while reflecting only very shortly on the term *zẖ3.w* or on the ancient Egyptian conceptualizations of writing practices. Notwithstanding its methodological flaws, the book presents an important attempt to rethink the place we ascribe literacy in the ancient Egyptian society.
7 See, for example, the extensive study of Old Kingdom scribes in Piacentini 2002.
8 One of the most popular personalities of New Kingdom Egypt in both Egyptian and Egyptological tradition (compare Vinson 2010 and 2011), but also one among the most complex to characterize consistently and meaningfully, is the son of Ramesses II, prince and priest Khaemwaset, cf. recent catalogue *Savoir et pouvoir à l'époque de Ramsès II, Khâemouaset, le prince archéologue*, published to accompany an exhibition in Arles in 2016–17. The catalogue, which appeared just as the present book was being typeset, also contains more general relevant references to artefacts of written culture and scribal social practices, and to the figure of draughtsman Dedia (see chapter 7).

Prologue – Writing Tools and Hands

1 See Eyre 2013: 17–54 on the 'physical form of writing' with further references.

2 Parkinson 1999: 46–55.

3 For the historical development of the Egyptian see Loprieno 1995, Parkinson 1999: 46–55 and Allen 2010. There is Old Egyptian, Middle Egyptian, Late Egyptian, Demotic and Coptic. The last two used specific writing systems, demotic being based on abnormal cursive hieratic and Coptic using Greek alphabet with a selection of signs from Demotic. Major grammars of different phases of development of the Egyptian are by E. Edel, A.H. Gardiner, J.P. Allen, J. Winand, F. Neveu, F. Junge, J.H. Johnson, T.O. Lambdin, B.O. Layton.

4 Černý 1952: 12, Tait 1988.

5 See also Allon 2013 and further in this volume.

6 For scribal iconography overview including, but not limited to positions, attire and tools see Vandier 1964: 193–216. A sculptor decorating a statue whilst holding a palette with pigments ibid., fig. on 715.

7 Made of *Cyperus papyrus,* on the plant, outline of harvest and manufacturing and characteristics of the resulting product see Parkinson and Quirke 1995, detailed analysis Leach and Tait 2000.

8 Parkinson and Quirke 1995: 16.

9 Černý 1952: 16, but cf. Baines 2007: 161–3 on possible aesthetic/performative aspects of operating a large roll in a ceremonial context.

10 Bierbrier 2012: 273.

11 Černý 1952: 11.

12 Quirke 2004b: 16–19.

13 Ibid.: 17–18.

14 Editio princeps J. Barns 1952; on the text R.B. Parkinson 1997, on reading of *Sinuhe* Parkinson 2002: 149–67, Parkinson 2009: 171–207 including an analysis of the Ashmolean copy.

15 As did many other literary ostraca, Parkinson 2009: 171–207.

16 Gasse 2005, Peust 2006 with further references, also Mathieu and Ritter 2008, Kaper 2010, Petersmarck 2012, Goelet 2013.

17 As suggested by G. Andreu-Lanoë.

18 On the division of writing materials, sites with most finds of specific types, see also Hagen 2012: 64–77, Eyre 2013. On New Kingdom writing boards in detail Hagen 2013b.

19 List of preserved manuscripts Quirke 1996: 392, Hagen 2013b.

20 Galán 2007.

21 Les artistes 2002: 224–5, http://www.louvre.fr/en/oeuvre-notices/tablet-apprentice-scribe with further references.

22 Although, for example, a limestone board from Abydos is of a later date, no. E 580, Brussels, see Janssen and Janssen 1990: 77, fig. 30.

23 Gardiner 1916, Newberry 1913, Dévaud 1916.

24 No. BM EA 5646, wooden writing board probably from Thebes, Eighteenth Dynasty, Parkinson 1999, 148–9. The board is inscribed with a hymn to Thoth.

25 Barbotin 1997 for AF 497.

26 An almost complete board MMA 14.108 with a plan of a garden. There are also a number of earlier, Middle Kingdom boards and board fragments e.g. MMA 27.3.49a.

27 Prague Náprstek Museum, P 7228, literary text (Instructions of Amenemhat I). Wood, 15.3 × 11.3 centimetres, thickness 1.2 centimetres. Inscribed on one side, 7 lines in black and red ink, Eighteenth Dynasty, Western Thebes.

28 Eyre 2013: 26–7, based on Janssen 1975.

29 Discussion Donker van Heel and Haring 2003 including previous references, McDowell 1990: 6.

30 Rzepka 2014, Dorn 2014 with further references, and GMT.

31 Ragazzoli and Frood 2013, Jacquet Gordon 2003, Navratilova 2010.

32 E.g. Darnell 2002, 2014.

33 Tosh 2009: 90–100, Jan Assmann defined the twofold aspect of sources as 'Spuren und Botschaften', Assmann 1991, and found Egypt to be a prime case study.

1 Paheri

1 See Ragazzoli 2010.

2 For scholarship, canonization and social power in the New Kingdom, see Ragazzoli 2015.

3 Paheri's tomb was first published in Tylor and Griffith 1894. The tomb and its decoration were recently restudied and discussed in Davies 2009.

4 Tylor and Griffith 1894: 3

5 The hieroglyphic text could be found in *Urk IV*: 1–11. A translation of the text appears in Lichtheim 2006: II. 12–15.

6 Ancient Egyptian texts and battle reliefs depict the cutting and counting of dead enemies' hands, see Helck 1975. Recently, two pits with altogether fourteen cut off right hands were found in the excavations at Avaris, see Bietak et al. 2012–13: 31–2.

7 Tylor and Griffith 1894: 3

8 On the similarity between the tombs, see Manniche 1988: 62–87. Laboury suggests direct acquaintance between Wensu and Pahery, see Laboury 2016.

9 l. 31–4.

10 The half missing phrase appears in the tomb of Rekhmire, see *Urk IV*: 1081 and *DZA* 24.228.980.

11 l. 23–24; lph is an abbreviation for life, health, prosperity, which is most often abbreviated in ancient Egyptian ꜥ(nḫ)-(w)ḏꜣ-s(nb).

12 See Haring 2009b.

13 See Papazian 2013.

14 Davies 2009: 154.

15 See important discussion on scribes and artists in Laboury 2013a, where this scene is discussed (ibid., 32).

16 See Davies 2009: fig. 7.

17 For on a discussion on this and other artists' 'signatures', see Laboury 2013b and Laboury 2016.

18 For discussion and newly found inscriptions identifying Paheri, see Davies 2009: 142.

19 Ibid.: 142.

20 The title only partially appears there, but the gap fits the missing signs.

21 nn zḫꜣ.w-ḳdw.t pw jn ḥꜣtj=f sšm=f sw. On his signatures, see Kruchten and Delvaux 2010: 199–223, pls. 16–17, 37, 65, 78; see also Laboury 2016.

2 Senenmut

1 An excellent summary of her reign and achievements was presented in Roehrig et al. 2005a. For an art-historical approach, see Tefnin 1979: viii–xi.

2 Gardiner 1964.

3 Polz 2007. For an overview of changing opinions, see Ratié 1979, Cooney 2014. A major watershed was represented by works of Ratié 1979 and Tefnin 1979.

4 Gardiner 1964: 184.

5 See also Roehrig 1990. For a list of courtiers of Hatshepsut, see Ratié 1979: 243–73.

6 E.g. from the circles of royal nurses as tutors, see statue of Hatshepsut's nurse Sitre, Roehrig 2002, also Winlock 1932: 5, 10.

7 See also Keller 2005c.

8 Meyer 1982.

9 Bedman and Martín-Valentín 2004: 184–5.

10 Careful analysis Schulman 1969–70, also Dorman 1988.

11 Schulman 1969–70: 29.

12 Yoyotte 2013 and Keller 2005b.

13 Brunner-Traut, Maus, LÄ III: 1250–2.

14 Dorman 1988, also Ratié 1979: 251–2.

15 Cf also Dorman 1988: 203–12.

16 See Dorman 1991, also Bedman and Martín-Valentín 2004, photographs from the tomb illustrate the volume, see also Bedman and Martín-Valentín 2011.

17 Stela Berlin 2066, Dorman 2005b: 132–3.

18 Berlin 2296, BM 174, BM 1513, Cairo CG 579, Cairo CG 42114, CG 42115, CG 42116, CG 42117, JE 34582, JE 47278, Chicago Field Museum 173800, MMA 48.149.7, 'Sheikh Labib', 'Naville' statue fragment, statue from the temple of Thutmose III, Djeser akhet and the statue above his tomb no TT 71, to name just those connected with the Theban region. For a complete list see Dorman 1988: 188–97.

19 See also his list of monuments in Ratié 1979: 253.

20 Monuments of Senenmut on Silsila, Kucharek 2010 and Caminos and James 1963.

21 Indeed he is one of the Dynasty Eighteen courtiers for whom an outline of an actual biography may be written, see Bedman and Martín-Valentín, 2004.

22 See also Bedman and ibid.: 24–5.

23 E.g. Dorman 1991: 32.

24 Dorman 2005c: 107.

25 Dorman 2005b.

26 See Roehrig 1990 and also Roehrig 2005.

27 Dorman 2005c: 107.

28 *Urk IV*: 34–5.

29 See Roehrig 2005: 112–13 and Keller 2005a.

30 Musée du Louvre E 11057; Keller 2005d: 122–3, also context in Dorman 1988.

31 Dorman 2005c: 108.

32 Their names were found on Deir el-Bahri ostraca relatively frequently, Senenmut's far less so.

33 On the architecture and art of Hatshepsut's time Cwiek 2014, Galán, Bryan, Dorman eds. 2014. On a relationship of Hatshepsut and Nebhepetre Dodson 1989.

34 Bickel ed. 2013, Galán, Dorman, Bryan eds. 2014.

35 Dorman 1988, Keller 2005a.

36 Mentioned in nearly every Senenmutian study, see Ratié 1979: 255–6 with further references.

37 Dorman 1988: 125, Meyer 1982: 169–70.

38 CG 42114, l. 12, translation Dorman 1988: 125.

39 See also comments by Bedman and Martín-Valentín 2004: 184–5.

40 The Field Museum of Natural History, Gift of Stanley Field and Ernest Graham, no. 173800; see Ross 2002: 454.

41 Trans. R. Parkinson, Parkinson 1997: 240, the loyalist teaching.

42 Although opposite opinions would have Neferure outlive also Hatshepsut, e.g. Cooney 2014.

43 Schulman 1969–70: 47–9.

44 Schulman 1969–70: Dorman 1988, Dorman 2005.

45 Bedman and Martín-Valentín 2004: 197, Bedman and Martín-Valentín 2011: 71.

46 Burke 1992.

47 CG 34012, JE 15116, JE 27491, *Urk. IV* 833–8; Lacau 1909: 24–5. Klug 2002: 90ff., with further bibliography.

48 Lacau 1909: 25.

49 Morales 2014.

50 As shown in temple reliefs of Semna. See also Laboury 1998.

51 Compare Tefnin 1979, Laboury 1998.

52 Burke 1992: 197.

53 See also Morales 2014.

54 Loprieno 1996.

55 See most recently on Thutmoside wars in Syria Redford 2003.

56 Gnirs 2009.

57 Tombs with tribute scenes include Senenmut's tombs, and a number of Eighteenth Dynasty memorials, e.g. TT 40, TT 55, TT 63, TT 76, TT 78, TT 81, TT 85, TT 89, TT 91, TT 100, TT 131, TT 155, large percentage of which is dated to the era of Thutmose I to Thutmose III, i.e. Senenmut's era.

58 *Urk. IV.*

59 *Urk. IV*, 495–516.

60 On his texts Di Biase-Dyson 2014 with further references and Manassa 2013a.

61 *Urk. IV*, 409.

62 Bologna, Museo Civico Archeologico (KS 1822).

63 *Urk IV*, 504 and following.

64 Tr. Keller 2005c. Chief mouth also translated as chief spokesman, see Simpson, Senenmut, LÄ V, 849–51.

65 Statue PM II, 280; BM EA 1513; CG 579; *Urk IV*, 411.

66 Jansen Winkeln 2004.

67 See Junge 2003: 153–4, 158–9. The habitus formation concerns here both the Middle Kingdom, when autobiography flourishes and instruction texts like Ptahhotep might have been composed, and the Eighteenth Dynasty, when autobiography develops further and instruction texts are frequently copied (see also Hagen 2012: 41–2).

68 Hagen 2012.

69 Or: craftsman, *ḥmw*, Ptahhotep, 367; Žába 1956, 45 (transcription), 91 (translation), 150 (commentary, reference to a parallel in Instruction for Merikare); Junge (2003, 199) translated as 'master' (of good speech). Note the figural use of the word that originally identifies a master craftsman to denote a master of the 'craft' of speech.

70 Trans. Parkinson 1997: 258.

71 Erasmus, On Ennius in Adagia see Miller 2006.

72 Parkinson 2002: 257–8, although he is more dismissive concerning the value of teachings.

73 Compare Junge 2003: 140–7, 148–54.

74 Gnirs 2009.

75 Bedman and Martín-Valentín 2011: 69–70, but compare Dorman 1991:146–7.

76 Caminos and James 1963: 53.

77 Dorman 1988: 163–4, see Keller 2005c, Ratié 1979.

78 See also chapter Dedia, and Kampp 1996: 117–19, Salvador 2014: 153–67, containing references to preceding studies.

79 Where Bedman and Martín-Valentín see a proof of his quasi real status, see Bedman and Martín-Valentín 2004: 185. This may be excessive perhaps.

3 Tjanuni

1 On a survey of Egypt's military campaigns during the New Kingdom, see Spalinger 2005. More specifically on Egypt's foreign policy in Nubia, see Morris 2005.

2 Employing here Heike Guksch's term to describe the importance of the relationship to the king in autobiographies of the Eighteenth Dynasty, see Guksch 1994.

3 On the Hyksos, see Bietak 2010.

4 Manassa 2013a.

5 See Ikram and Dodson 1998: 117–18; Shaw 2009.

6 These events were narrated in the autobiographical text of Ahmose son of Ibana, see chapter 1.

7 Spalinger 2005: 17

8 On chariots in ancient Egypt see Díaz Hernández 2014, and the collected papers in Veldmeijer & Ikram 2013.

9 Allen 2005.

10 Allen 2005: 262. Ann Macy Roth suggests, however, that Thutmose III's stature was not measured correctly, as it did not take into account the mummy's missing feet, see Keller 2005b.

11 The tomb and objects that relate to it were published in Brack and Brack 1977.

12 The rectangular brackets mark the sections of the text which could not be seen in the tomb when published in 1977, but which appear in the Champollion's copy of the text, see Brack and Brack 1977: 46–7.

13 For scribes and education see chapters Hori and Inena, also Amenemhat.

14 See Jäger 2004.

15 These examples come from *The Teaching of Khety*. For a translation, see Parkinson 1997: 273–83.

16 Borchardt 1907: 59.

17 Brack and Brack 1977: 40–1, pl. 28a.

18 Ibid. 43–44, pl. 29a.

19 On censuses in ancient Egypt, see Wilkinson 2000: 64; Kóthay 2013: 510–18.

20 See in general Redford 1986, Baines 2008, both with further references. On Eighteenth Dynasty, see Popko 2006 with further references.

21 On ancient Egyptian daybooks, see Redford 1986: 97–126. On daybooks in the military context, see Hsieh 2012.

22 See Redford 1986: 122–5.

23 *Sanā al-barq al Shami,* in Rabbat 2001: 145. Elsewhere in the text, the protagonist says to Saladin: 'I am a man of the pen and do not compete with swords. I announce victories but do not cause deaths' (Rabbat 2001: 153).

24 On the life of 'Imād al-Dīn and his autobiography, see Richards 1993 and Rabbat 1997.

4 Amenemhat

1 Ranke 1935–77: I, 28, 8.

2 See Parkinson 2002: 241–8.

3 Abbreviation used also for the Middle Kingdom ruler, King Amenemhat I.

4 Most of New Kingdom graffiti in his pyramid complex name Netjerikhet as Djoser. Also the Royal Canon of Turin, a major New Kingdom kings-list, gives the name Djoser, written in red ink. See also Gundacker 2015.

5 Edition Navratilova 2015a: 156–61.

6 See also further.

7 See e.g. Navratilova 2015a: 91–3.

8 Badawi 1948, Kitchen 1991, Evans ed. 2012.

9 Kitchen 1991.

10 The most recent outline in Eyre 2013.

11 Compare resources in Pasquali 2011.

12 Moreno García 2013, passim with further references to the changing roles of the vizier.

13 Duties of the vizier were described in several New Kingdom vizieral tombs, best known from Rekhmire, TT 100.

14 Travel as elite and beyond elite experience was investigated by Baines 2013b and Köpp-Junk 2013.

15 Polz 1991 with further references.

16 Navratilova 2015a: 63–4.

17 Gunn 1926, Cwiek 2014: 24.

18 Although the prehistorical, or indeed perhaps Archaic periods, might have still seen a steppe character surviving in parts of the later desert biotope.

19 The most extensive schooling texts are preserved from the Ramesside era, but possibly had predecessors in an oral form, and certainly there were written classics

already in the early Eighteenth Dynasty – the Satire of Trades by a respected writer known as Khety, literary works such as the story of Sinuhe, etc. Compare Parkinson 2002, also Widmaier 2013.

20 Parkinson 1997: 29.

21 Darnell 2014, Förster and Riemer eds 2013: 42.

22 Darnell 2014, 81–2.

23 Investigated in Zivie 2007.

24 Raven 2014.

25 See chapters Dedia and Djehutimose.

26 Posener-Kriéger 1981, KRI VII, 263–8.

27 Van Dijk 1993. See also Raven 2014 for two latest decades.

28 Popko 2006.

29 Cwiek 2014, Bickel ed. 2013, Bryan, Dorman, Galán eds 2014.

30 Oppenheim 2011.

31 Janák 2011.

32 Frood 2013.

33 Helck 1952, Wildung 1972, Philips 1980, Navratilova 2015a, Verhoeven 2012a.

34 Navratilova 2013, Navratilova 2015b.

35 Underlined expressions mark narrative forms *iw.t pw irw n, sdm.n=f* form of verb *gm*) and *ʿhʿ n dd*. See also Ragazzoli 2013 and Navratilova 2015a.

36 The entire graffito is *mk hm,* Discussion with alternatives Navratilova 2015a: 67–9.

37 Verhoeven 2009.

38 Reisner 1971.

39 Wente 1984, new publication by Ragazzoli, forthcoming.

40 Guksch 1994: 88–9. Compare also Gnirs 2009.

41 A problematic term analysed Fischer-Elfert 2005, with further references.

42 Self-fashioning is a concept introduced by Stephen Greenblatt and applicable within Egyptology; see Ragazzoli 2010, and others – Renaissance studies inspiration applied by Hagen 2013a, 2012, also Parkinson 2009.

43 Opinions discussed in Parkinson 2002, 2009, Baines 2013b with further references. But compare recently also Pinarello 2015.

44 Parkinson 2005, Effland 2003.

45 Allen 2003, Burkard and Thissen 2008: 141–55, Fischer-Elfert 1983, Fischer-Elfert 1986, Gardiner 1911, Schad 2006: 11–40, Select Papyri 1842: pls. 35–62, Wente 1990: 98–110.

46 Fischer-Elfert 1986: 288–9.

47 Edition Gardiner 1911.

48 For characteristics of professions see Jäger 2004, their humorous effect was discussed by Houlihan, 2001: 12–13.

49 Appearing in teachings of Ptahhotep or Ani, or indeed in Anastasi I too see chapter 9.

50 Houlihan 2001, with further references.

51 Allon 2013: 110–11, with further references.

52 Darnell 2014, 51–3. Baines 2015.

53 Navratilova 2015a: 216.

54 Fischer-Elfert 2005.

55 Sweeney UEE, Toivari Viitala 2001.

56 Indirect participation was a different aspect cf. For the community of Deir el-Medina see Toivari Viitala 2001 and Černý 1973a.

57 Moot point of female literacy, compare Bryan 1984, Eyre 2011, also chapter 5.

58 Cf. Allon 2013.

59 Cf. Peden 2001: xxi.

60 Gunn Mss. Notebook 31, p.75.

5 Tutankhamun

1 The photographs of Burton are kept in the archives of the Metropolitan Museum of Art and the Griffith Institute, University of Oxford; see On Burton's mission, see Allen 2006.

2 JE 62079; Carter registered the palette under no. 262.

3 Scholars debate on the exact kinship relationship between Meriaten and Tutankhamen, especially around the identity of his other. As with many other questions that relate to the succession of kings following Akhenaten, the literature is extensive. For a recent discussion with further bibliography, see Eaton-Krauss 2016: 1–11.

4 See Senenmut's image, fig. 2.2 a and b.

5 See for example the use of colour in the Funerary Papyrus of the Steward Sethnakht (The Metropolitan Museum of Art, Gift of Edward S. Harkness, 1935, 35.9.19a–e).

6 See, for example, Louvre E 3669.

7 For a critical review of palettes and their analysis as scribal tools, see Pinarello 2015. Note that he criticizes the modern fetishization of the palette-and-pen, but mostly ignores similar emphasis on these tools in ancient times.

8 On the cultural background of the choice of this specific image, see Goldwasser 1995b: 31.

9 For a selective critique of this conflation and its implications, see Pinarello 2015.

10 On Meritaten, see Green 1996: 10–11.

11 It seems that the palace was first built for Kiya, whose name and titles were erased and replaced with those of Meritaten, see Reeves 1988 and Spence 1999. Such an alternation might also be visible in MMA 1985.328.8, where the woman's Nubian wig was filled in with plaster. It was then modelled and recarved into the side lock of hair, which was worn by Akhenaten's daughters.

12 The gift and other correspondences appear in the so-called Amarna letters, a corpus of diplomatic letters found at the site. Interestingly, the letter mentions a gift of pigments or dyes sent for Meritaten, see letter EA 12.

13 On the Amarna succession, see Harris 1974; Samson 1979; Allen 2009; Falck 2012; Reeves 2001: 172–7.

14 Zivie 2009: 109–13.

15 The walls of her burial place in Amarna depict them mourning their daughter's untimely death, see van Dijk 2009.

16 The main discussions on female literacy are Baines and Eyre 1983, Bryan 1984, and most recently, Grajetzki 2009.

17 Černý 1939: 11, lines 5–6.

18 On the goddess Seshat, see Budde 2000.

19 The most recent discussion with the relevant bibliography is Grajetzki 2009.

20 On the debate, see Posener 1969; Fischer 1976: 70-72; Grajetzki 2009.

21 Bryan 1984. Baines challenges Bryan's analysis pointing out that the equipment belongs to the woman's husband, under whose chair there is no room to place any object (Baines 2007: 173). See, however, Bryan's example of TT 56, in which the equipment is clearly placed under than man's chair, and similarly in TT 194.

22 On some Egyptological interpretations of palettes, see Pinarello 2015.

23 The literature on Tutankhamun is extensive. See most recently, Reeves 1990, Hawass 2013, Eaton-Krauss 2016.

24 On royal literacy, see Baines 2007: 78–83, Zinn 2012: 3–4.

25 The Mastaba of Sennedjemib Inti was excavated by the Harvard University–Boston Museum of Fine Arts Expedition at Giza (tomb G2370).

26 The relevant line appears in *Urk I*, 60, l.9. The tomb records another royal letter.

27 BMFA 25.632, see Helck 1955.

28 Cairo JE 6307; The text was published in Helck 1983: 21–9. An English translation is available in Simpson 2003: 339–46.

29 KRI II, 346-47, see Eyre 2013: 280–1.

30 On the Ished tree, see Helck 1957: 117–40, Welvaert 1996.

31 On the *gn.wt* see Redford 1986, Baines 2008.

32 See Caminos 1998: 49–51.

33 See Street 1984 and 1993.

6 Haremhab

1 Haremhab's statue, The Metropolitan Museum of Art, Gift of Mr and Mrs V. Everit Macy, 1923 (23.10.1). The statue was first published by Winlock 1923; Winlock 1924. It was also collected and discussed along with other documents pertaining to Haremhab in Hari 1964.

2 On the so-called scribal statues, see Scott 1989; Allon 2013.

3 See the prologue to this book.

4 On Haremhab and his career, see Hari 1964 and quite recently Booth 2009.

5 For a short introduction into the Amarna Period and its aftermath, see van Dijk 2000.

6 The main features of the tomb were published in Martin 1989 and later in Raven et al. 2011.

7 See also the most recent discovery regarding the decoration of the First Courtyard in Johnson 2016.

8 For an interpretation of this disparity, see Baines 2007: 44.

9 On the obstacles in interpreting titles and epithets, see Quirke 2004b: 1–5.

10 See for example Fig. 1.1 from the tomb of Paheri.

11 Hartwig 2004: 49–51.

12 cf. Eyre 2013: 7–9.

13 The stela was studied in Martin 1989: 29–31, pls. 21–2.

14 CG 42129, see Hari 1964: figs. 7–10.

15 The most extensive survey of the scribal statue was in fact never published (Scott 1989). Further discussions appear in Allon 2013, Pinarello 2015 (on Old Kingdom statues).

16 Statue BMFA 34–4–1, see PM 1974: 146.

17 For discussions on Mentuhotep and his statues, see Sauneron 1975, Delange 1987: 55–65, 78, Simpson 1991, Verbovsek 2004: 392–415.

18 For example, Amenhotep son of Hapu's who commissioned a number of scribal statues (Luxor JE 44861, Luxor JE 44862, and others), see Varille 1968: 26–31

19 See Allon 2013.

20 Haremhab's decree of law received a thorough study in Kruchten 1981.

21 The Abydene stela was registered as CG 34162.

22 See Lorton 1986: 57; Bontty 2000; van den Boorn 1988: 166–70.

7 Dedia

1 History of the period may be found concisely in relevant chapters of Shaw 2000, also Lloyd 2010 with further references.

2 Montserrat 2000.

3 Stevens 2003, 2006; Stevens 2012, also Stevens 2015 at DOI: 10.1093/oxfordhb/9780199935413.013.31.

4 Brand 2001: 46.

5 Arnold 1974: 69 n. 205.

6 Such as Senenmut's tomb builders, as maybe some of the visitors' graffiti writers, see chapters 2 and 8.

7 Baines 1985: 283.

8 Baines 1985, compare also contributions in Davies 2001.

9 Compare also Baines 1994: 67–94.

10 Louvre N 168, see Landgrafova 2012: 80–2; Delange 2015.

11 http://www.metmuseum.org/about-the-museum/now-at-the-met/2015/showing-signs-hieroglyphs-and-palettes-in-stela-of-irtisen, text by Niv Allon, accessed 17 February, 2016.

12 Landgrafova 2012: 81–2.

13 Aldred 1991: 93–4.

14 Frood 2007: 126.

15 Compare in Laboury 2010: 33–46 and Laboury and Tavier 2010: 91–106.

16 Eaton-Krauss 2003: 197–8; 201 n. 35.

17 Eaton-Krauss 2003: 194–5. See also Gabolde 1998: 32–4.

18 Eaton-Krauss 2003: 194.

19 Gabolde 1998: 35.

20 Eaton-Krauss: 2003.

21 Spencer 1989: 15–16, 64–5.

22 Brand 2001: 46.

23 Brand 2001: 46–47. But see also Ratié 1986.

24 Compare Brand 2001: 66, with further references.

25 Brand 2001: 54–55, 109–110, 113.

26 Lowle 1976.

27 Frood 2007: 133 with further references.

28 KRI I 327–31, KRITA I, 265–9, RITANC I, 220–5 with further references.

29 RITANC I, 221.

30 On position of women Robins 1993, compare also Sweeney, UEE.

31 RITANC I, 223.

32 RITANC I, 222.

33 Published KRI I, 329, KRITA I, 267–9, RITANC I, 224–5, PM I/2:.656, both with further references.

34 Frood 2007: 18–19.

35 Zivie 2013.

36 Zivie 2013: 35.

37 Frood 2007: 126.

38 Lowle 1976, KRI VII, 24–6, KRITA VII, 19–21, Frood 2007: 133–6.

39 Presence in both royal and non-royal kinglists, Redford 1986.

40 Translated by K.A. Kitchen. KRITA VII, 19.

41 Line 12–13, KRITA VII, 19. Identification of temples names vs. sovereigns in Frood 2007: 243 n. 36.

42 Identification see Stadelmann, Totentempel III, LA VI, 710.

43 On memorial temples see further Ullmann 2002.

44 Kampp 1996: 49.

45 Frood 2007: 1–4.

46 Zivie 2013.

47 Brand 2001: 56–88.

48 Ibid.: 90, 93–102.

49 Ibid.: 90–1.

50 Ibid.: 103–5.

51 See also Baines 2013a.

52 Burkard 2003, Meskell 2000, Ventura 1986.

53 Černý 1973b.

54 Dorn 2011, Keller 1993, among others.

55 See in detail Haring 2006, Donker van Heel and Haring 2003.

56 Galán 2007.

57 Hayes 1942: ostraca nos. 5; 63 recto 7, and verso 1; 64 recto 6; 70. 3 and 4; 82.3 and 6; 83.6; 97.2; 130.1, 2. 'Scribes' are here differentiated from 'masons', cf. e.g. ostracon no.82.

58 Their titles differ, $s^c n \underline{h} u$ vs. $s\check{s}\ \underline{k}dw$.

59 Donker van Heel and Haring 2003, Haring 2006.

60 Compare Laboury 2010.

61 Compare Widmayer 2013: 512–527.

62 Goelet 2013, Widmaier 2013.

63 Ibid.: 539–545.

64 Compare chief sculptor, Dedia's contemporary, Userhat, KRI I, 361–2, RITA I, 296–9, and KRI VII, KRITA VII 20–2.

65 Frood 2007: 123–128.

66 Cf. above and Janssen 1992, Widmaier 2013.

8 Inena

1 Landgrafova and Navratilova 2009: 163–4.

2 On New Kingdom literature see Moers 2010. Burkard and Thissen 2008.

3 British Museum, EA 10183,10.

4 Lichtheim, 1974: 203–11, Burkard and Thissen 2008, Hollis 1990.

5 $z\underline{h}3.w$ 'Inn3 p3 nb n p3 $z\underline{h}3.w$ – literally lord of this written document. The $z\underline{h}3.w$ as document is provided with a classifier used for letters and similar.

6 Ses D'Orbiney 19, 7–10, Parkinson 1999: 168, Ragazzoli 2014: 225.

7 Parkinson 1997: 281.

8 For etymology of the Greek word, latinized, see James A[ugustus] H[enry] Murray, ed. (1888–1893). 'colophon, n'. *The Oxford English Dictionary: A New English*

Dictionary on Historical Principles Founded Mainly on the Materials Collected by the Philological Society [Vol. II, C–Czech]. Oxford: Clarendon Press. OCLC US 460661449. For Egyptian colophons see Lenzo 2004, Parkinson 1991, Luiselli 2003.

9 Egyptian papyrus rolls also have colophon-like statements as part of the title of a text composition, cf. The Rhind Mathematical Papyrus, BM EA 10057, cf. Eyre 2013: 304–5.

10 Quirke 2004a: 11, after Jan Assmann.

11 Compare Parkinson 2009: 61–8, Simon 2013.

12 Parkinson 1991.

13 An outline and analysis of the New Kingdom colophons Lenzo 2004.

14 Haring 2006, 107, n. 2, a group of ostraca from Deir el-Medina, Luiselli 2003, 347.

15 There are some differences between Middle Kingdom and later colophons, see Parkinson 1991 and Lenzo 2004.

16 Černý 1952: 29.

17 Parkinson 1991.

18 List of papyri and identification of Inena Ragazzoli 2014.

19 A full list with contents of the Chester Beatty papyri and related Deir el-Medina papyri in Hagen 2012: 104–111.

20 Quirke 2004a:19. Provenance of the Chester Beatty papyri and their relation to other manuscript is now being analysed by Stéphane Polis.

21 Hagen 2007, Ragazzoli 2011.

22 Caminos 1954: 113.

23 Ibid.: 125.

24 Ibid.: 150.

25 Ragazzoli 2014.

26 Ragazzoli 2011: 124–6.

27 On Inena in context of Treasury see also Ragazzoli 2011: 147–51; if Inena's letters on various papyri are taken as testimony to his work and situations he tackled as part of his Treasury job, then he might have had an interesting career as a Treasury employee responsible for certain Delta areas.

28 On Samut's 'signatures' Leblanc 2004: 99 n. 5, On son Amenwahsu Amer 2000: 1–5.

29 Ragazzoli and Frood 2013, Navratilova 2013.

30 See Andrássy, Budka, Kammerzell 2009, on non-textual New Kingdom Egyptian marks Haring 2009b.

31 Haring 2009b.

32 Compare comments Parkinson 1991, Luiselli 2008, Lenzo 2004 and Ragazzoli 2014.

33 Janssen and Janssen 1990: 72–6.

34 Goelet 2013.

35 On *Kemit* (also transcribed *Kemyt*) in detail see Goelet 2013: 111–21, and Parkinson 2002: 322–5.

36 Baines 1983: 583.

37 Posener 1951; Hagen 2007.

38 Galán 2007.

39 Petersmarck 2012 with further references, and Parkinson 2002: 322–5.

40 Goelet 2013: 115.

41 An Arab-French toponym used at the excavation for a mound in the south part of the site.

42 An attempted well near the village that never reached the water table, hence remained a great waterless pit, later used as a dump.

43 Parkinson 2009.

44 Goelet 2013.

45 See discussion in Widmaier 2013.

46 Such as who paid for the schooling, could gifted youngsters enter a school sponsored by a temple or an office, and so on.

47 See most recently Eyre 2013.

48 Eyre 2013: 56–7.

49 = P BM EA9994, 7; E.A.W. Budge 1923, pls. 15–30, Gardiner 1937: xviii, 99–116, Caminos 1954: 373–428, Lichtheim 1974: 168–75, Moers 2001.

50 = P. BM EA 9994, 7,6–8,7; A.H. Gardiner assumed this might have been a Theban papyrus (Gardiner 1937: xviii).

51 I.e. tired by physical work, ready for being slaughtered? Caminos 1954: 397.

52 See Ragazzoli 2010.

53 For Egyptian 'job descriptions' in general see Jäger 2004.

54 Typical warnings of disadvantages e.g. in P. Anastasi II, P. Sallier I, P. Chester Beatty IV and V.

55 See P. Anastasi V, 15,6–17,3, Caminos 1954: 247.

56 After Caminos 1954: 164.

57 Hagen 2007.

58 Demarée 2008, Ryholt 2013, Hagen forthcoming.

59 Leblanc 2004.

60 Compare Janssen and Janssen 1990: 77.

61 Description and analyses of the house of life range from Gardiner 1938 to Eyre 2013: 311–15 with further references.

62 On storage of records see also Eyre 2013: 309–15.

63 Parkinson and Quirke 1995: 58–9, Eyre 2013.

64 See also Eyre 2013, passim, Parkinson and Quirke 1995: 60–1.

65 See Traunecker 2014.

66 Galán 2005: 9.

67 Fischer-Elfert 2003.

68 Janssen 1982a, also Toivari-Viitala 2001: 171–2.

69 See Burkard and Thissen 2008: 127–31, Černý and Gardiner 1957, pls. 78–9, Fischer-Elfert 2006, Foster 1984, Guglielmi 1983, Goedicke 1987, KRI VI, 215–17, Parkinson 2009: 209–210, also Janssen 1982b.

70 Parkinson 2009: 209–210.

71 Compare Sweeney 2001: 4.

72 Sweeney 2001: 14.

73 See Parkinson 2002, 81–5, see also Quirke 2004a: 24–5

74 Morenz 1998: 73–81, see also Frood 2007: 84–91.

75 See Ragazzoli 2011: 571–2.

9 Hori

1 Papyrus Anastasi I (pBM EA 10247), 1,1. The main editions of the texts are Gardiner 1911: 1*–34* and 2–81, Fischer-Elfert 1986; Fischer-Elfert 1992. The most recent transliteration and translation of the text appear in *Thesaurus Linguae Aegyptiae* (Dils 2016); A partial English translation can be found in Allen 2003.

2 The word is *pnꜥ*, 'to turn upside down', which is written with a classifier of a turned boat, see Wb 1, 508.11–509.9. This quote translates P. Anastasi I, 4,7–5,1.

3 See list of sources in Fischer-Elfert 1992: 1–4.

4 The handwriting shares a few features with that of Inena, the scribe of chapter 8, see Gardiner 1911: 1*. A correction seems to appear, for example, above the third column of P. Anastasi I.

5 On school texts and literature in the Ramesside Period, see Osing 1997, who includes P. Anastasi I in his discussion of Late Egyptian texts.

6 As in many ancient Egyptian texts, the author himself remains unnamed, but his protagonist Hori, serves for him as a voice.

7 Ragazzoli 2011.

8 See Jäger 2004: 258–93.

9 A full account of the text and its scholarly history may be found in Gardiner 1911: 2*–4*.

10 Bierbrier 2012:19–20.

11 Among the pieces that came from the Anastasi collection is a statue in the British Museum (BM EA 36). The identity of the statue's owners was only recently revealed, when a fragment found in the tomb of Haremhab in Saqqara (see chapter 6) was found to come from the British Museum statue, before it was removed from the site, see Walsem and Raven 2011: 375–80.

12 Birch 1842.

13 Goodwin 1858; Goodwin and Chabas 1866.

14 Brugsch 1867.

15 Lauth 1868.

16 On epistolary formulae in ancient Egypt, see Bakir 1970.

17 For Menna's text, see Fischer-Elfert 2006, and in this book's chapter on Inena; for Wenamun see Schipper 2005; See also Quack 2001. For the epistolary genre in the literary realm, see Schad 2006.

18 On the history of the reception of the text in Egyptology, see Schipper 2005: 7–40.

19 Erman 1885: 508–13.

20 Fisher-Elfert 1992.

21 Gardiner 1911: 5*.

22 P. Anastasi I, 17.2–3.

23 Ibid., 1.1.

24 Or good wine mixed with that of low quality, see Fischer-Elfert 1986: 51, note e.

25 P. Anastasi I, 8.1.

26 See Goldwasser 1990.

27 P. Anastasi I, 5.4–6.5.

28 Ibid., 7.5–6.

29 Following Parkinson's translation in Parkinson 1998: 146. For a discussion of the text, see Parkinson 2002: 200–4.

30 P. Anastasi I, 8.7–8.

31 Ibid., 9.3–4.

32 pBM EA 10474, 24. 8–12. For a discussion on the text and further bibliography, see Laisney 2007. A translation may be found in Lichtheim 2006: II. 160.

33 Sometimes called in the literature Djedefhor and Hordedef, see Parkinson 2002: 49–50, 313–14.

34 P. Anastasi I, 11.1–3.

35 This section appears in ibid., 13.5–18.4.

36 Ibid., 14.5.

37 Ibid., 18.4.

38 On *mhr*, see Rainey 1967; Zorn 1991.

39 On *maryannu* see O'Callaghan 1951: 309–24, Rainey 1965: 19–21.

40 P. Anastasi I, 18.3–6.

41 Ibid., 20.7–21.1.

42 Ibid. 23.6–7.

43 Ragazzoli sees the text as a realization of the potential presented in *Late Egyptian Miscellanies*, see Ragazzoli 2011: 205–9. It might be interesting to note that the texts also differ in their scope. Most of the *Late Egyptian Miscellanies* texts present hierarchal differences between writer and addressee, especially when related to the scribal profession. P. Anastasi I, however, presents a case in which the two scribes are colleagues.

44 P. Chester Beatty IV = pBM EA 10684, Vs 5.6–6.3.

10 Djehutimose Tjaroy

1 See also Parkinson 1999: 160, about his son Butehamun, Davies 1997, Verhoeven 2012b.

2 Bibliography: Erman 1923, Černý 1939, no. 33, Wente 1967: 53–54; Černý 1973a: 381, Thijs 2003: 301–3, photographs also in Janssen 1991: pls. 50–2.

3 Olsen 2013: 145–56.

4 Michaux-Colombot 2013.

5 Olsen 2013 with further references. Gabler 2012.

6 Gabler 2012, Černý 1973a: 261–84, Müller-Wollermann 2004: 274–7, McDowell 1990: 51–4.

7 Compare Gabler 2012 and McDowell 1990.

8 Interestingly, one modern pop culture reading of the Medjay includes brave warriors resembling the Tuaregs in Sommers' *Mummy* films. On reinterpreting these 'guardians of Hamunaptra' in the fantasy universe versus select historical evidence see *Alisha Jourdenais, Medjai* at http://amra-bey.narod.ru/medjai.html, accessed 29 February 2016. These Medjay, however, belong to the history of Egyptomania.

9 A. Erman called the case in German 'ein Fall abgekürzter Justiz' – a case of shortcut justice.

10 Valbelle 1985: 216–20, about late Ramesside activities.

11 Gabler 2012.

12 Valbelle 1985: 219 with further references.

13 Fluctuations see Davies 1999: xix, Valbelle 1985: Table III following p. 105.

14 Valbelle 1985: 219, with further references.

15 Compare Haring 2006.

16 Gardiner 1941: 220.

17 Valbelle 1985: 221.

18 Eyre 2013: 175.

19 Ibid.: 175–6.

20 Late Ramesside letters sequence in Wente 1967.

21 Gardiner 1941.

22 Vinson 1995: 93–102.

23 P. BM 10375, Ritner 2009: 104–9.

24 Černý 1973a: 364 renders 'despaired'.

25 Mobility of Egyptian dignitaries was part of their job, as is often seen in biographies. In the Ramesside texts, the absence from one's city is also thematised in the praises of the cities, analysed by Ragazzoli 2008: 143–5, 170–8.

26 The graffiti research outline in Bouvier and Bouvier 2006, early work Spiegelberg 1921, Černý 1956, editio princeps of most graffiti GMT, latest developments including work of Swiss and Polish teams Dorn 2014, Rzepka 2014.

27 Bouvier and Bouvier 2006, Jansen-Winkeln 1995, Graefe 2003.

28 Gabler 2012.

29 Bouvier and Bouvier 2006.

30 See Davies 1999: 76–7.

31 Identifying their individual hands is a standing task in Deir el-Medina studies, see Janssen 1987, Bouvier 2002, or Burkard 2013.

32 Haring 2006 with further references.

33 Outline of the community administration in Häggman 2002.

34 Haring 2006: 110–11, with further references.

35 Details Davies 1999: 79–80.

36 Davies 1999, op. cit Kitchen 1982: 193–4.

37 Caminos 1954: 82.

38 Pinch 1993: 235, 242, Caminos 1954: 82.

39 See Shoemaker 2002; Cornelius 2004.

40 Kitchen 1982: 194–5.

41 Černý 1973a: 329 ff., Caminos 1954: 86, Parkinson 1999: 154–6, Hagen 2012: 103–13.

42 Černý 1973a: 334–6. On P. Chester Beatty see Pestman 1982, Hagen 2012: 104–11, also Ragazzoli 2011: 180–1.

43 Černý 1973a: 334–5.

44 Draughtsman Prehotep ODeM 303, KRI III/17, 534.

45 P. Salt 124, Janssen 1982a.

46 Caminos 1954: 105f.

47 Černý 1973a: 347.

48 Bickel and Mathieu 1993: 38, Parkinson 1999: 157, Burkard 2013.

49 Janssen 1982.

50 Bickel and Mathieu 1993: 31–51.

51 Ibid: 48.

52 See also Moers 2010.

53 Archive as defined by Quirke 1996.

54 Bickel and Mathieu 1993: 48.

55 Caminos 1954: 114, with further references.

56 Caminos 1954: 136.

57 About relations of Khaemhedjet (i) Davies 1999: 30, 54, 70, 116, 117, 121, 133, 137, 221, 282.

58 Caminos 1954: 136–8.

59 Compare Bickel and Mathieu 1993, Koenig 1981 and Pestman 1982. Also Hagen 2012: 103–12.

60 P. Leiden I 370, vol. 4–5, Černý, 1939: 10, 13–14.

61 Caminos 1954: 139, Davies 1997: 64.

62 Bickel and Mathieu 1993: 48f.

63 Černý 1939, Wente 1990, Janssen 1991.

64 Haring 2009a.

65 Sweeney 2001.

66 Bakir 1970, Wente 1990, Haring 2009a.

67 Janssen 1991: 12. However, the dispatch might have concerned an answering letter as well as an official task.

68 See objects connected with Butehamun in the Turin Museum, Verhoeven 2012b.

69 Černý 1973a: 357–8 with a list of monuments attesting the family relations. A detailed discussion of the family relations of Butehamun Davies 1997.

70 Černý 1973a: 363–366.

71 Černý 1973a: 358–60, family histories.

72 Gardiner and Černý 1956: pl. 80–80A. O. Louvre 698, the text is written entirely in red, with red, then changed to black, verse points. Texts entirely in red, whether on ostraca or on graffiti, appear throughout the New Kingdom, but are relatively scarce. Might they have been true drafts? For example, another instance is a red ink ostracon from DeM Prague 3809, a record of an oath. On text see also Goldwasser 1995a.

73 Černý 1973a: 367.

74 Compare Janssen 1991: 8–9.

75 Compare Caminos 1954.

76 Ragazzoli 2008.

77 Frood 2007: 20–22, 24–26.

Epilogue

1 Vike 2011.

2 Compare comments by Korostovtsev 1962, followed e.g. by Quirke 2004a: 15–16.

3 Baines 2013a: 245.

4 Complex adaptive character especially of New Kingdom administration was discussed by Shirley (2013: 574–6) based on observations by M. Lehner and B. J. Kemp.

Bibliography

Aldred, C. 1991. *Akhenaten, King of Egypt*, London.

Allam, S. 1968. Sind die Schriftostraka Brouillons? *Journal of Egyptian Archaeology* 54: 121–28.

Allen, J.P. 2002. *The Heqanakht Papyri*. Publications of the Metropolitan Museum of Art Egyptian Expedition 27. New York.

Allen, J.P. 2003. The Craft of the Scribe (Papyrus Anastasi I). In W.W. Hallo and K. Lawson Younger, Jr., *The Context of Scripture. Archival Documents from the Biblical World* vol. III. 9–14. Leiden.

Allen, J.P. 2005. After Hatshepsut: The Military Campaigns of Thutmose III. In C.H. Roehrig et al. (eds), *Hatshepsut: from Queen to Pharaoh*. 261–2. New York.

Allen, J.P. 2006. Introduction. In S.J. Allen (ed.), *Tutankhamun's Tomb: The Thrill of Discovery*. H. Burton (photographs). New York.

Allen, J.P. 2009. The Amarna Succession. In P.J. Brand and L. Cooper (eds), *Causing His Name to Live: Studies in Egyptian Epigraphy and History in Memory of William J. Murnane*. Culture and History of the Ancient Near East 37. 9–21. Leiden, Boston.

Allen, J.P. 2010. Language, Scripts, and Literacy. In A.B. Lloyd (ed.), *A Companion to Ancient Egypt* 2. 641–62. Chichester, Malden, MA.

Allon, N. 2013. The Writing Hand and the Seated Baboon: Tension and Balance in Statue MMA 29.2.16. *Journal of the American Research Center in Egypt* 49: 93–112.

Amer, A.M.A. 2000. The Scholar-Scribe Amenwahsu and his Family. *Zeitschrift für ägyptische Sprache und Altertumskunde* 127: 1–5.

Andrassy, P., J. Budka and F. Kammerzell (eds). 2009. *Non-Textual Marking Systems, Writing and Pseudo Script from Prehistory to Present Times*. Lingua aegyptia. Studia monographica 8. Göttingen.

Arnold, D. 1974. *Der Tempel des Königs Montuhotep von Deir el Bahari, Architektur und Deutung*. Archäologische Veröffentlichungen 8. Mainz.

Assmann, A. 1991. Gebrauch und Gedächtnis. Die zwei Kulturen des pharaonischen Ägypten. In A. Harth and A. Assmann (eds), *Kultur als Lebenswelt und Monument*. 135–52. Frankfurt.

Assmann, A. 1997. Traum-Hieroglyphen von der Renaissance bis zur Romantik. In G. Benedetti and E. Hornung (eds), *Die Wahrheit der Träume*. 119–44. München.

Assmann, A. 2010. *Erinnerungsräume. Formen und Wandlungen des kulturellen Gedächtnisses*. Munich.

Badawi, A. 1948. *Memphis als zweite Landeshauptstadt im Neuen Reich*. Cairo.

Baines, J. 1983. Literacy and Ancient Egyptian Society. *Man*, New Series, 18/3: 572–99.

Baines, J. 1985. Color Terminology and Color Classification: Ancient Egyptian Color Terminology and Polychromy. *American Anthropologist, New Series*, 87.2: 282–97.

Baines, J. 1994. On the Status and Purposes of Ancient Egyptian Art. *Cambridge Archaeological Journal* 4.1: 67–94.

Baines, J. 2007. *Visual and Written Culture in Ancient Egypt*. Oxford.

Baines, J. 2008. On the Evolution, Purpose, and Forms of Egyptian Annals. In E.-M. Engel et al. (eds), *Zeichen aus dem Sand: Streiflichter aus Ägyptens Geschichte zu Ehren von Günter Dreyer*. 19–40. Wiesbaden.

Baines, J. 2013a. Ancient Egypt. In A. Feldherr and G. Hardy (eds), *The Oxford History of Historical Writing, Volume 1: Beginnings to AD 600*. 53–75. Oxford.

Baines, J. 2013b. *High Culture and Experience in Ancient Egypt*, Sheffield.

Baines, J. 2015. On the Old Kingdom Inscriptions of Hezy: Purity of Person and Mind; Court Hierarchy. In H. Amstutz, A. Dorn, M. Müller, M. Ronsdorf and S. Uljas (eds), *Fuzzy Boundaries: Festschrift für Antonio Loprieno* 2. 519–36. Hamburg.

Baines, J. and Ch. Eyre. 1983. Four Notes on Literacy. *Göttinger Miszellen* 61: 65–96.

Bakir, A. 1970. *Egyptian Epistolography from the Eighteenth to the Twenty-first Dynasty*. Bibliothèque d'étude 48. Cairo.

Barbotin, Ch. 1997. Une nouvelle attestation de *Kémit*. *Revue d'égyptologie* 48: 247–50.

Barns, J.W.B. 1952. *The Ashmolean Ostracon of Sinuhe*. London.

Bedman T. and F. Martín-Valentín. 2004. *Sen-en-mut. El hombre que pudo ser rey de Egipto*. Madrid.

Bedman T. and F. Martín-Valentín. 2011. New Considerations Regarding Senenmut's TT353 at Deir el-Bahari. *KMT* 22 (3): 58–74.

Bell, L. 1986. The Epigraphic Survey: Philosophy of Egyptian Epigraphy After Sixty Years' Practical Experience. In J. Assmann, V. Davies and G. Burkard (eds), *Problems and Priorities in Egyptian Archaeology*. 43–55. London, New York.

Bell, L. 1996. New Kingdom Epigraphy. In N. Thomas (ed.), *The American Discovery of Ancient Egypt: Essays*. 96–109. Los Angeles, New York.

Bellion, M. 1987. *Catalogue des manuscrits hiéroglyphiques et hiératiques et des dessins sur papyrus, cuir ou tissu publiés ou signalés*. Paris.

Berlev, O. 1997. Bureaucrats. In S. Donadoni (ed.), *The Egyptians*. 87–119. Chicago, London.

Bickel, S. (ed.). 2013. *Vergangenheit und Zukunft Studien zum historischen Bewusstsein in der Thutmosidenzeit*. Aegyptiaca Helvetica 22. Basel.

Bickel, S., and B. Mathieu. 1993. L'écrivain Amennakht et son Enseignement, *Bulletin de l'Institut Français d'Archéologie Orientale* 93: 31–5.

Bierbrier, M. (ed.). 2012. *Who was Who in Egyptology*. 4th ed. London.

Bietak, M. 2010. From Where Came the Hyksos and Where Did They Go? In M. Marée (ed.), *The Second Intermediate Period (Thirteenth–Seventeenth Dynasties): Current Research, Future Prospects*. 139–81. Leuven.

Bietak, M. et al. 2012–13. Report on the excavations of a Hyksos palace at Tell el-Dab'a/ Avaris (23 August–15 November 2011). *Ägypten und Levante* 22–3: 17–53.

[Birch, S.] 1842. *Select Papyri in the Hieratic Character from the Collection of the British Museum*, vol. I.

Bontty, M. 2000. Images of Law and the Disputing Process in the *Tale of the Eloquent Peasant*. In A.M. Gnirs (ed.), *Reading the* Eloquent Peasant: *Proceedings of the International Conference on* The Tale of the Eloquent Peasant *at the University of California, Los Angeles, March 27–30, 1997*: 93–107. Göttingen.

Booth, Ch. 2009. *Horemheb: The Forgotten Pharaoh*. Stroud.

Boorn, G.P.F. van den. 1988. *The Duties of the Vizier: Civil Administration in the Early New Kingdom*. Studies in Egyptology. London, New York.

Borchardt, L. 1907. Das Dienstgebäude des auswärtigen Amtes under den Ramessiden. *Zeitschrift für Ägyptische Sprache und Altertumskunde* 44: 59–61.

Bouvier, G. 2002. Quelques remarques sur l'identification des 'mains' dans les documents hiératiques de l'époque ramesside. *Annales de la Fondation Fyssen* 17: 13–14.

Bouvier, G., Bouvier K. 2006. L'activité des gens de la nécropole à la fin de la XXe et à la XXIe dynastie, d'après les graffiti de la montagne thébaine: le transfert des momies royales. In A. Dorn and T. Hofmann (eds), *Living and writing in Deir el-Medine: Socio-historical Embodiment of Deir el-Medine Texts*. 21–9. Basel.

Brack, A., and A. Brack. 1977. *Das Grab Des Tjanuni: Theben Nr. 74*. Archäologische Veröffentlichungen 19. Mainz am Rhein.

Brand, P.J. 2001. *Monuments of Seti I*. Leiden.

Bresciani, E. 1999. *Letteratura e poesia dell'antico Egitto: cultura e società attraverso i testi*. Milano.

Browarski, E. 1996. Epigraphic and Archaeological Documentation of Old Kingdom Tombs and Monuments at Giza and Saqqara. In N. Thomas (ed.), *The American Discovery of Ancient Egypt. Essays*. 25–44. Los Angeles, New York.

Brugsch, H. 1868. Examen critique du livre de M. Chabas intitulé Voyage d'un Egyptien en Syrie, en Phénicie, en Palestine, etc. Paris.

Brunner-Traut, E. Maus, *LÄ* III, 1250–52.

Bryan, B. 1984. Evidence for female literacy from Theban tombs of the New Kingdom. *Bulletin of the Egyptological Seminar* 6: 17–32.

Budde, D. 2000. *Die Göttin Seschat*. Kanobos: Forschungen zum griechisch-römischen Ägypten 2. Leipzig.

Budge, E.A.W. 1923. *Egyptian Hieratic Papyri in the British Museum*, Second Series. London.

Burkard, G. 2003. 'Oh diese Mauern Pharaos'. Zur Bewegungsfreiheit der Einwohner von Deir el-Medine. In *Mitteilungen des Deutschen Archäologischen Instituts, Abteilung Kairo*, 59. 11–39.

Burkard, G. 2013. Amunnakht, Scribe and Poet of Deir el-Medina: A Study of Ostrakon O. Berlin P 14262. In V. Lepper and R. Enmarch, *Ancient Egyptian Literature. Theory and Practice*. 65–82. Oxford.

Burkard, G., H.-J. Thissen. 2008. *Einführung in die altägyptische Literaturgeschichte* II, *Neues Reich*. Berlin.

Burke, P. 1992. *The Fabrication of Louis XIV*. New Haven, London.

Caminos, R. 1954. *Late-Egyptian Miscellanies*. Brown Egyptologicial Studies 1. London.

Caminos, R. 1998. *Semna-Kumma I: The Temple of Semna*. Archaeological survey of Egypt 37. London.

Caminos, R.A. and T.G.H. James. 1963. *Gebel es-Silsilah* I: *The Shrines*. Archaeological Survey of Egypt 31. London.

Černý, J. 1931. Les ostraca hiératiques, leur intêret et la necessité de leur étude. *Chronique d'Egypte* 12: 212–24.

Černý, J. 1939. *Late Ramesside Letters*. Bruxelles.

Černý, J. 1952. *Paper and Books in Ancient Egypt*. London.

Černý, J. 1956. *Graffiti hiéroglyphiques et hiératiques de la nécropole thébaine, Nos. 1060–1405*. Le Caire.

Černý, J. 1973a. *The Community of Workmen at Thebes in the Ramesside Period*. Le Caire.

Černý, J. 1973b. *The Valley of the Kings. Fragments d'un manuscrit inachevé*. Le Caire.

Černý, J. and A.H. Gardiner. 1956. *Hieratic Ostraca*. London.

Chabas, F. 1873. *Mélanges égyptologiques* II. Paris.

Cooney, K. 2014. *The Woman Who Would Be King*. New York.

Cornelius, I. 2004. The Many Faces of the Goddess: The Iconography of the Syro-Palestinian Goddesses Anat, Astarte, Qedeshet and Asherah c. 1500–1000 BCE. *Orbis Biblicus et Orientalis* 204. Freiburg, Göttingen.

Cwiek, A. 2014. Old and Middle Kingdom Tradition. In the Temple of Hatshepsut at Deir el-Bahari. *Études et Travaux* XXVII (2014): 20–51.

Darnell, J.C. et al. 2002. *Theban Desert Road Survey in the Egyptian Western Desert* I. Chicago.

Darnell, J.C. et al. 2014. *Theban Desert Road Survey II – The Rock Shrine of Pahu, Gebel Akhenaton, and Other Rock Inscriptions from the Western Hinterland of Qamula*. New Haven.

Davies, B.G. 1997. Two Many Butehamuns? Additional Observations on Their Identity. *Studien zur Altägyptischen Kultur* 24: 49–68.

Davies, B.G. 1999. *Who's Who at Deir el-Medina. A Prosopographic Study of the Royal Workmen's Community*. Leiden.

Davies, W.V. (ed.). 2001. *Colour and Painting in Ancient Egypt*. London.

Davies, W.V. 2009. The Tomb of Ahmose Son-of-Ibana at Elkab: Documenting the Family and Other Observations. In W. Claes et al. (eds.), *Elkab and Beyond*. 139–75. Leuven.

Day, J. 2015. Repeating Death: The High Priest Character in Mummy Horror Films. In W. Carruthers (ed.), *Histories of Egyptology: Interdisciplinary Measures*, 215–26. New York, London.

Delange, E. 1987. *Catalogue des statues égyptiennes du Moyen Empire 2060–1560 avant J.-C*. Paris.

Delange, E. 2015. Stela of the Overseer of Artisans Irtisen. In A. Oppenheim et al. (eds), *Ancient Egypt Transformed: The Middle Kingdom*. 152–3. New York.

Demarée, R.J. 2008. Letters and Archives from the New Kingdom Necropolis at Thebes. In L. Pantalacci (ed.), *La lettre d'archive: communication administrative et personelle dans l'antiquité proch-orientale et égyptienne*. 43–52. Cairo.

Demarée R.J. and A. Egberts (eds). 1992. *Village Voices. Proceedings of the Symposium 'Texts from Deir el-Medîna and their interpretation', Leiden, 31 May–1 June 1991* (CNWS Publications 13). Leiden.

Der Manuelian, P. 1998. An Approach to Streamlining Egyptological Epigraphic Method. *Journal of the American Research Center in Egypt* 35: 97–113.

Derchain, P. 1999. 'Quand'elles écrivaient', *Bulletin de la Société d'Egyptologie Genéve*, 23: 28–9.

Dévaud, E. 1916. *Les maximes de Ptahhotep d'après le Papyrus Prisse, les papyrus 10371/10435 et 10509 du British Museum et la Tablette Carnarvon*. Fribourg.

Di Biase-Dyson, C. 2014. Amenemheb's Excellent Adventure in Syria: New Insights from Discourse Analysis and Toponymics. In G. Neunert, H. Simon, A. Verbovsek and K. Gabler (eds), *Text: Wissen – Wirkung – Wahrnehmung: Beiträge des vierten Münchner Arbeitskreises Junge Ägyptologie (MAJA 4), 29.11. bis 1.12.2013*. 121–50. Wiesbaden.

Díaz Hernández, R.A. 2014. The Role of the War Chariot in the Formation of the Egyptian Empire in the Early 18th Dynasty. *Studien zur Altägyptischen Kultur* 43: 109–22.

Dijk, J. van. 1993 *The New Kingdom Necropolis of Memphis. Historical and Iconographical Studies*. Groningen.

Dijk. J. van. 2000. The Amarna Period and the Later New Kingdom (*c.* 1352–1069 BC). In I. Shaw (ed.), *The Oxford History of Ancient Egypt*, 265–307. Oxford, New York.

Dijk, J. van 2009. The Death of Meketaten. In P.J. Brand and L. Cooper (eds), *Causing His Name to Live: Studies in Egyptian Epigraphy and History in Memory of William J. Murnane*, Culture and History of the Ancient Near East 37. 83–88. Leiden, Boston.

Dodson, A. 1989. Hatshepsut and 'Her Father' Mentuhotpe II. *Journal of Egyptian Archaeology* 75: 224–6.

Donker van Heel, K. and B.J.J. Haring. 2003. *Writing in a Workmen's Village. Scribal Practice in Ramesside Deir el-Medina*. Leiden.

Dorman, P.F. 1988. *The Monuments of Senenmut: Problems in Historical Methodology*. London, New York.

Dorman, P.F. 1991. *The Tombs of Senenmut: The Architecture and Decoration of Tombs 71 and 353*. Publications of the Metropolitan Museum of Art Egyptian Expedition 24. New York.

Dorman, P. F. 2005. The Career of Senenmut. In C.H. Roehrig et al. (eds), *Hatshepsut: from Queen to Pharaoh*. 107–9. New York.

Dorman, P.F. 2005a. False Door Stela. In C.H. Roehrig et al. (eds), *Hatshepsut: from Queen to Pharaoh*. 132–3. New York.

Dorman, P.F. 2005b. The Tomb of Ramose and Hatnefer. In C.H. Roehrig et al. (eds), *Hatshepsut: from Queen to Pharaoh.* 91–2. New York.

Dorman, P.F. 2008. Epigraphy and Recording. In R.H. Wilkinson (ed.), *Egyptology Today.* 77–97. Cambridge, New York.

Dorn, A. 2006. *M33-nḥt.w-f,* ein einfacher Arbeiter, schreibt Briefe. In A. Dorn and T. Hofmann (eds), *Living and Writing in Deir el-Medine, Aegyptiaca Helvetica* 19. 67–85. Basel.

Dorn, A. 2011. *Arbeiterhütten im Tal der Könige Ein Beitrag zur altägyptischen Sozialgeschichte aufgrund von neuem Quellenmaterial aus der Mitte der 20. Dynastie (ca. 1150 v. Chr.).* Aegyptia Helvetica 23. Basel.

Dorn, A. 2014. Von Graffiti und Königsgräbern des Neuen Reiches. In B.J.J. Haring, O.E. Kaper and R. van Walsem (eds), *The Workman's Progress. Studies in the Village of Deir el-Medina and Other Documents from Western Thebes in Honour of Rob Demarée,* 57–71. Leiden.

Drower, M.S. 1985. *Flinders Petrie. A Life in Archaeology.* London.

Eaton-Krauss, M. 2003. Restorations and Erasures in the Post-Amarna Period. In Z. Hawass (ed.), *Egyptology at the Dawn of the Twenty-first Century. Proceedings of the Eighth International Congress of Egyptologists.* Cairo 2000, II. 194–202. Cairo, New York.

Eaton-Krauss, M. 2016. *The Unknown Tutankhamun.* Bloomsbury Egyptology. London.

Effland, U. 2003. Aggression und Aggressionskontrolle im alten Ägypten. In N. Kloth, K. Martin and E. Pardey (eds), *Es werde niedergelegt als Schriftstück: Festschrift für Hartwig Altenmüller zum 65. Geburtstag,* 71–81. Hamburg.

el-Daly, O. 2005. *Egyptology: The Missing Millennium. Ancient Egypt in Medieval Arabic Writings.* London.

Erman, A. 1885. *Aegypten und aegyptisches Leben im Alterthum.* Tübingen.

Erman, A. 1923. *Die Literatur der Ägypter.* Leipzig.

Erman A. and H.O. Lange. 1925. *Papyrus Lansing. Eine ägyptische Schülerhandschrift der 20. Dynastie.* Kobenhavn.

Evans, L. (ed.). 2012. *Ancient Memphis 'Enduring is the Perfection'. Proceedings of the International Conference held at Macquarie University of Sydney on August 14–15, 2008.* Leuven.

Eyre, C. 2009. On the Inefficiency of Bureaucracy. In P. Piacentini and C. Orsenigo (eds), *Egyptian Archives: Proceedings of the First Session of the International Congress Egyptian Archives/Egyptological Archives, Milano, September 9–10, 2008.* 15–30. Milano.

Eyre, C. 2011. Source Mining in Egyptian Texts: The Reconstruction of Social and Religious Behaviour in Pharaonic Egypt. In A. Verbovsek, B. Backes and C. Jones (eds), *Methodik und Didaktik in der Ägyptologie: Herausforderungen eines kulturwissenschaftlichen Paradigmenwechsels in den Altertumswissenschaft*en. 599–615. Munich.

Eyre, C. 2013. *The Use of Documents in Pharaonic Egypt.* Oxford.

Falck, M. von. 2012. Zwischen Echnaton und Tutanchamun: eine neu nachgezeichnete Skizze. *Sokar* 25: 87–97.

Fischer, H.G. 1976. *Varia*. Egyptian Studies 1. New York.

Fischer-Elfert, H.-W. 1983. Morphologie, Rhetorik und Genese der Soldatencharakteristik. *Göttinger Miszellen* 66: 45–65.

Fischer-Elfert, H.-W. 1986. *Die Satirische Streitschrift des Papyrus Anastasi I. Übersetzung und Kommentar*. Wiesbaden.

Fischer-Elfert, H.-W. 1992. *Die satirische Streitschrift des Papyrus Anastasi I*. 2nd revised ed. Kleine ägyptische Texte [7]. Wiesbaden.

Fischer-Elfert, H.-W. 2003. Representations of the Past in New Kingdom Literature. In J. Tait (ed.), *'Never Had the Like Occurred': Egypt's View of its Past*. 119–37. London.

Fischer-Elfert, H.-W. 2005. *Abseits von Maat*. Würzburg.

Fischer-Elfert, H.-W. 2006. Literature as a Mirror of Private Affairs: The Case of Menna (i) and his Son Merj-Sachmet (iii). In A. Dorn and T. Hofmann (eds), *Living and Writing in Deir el-Medina*. 87–92. Basel.

Förster, F., and H. Riemer (eds). 2013. *Desert Road Archaeology in Ancient Egypt and Beyond*. Africa praehistorica 27. Köln.

Foster, J.H. 1984. Oriental Institute Ostracon No. 12074: 'Menna's Lament' or 'Letter to a Wayward Son'. *Journal of the Society of the Study of Egyptian Antiquities* 14: 88–99.

Frood, E. 2007. *Biographical Texts from Ramessid Egypt*. Atlanta.

Frood, E. 2013. Egyptian Temple Graffiti and the Gods: Appropriation and Ritualization in Karnak and Luxor. In D. Ragavan, ed., *Heaven on Earth. Temples, Ritual and the Cosmic Symbolism in the Ancient World*. 285–318. Chicago.

Gabler, K. 2012. *Mnṯw-ms*, der 'Muster-*mḏꜣj*'? Ein prominenter Titelträger im Vergleich mit der Berufsgruppe der Medja von Deir el-Medine. In G. Neunert, K. Gabler and A. Verbovsek (eds), *Sozialisationen: Individuum – Gruppe – Gesellschaft: Beiträge des ersten Münchner Arbeitskreises Junge Aegyptologie (MAJA 1), 3. bis 5.12.2010*. 81–96. Wiesbaden.

Gabolde, L. 1998. *D'Akhenaten à Toutânkhamon*. Lyon, Paris.

Galán, J.M. 2005. Four Journeys in Ancient Egyptian Literature. *Lingua Aegyptia, Studia Monographica* 5. Göttingen.

Galán, J.M. 2007. An Apprentice's Board from Dra Abu El-Naga. *The Journal of Egyptian Archaeology*, 93: 95–116.

Galán, J.M., B.M. Bryan, P.F. Dorman (eds). 2014. *Innovation and Creativity in the Reign of Hatshepsut*. Studies in Ancient Oriental Civilization 69. Chicago.

Gange, D. 2013. *Dialogues with the Dead: Egyptology in British Culture and Religion, 1822–1922. Classical Presences*. Oxford.

Gardiner, A.H. 1911. *Egyptian Hieratic Texts. Series 1: Literary Texts of the New Kingdom. Pt. 1, The Papyrus Anastasi I and the Papyrus Koller Together with the Parallel Texts*. Leipzig.

Gardiner, A.H. 1916. The Defeat of the Hyksos by Kamōse: The Carnarvon Tablet, no. 1. *Journal of Egyptian Archaeology* 3 (2/3): 95–110.

Gardiner, A.H. 1920. Graffiti. In: N. de G. Davies and A.H. Gardiner, *The Tomb of Antefoker, Vizier of Sesostris I, and of his Wife Senet (No. 60)*. London.

Gardiner, A.H. 1925. The Autobiography of Rekhmereʿ. *Zeitschrift für ägyptische Sprache und Altertumskunde* 60: 62–76.

Gardiner, A.H. 1937. *Late Egyptian Miscellanies, Bibliotheca Aegyptiaca* 7. Brussels.

Gardiner, A.H. 1938. The House of Life. *Journal of Egyptian Archaeology* 21: 157–79.

Gardiner, A.H. 1941. Ramesside Texts Relating to the Taxation and Transport of Corn. *Journal of Egyptian Archaeology* 27: 19–73.

Gardiner, A.H. 1964. *Egypt of the Pharaohs: An Introduction*. Oxford.

Gasse, A. 2005. *Catalogue des ostraca littéraires de Deir Al-Medîna. Tome V, Nos 1775–1873 et 1156*. Le Caire.

Gertzen, T.L. 2013. *École de Berlin und 'Goldenes Zeitalter' (1882–1914) der Ägyptologie als Wissenschaft: das Lehrer-Schüler-Verhältnis von Ebers, Erman und Sethe*. Berlin.

Gnirs, A.M. 2009. In the King's House: Audiences and Receptions at Court. In R. Gundlach and J.H. Taylor (eds), *Egyptian Royal Residences: 4. Symposium zur ägyptischen Königsideologie/4th Symposium on Egyptian Royal Ideology. London, June, 1st–5th 2004*: 13–43. Wiesbaden.

Goedicke, H. 1987. Menna's Lament. *Revue d'Égyptologie* 38: 63–80.

Goelet Jr., O. 2013. Reflections on the Format and Paleography of the Kemyt: Implications for the Sitz im Leben of Middle Egyptian Literature in the Ramesside period. In G. Moers et al. (eds), *Dating Egyptian Literary Texts*. 111–21. Hamburg.

Goldbrunner, S. 2006. *Der Verblendete Gelehrte: der erste Setna-Roman (P. Kairo 30646)*. Demotische Studien 13. Sommerhausen.

Goldwasser, O. 1990. On the Choice of Registers: Studies on the Grammar of Papyrus Anastasi I. In S. Israelit-Groll (ed.), *Studies in Egyptology Presented to Miriam Lichtheim*. 1200–40. Jerusalem.

Goldwasser, O. 1995a. On the Conception of the Poetic Form: A Love Letter to a Departed Wife: Ostracon Louvre 698. In S. Izreʾel and R. Drory (eds), *Language and Culture in the Near East*. 191–205. Leiden, New York, Köln.

Goldwasser, O. 1995b. From Icon to Metaphor: Studies in the Semiotics of the Hieroglyphs. Orbis Biblicus et Orientalis 142. Freiburg (Schweiz), Göttingen.

Goodwin, C.W. 1858. Hieratic Papyri. *Cambridge Essays* 4: 226–82.

Goodwin, C.W. and F. Chabas. 1866. *Voyage d'un Égyptien en Syrie, en Phénicie, en Palestine, &c. au XIVme siècle avant notre ère: traduction analytique d'un papyrus du Musée Britannique, comprenant le fac-simile du texte hiératique et sa transcription complète en hiéroglyphes et en lettres coptes*. Paris.

Graefe, E. 2003. The Royal Cache and the Tomb Robberies. In N. Strudwick and J.H. Taylor (eds), *The Theban Necropolis. Past, Present and Future*. 74–82. London.

Grajetzki, W. 2009. Women and Writing in the Middle Kingdom: Stela Louvre C 187. *Revue d'égyptologie* 60: 209–14.

Green, L. The Royal Women of Amarna: Who was Who. In D. Arnold, *The Royal Women of Amarna. Images of Beauty from Ancient Egypt*. 7–15. New York.

Guglielmi, W. 1983. Eine 'Lehre' für einen reiselustigen Sohn (Ostrakon Oriental Institute 12074). *Welt des Orients* 14: 147–66.

Guksch, H. 1994 *Selbstdarstellung der Beamten in der 18. Dynastie. Studien zur Archäologie und Geschichte Altägyptens 11.* Heidelberg.

Gundacker, R. 2015. The Chronology of the Third and Fourth Dynasties According to Manetho's Aegyptiaca. In P. der Manuelian and T. Schneider (eds), *Towards a New History for the Egyptian Old Kingdom.* 76–199. Cambridge MA.

Gunn, B.G. 1926. A Shawabti-figure of Puyamrẹ̃' from Saqqara. *Annales du Service des Antiquités de l'Égypte* 26: 157–9.

Hagen, F. 2006. Literature, Transmission, and the Late Egyptian Miscellanies. In R.J. Dann (ed.), *Current Research in Egyptology 2004: Proceedings of the Fifth Annual Symposium which took place at the University of Durham January 2004*: 84–99. Oxford.

Hagen, F. 2007. Ostraca, Literature and Teaching at Deir el-Medina. In R. Mairs and A. Stevenson (eds), *Current Research in Egyptology 2005.* 38–52. Oxford.

Hagen, F. 2012. *An Ancient Egyptian Literary Text in Context. The Instruction of Ptahhotep.* Orientalia Lovaniensia Analecta 218. Leuven.

Hagen, F. 2013a. Constructing Textual Identity: Framing and Self-reference in Egyptian Texts. In R. Enmarch and V.M. Lepper (eds), *Ancient Egyptian Literature: Theory and Practice.* 185–209. Oxford.

Hagen, F. 2013b. An Eighteenth Dynasty Writing Board (Ashmolean 1948.91) and The Hymn to the Nile. *Journal of the American Research Center in Egypt* 49: 73–91.

Hagen, F. forthcoming, Libraries in Ancient Egypt *c.* 1600–1000 BC. In K. Ryholt and G. Barjamovic (eds), *Libraries Before Alexandria.* Oxford.

Häggman, S. 2002. *Directing Deir el-Medina, The External Administration of the necropolis.* Uppsala.

Hari, R. 1964. *Horemheb et la reine Moutnedjemet ou la fin d'une dynastie.* Genève.

Haring, B.J.J. 2006. Scribes and Scribal Activity at Deir el-Medina. In A. Dorn and T. Hofmann (eds), *Living and Writing in Deir el-Medina.* 107–12. Basel.

Haring B.J.J. 2009a. 'In Life Prosperity, Health' Introductory Formulae in Letters from the Theban Necropolis. In D. Kessler, et al. (eds), *Texte-Theben-Tonfragmente. Festschrift für Günter Burkard* [Ägypten und Altes Testament 76]. 180–91. Wiesbaden.

Haring, B.J. 2009b. On the Nature of Workmen's Marks of the Royal Necropolis Administration in the New Kingdom. In P. Andrássy, J. Budka, F. Kammerzell (eds), *Non-textual Marking Systems, Writing and Pseudo Script from Prehistory to Present Times.* 123–35, Wiesbaden.

Haring, B.J.J. 2009c. Economy. In E. Frood and W. Wendrich (eds). *UCLA Encyclopedia of Egyptology.* Los Angeles. http://escholarship.org/uc/item/2t01s4qj

Harris, J.R. 1974. Nefernefruaten regnans. *Acta Orientalia* 36: 11–21.

Hartwig, M. 2004. *Tomb Painting and Identity in Ancient Thebes 1419–1372 BCE.* Monumenta Aegyptiaca X. Turnhout.

Hawass, Z. 2013. *Discovering Tutankhamun: From Howard Carter to DNA*. Cairo.

Hayes, H.E. 1942. *Ostraka and Name Stones from the Tomb of Sen-mut (no. 71) at Thebes*. New York.

Helck, W. 1952. Die Bedeutung der ägyptischen Besucherinschriften. *Zeitschrift des Deutschen Morgeländischen Gesellschaft* 102: 39–46.

Helck, W. 1955. Eine Stele des Vizekönigs Wsr-St.t. *Journal of Near Eastern Studies* 14 (1): 22–31.

Helck, W. 1957. Ramessidische Inschriften aus Karnak, I: eine Inschrift Ramses' IV. *Zeitschrift für ägyptische Sprache und Altertumskunde* 82: 98–140.

Helck, W. 1975. Abgeschlagene Hände als Siegeszeichen. *Göttinger Miszellen* 18: 23–24.

Helck, W. 1983. *Historisch-biographische Texte der 2. Zwischenzeit und neue Texte der 18. Dynastie*, 2nd revised ed. Kleine ägyptische Texte [6 (1)]. Wiesbaden.

Hollis, S. 1990. *The Ancient Egyptian 'Tale of the Two Brothers': The Oldest Fairy Tale in the World*. Norman, London.

Houlihan, P. 2001. *Wit and Humour in Ancient Egypt*. London.

Hsieh, J. 2012. Discussions on the Daybook Style and the Formulae of Malediction and Benediction Stemming from Five Middle Kingdom Rock-cut Stelae from Gebel el-Girgawi. *Zeitschrift für ägyptische Sprache und Altertumskunde* 139 (2): 116–35.

Humbert, J. M. 1989. *L'Egyptomanie dans l'art occidental*. Paris.

Ikram, S. and A. Dodson. 1998. *The Mummy in Ancient Egypt: Equipping the Dead for Eternity*. London.

Innis, M.A. 2007. *Empire and Communications*. Toronto.

Jacquet-Gordon, H. 2003. *The Temple of Khonsu. Vol. 3: The Graffiti on the Khonsu Temple Roof at Karnak. A Manifestation of Personal Piety*. Oriental Institute Publications 123. Chicago.

Jäger, S. 2004. *Altägyptische Berufstypologien*. Lingua Aegyptia Studia monographica 4. Göttingen.

Janák, J. 2011. Spotting the Akh: The Presence of the Northern Bald Ibis in Egypt and its Early Decline. *Journal of the American Research Center in Egypt* 46: 17–31.

Jansen-Winkeln, K. 1995. Die Plünderung der Königsgräber des Neuen Reiches. *Zeitschrift für ägyptische Sprache und Altertumskunde* 122: 62–78.

Jansen-Winkeln, K. 2004. Lebenslehre und Biographie. *Zeitschrift für ägyptische Sprache und Altertumskunde* 131: 59–72.

Janssen, J.J. 1975. *Commodity Prices from the Ramessid Period: An Economic Study of the Village of Necropolis Workmen at Thebes*. Leiden.

Janssen, J.J. 1982a. Two Personalities. In R.J. Demarée and J.J. Janssen (eds), *Gleanings from Deir el-Medina*. 113–15. Leiden.

Janssen, J.J. 1982b. A Draughtsman Who Became Scribe of the Tomb: Harshire, Son of Amennakhte. In R.J. Demarée and J.J. Janssen (eds) *Gleanings from Deir el-Medina*. 149–53. Leiden.

Janssen, J.J. 1987. On Style in Egyptian Handwriting. *Journal of Egyptian Archaeology* 73: 161–7.

Janssen, J.J. 1991. *Late Ramesside Letters and Communications. HPBM* VI. London.

Janssen, J.J. 1992. Literacy and Letters at Deir el-Medina. In R.J. Demarée and A. Egberts (eds), *Village Voices. Proceedings of the symposium 'Texts from Deir el-Medina and their interpretation', Leiden, May 31–June 1, 1991* (CNWS Publications 13). 81–94. Leiden.

Janssen, J.J. and R. Janssen. 1990. *Growing Up in Ancient Egypt.* London.

Johnson, W.R. 2016. Horemheb's Saqqara Tomb: A New Discovery. In P. Giovetti and D. Picchi (eds), *Egypt: Millenary Splendour: the Leiden Collection in Bologna.* 228–33. Milano.

Junge, F. 2003. *Die Lehre Ptahhoteps und die Tugenden der ägyptischen Welt.* Freiburg, Göttingen.

Kampp, F. 1996. *Die Thebanische Nekropole* I. Mainz.

Kaper, O.E. 2010. A Kemyt Ostracon from Amheida, Dakhleh Oasis. *Bulletin de l'Institut Français d'Archéologie Orientale* 110: 115–26.

Keller, C.A. 1993. Royal Painters: Deir el-Medina in Dynasty XIX. In E. Bleiberg, and R.E. Freed (eds), *Fragments of a Shattered Visage: The Proceedings of the International Symposium of Ramesses the Great.* 50–86. Memphis.

Keller C.A. 2005a. Hatshepsut's Reputation in History. In C.H. Roehrig et al. (eds), *Hatshepsut: From Queen to Pharaoh.* 294–9. New York.

Keller, C.A. 2005b. Double Portrait of Senenmut. In C.H. Roehrig et al. (eds), *Hatshepsut: From Queen to Pharaoh.* 120–1. New York.

Keller, C.A. 2005c. The Statuary of Senenmut. In C.H. Roehrig et al. (eds), *Hatshepsut: From Queen to Pharaoh.* 117–19. New York.

Keller, C.K. 2005d. Senenmut Kneeling with Surveyor's Cord. In C.H. Roehrig, R. Dreyfus and C.A. Keller (eds), *Hatshepsut: From Queen to Pharaoh.* 122–4. New York, New Haven.

Kitchen, K.A. 1982. *The Pharaoh Triumphant.* Warminster.

Kitchen, K.A. 1991. Towards a Reconstruction of Ramesside Memphis. In E. Bleiberg and R.E. Freed (eds), *Fragments of a Shattered Visage: The Proceedings of the International Symposium of Ramesses the Great.* 87–104. Memphis.

Kjølby, A. 2009. 'Material Agency, Attribution and Experience of Agency in Ancient Egypt: The Case of New Kingdom Private Temple Statues'. In Nyord, R. and A. Kjølby (eds), *'Being in Ancient Egypt': Thoughts on Agency, Materiality and Cognition: Proceedings of the Seminar held in Copenhagen, September 29–30, 2006.* 31–46. Oxford.

Klug, A. 2002. *Königliche Stelen in der Zeit von Ahmose bis Amenophis III. Monumenta Aegyptiaca* 8. Bruxelles, Turnhout.

Koenig, Y. 1981. Notes sur la découverte des papyrus Chester Beatty. *Bulletin de l'Institut Français d'Archéologie Orientale* 81: 41–3.

Köpp Junk, H. 2013. Travel. In E. Frood and W. Wendrich (eds), *UCLA Encyclopedia of Egyptology.* Los Angeles. http://escholarship.org/uc/item/3945t7f7

Kóthay, K. 2013. Categorisation, Classification, and Social Reality: Administrative Control and Interaction with the Population. In J. Moreno-García (ed.), *Ancient Egyptian Administration.* 479–520. Leiden, Boston.

Korostovtsev, M.A. 1962. *Pistsy drevnego Egipta.* Moskva.

Krall, J. et al. 1894. *Papyrus Erzherzog Rainer: Führer durch die Ausstellung.* Wien.

Kruchten, J.-M. 1981. *Le Décret d'Horemheb. Traduction, commentaire épigraphique, philologique et institutionnel.* Université Libre de Bruxelles. Faculté de Philosophie et Lettres, 82. Bruxelles

Kruchten, J.-M. and L. Delvaux. 2010. *Elkab VIII: La tombe de Sétaou.* Publications du comité des fouilles belges en Égypte. Turnhout.

Kucharek, A. 2010. Senenmut in Gebel es-Silsilah. *Mitteilungen des Deutschen Archäologischen Instituts, Abteilung Kairo* 66: 143–59.

Laboury, D. 1998. *La statuaire de Thoutmosis III: essai d'interprétation d'un portrait royal dans son contexte historique. Aegyptiaca Leodiensia* 5. Liège.

Laboury, D. 2010. Les artistes des tombes privées de la nécropole thébaine sous la XVIII dynastie: bilan et perspectives. *Égypte.Afrique et Orient* 59: 34–46.

Laboury, D. 2013a. L'artiste égyptien, ce grand méconnu de l'égyptologie. In G. Andreu-Lanoë (ed.), *L'art du contour: le dessin dans l'Égypte ancienne.* 28–35. Paris.

Laboury, D. 2013b. De l'individualité de l'artiste dans l'art égyptien. In G. Andreu-Lanoë, (ed.), *L'art du contour: le dessin dans l'Égypte ancienne.* 36–41. Paris.

Laboury, D. 2016. Le scribe et le peintre à propos d'un scribe qui ne voulait pas être pris pour un peintre. In P. Collombert et al. *Aere perennius. Mélanges égyptologiques en l'honneur de Pascal Vernus,* 371–96. Orientalia Lovaniensia Analecta 242. Leuven, Paris, Bristol, CT.

Laboury, D., and H. Tavier. 2010. À la recherche des peintres de la nécropole thébaine sous la 18e dynastie. Prolégomènes à une analyse des pratiques picturales dans la tombe d'Amenemopé (TT 29). In E. Warmenbol and V. Angenot (eds), *Thèbes aux 101 portes. Mélanges à la mémoire de Roland Tefnin.* 91–106, pl. 8–22. Turnhout.

Lacau, P. 1909. *Stèles de la XVIIIe dynastie. Tome premier – Troisième fascicule, Le Caire, Imprimerie de l'Institut français d'Archéologie orientale, 1957 (25 x 35.2 cm; pp. 233–61)* = Catalogue général des antiquités égyptiennes du Musée du Caire. Nos 34065–34189: 24–5.

Laisney, V.P.-M. 2007. *L'Enseignement d'Aménémopé.* Studia Pohl, series maior 19. Roma.

Landgrafova, R. 2012. *It is My Good Name that You Should Remember.* Prague.

Lauth, F.J. 1868. *Moses der Ebräer: nach zwei ägyptischen Papyrus-Urkunden in hieratischer Schriftart.* München.

Leach, B., and J. Tait. 2000. Media Used on Papyrus. In P.T. Nicholson and I. Shaw (eds), *Ancient Egyptian Materials and Technology.* 238–9. Cambridge.

Leblanc, Ch. 2004. L'école du temple (*ât-Sebaït*) et le *per-ankh* (maison de vie): à propos de récentes découvertes effectuées dans le contexte du Ramesseum. *Memnonia* 15. 93–101.

Lenzo, G. 2004. Les colophons dans la littérature égyptienne. *Bulletin de l'Institut Français d'Archéologie Orientale* 114. 359–76.

Les artistes de Pharaon, Deir El-Medineh et la vallée des rois. 2002. Paris.

Lesko, L.H. 1994. Literature, Literacy, and Literati. In L. H. Lesko (ed.) *Pharaoh's Workers. The Villagers of Deir el-Medina*. 131–44. Ithaca.

Lichtheim, M. 2006. *Ancient Egyptian Literature: A Book of Reading*. With forewords by H.-W. Fischer-Elfert, A. Loprieno and J.G. Manning. Berkley, Los Angeles, London.

Lloyd, A.B. (ed.). 2010. *A Companion to Ancient Egypt*, Oxford, also as *A Companion to Ancient Egypt, Oxford, Blackwell Reference Online*.

Loprieno, A. 1995. *Ancient Egyptian: A Linguistic Introduction*. Cambridge.

Loprieno, A. 1996. The King's Novel. In A. Loprieno (ed.), *Ancient Egyptian Literature. History and Forms*. Probleme der Ägyptologie, 10. Leiden.

Loprieno, A. 2001. *La pensée et l'écriture: pour une analyse sémiotique de la culture égyptienne. Quatre séminaires à l'École Pratique des Hautes Études, Section des Sciences religieuses*. Paris.

Lorton, D. 1986. The King and the Law. *Varia Aegyptiaca* 2 (1): 53–62.

Lowle, D. 1976. A Remarkable Family of Draughtsmen from Nineteenth Dynasty Thebes. *Oriens Antiquus*, 15: 91–106.

Luiselli, M. 2003. The Colophon as an Indication of the Attitudes Toward the Literary Tradition in Egypt and Mesopotamia. *Basel Egyptology Prize* 1. 343–60. Basel.

Magen, B. 2009. Tatort Ägypten: die 'Lehre des Ptahhotep'. In Agatha Christies Kriminalroman 'Death Comes as the End'. In D. Kessler et al. (eds), *Texte – Theben – Tonfragmente: Festschrift für Günter Burkard*. 312–18. Wiesbaden.

Malek, J. 1995. The Archivist as a Researcher. In J. Assmann et al. (eds), *Thebanische Beamtennekropolen: neue Perspektiven archäologischer Forschung. Internationales Symposion, Heidelberg, 9.-13.6.1993*. 43–8. Studien zur Archäologie und Geschichte Altägyptens, 12. Heidelberg.

Malek, J. 2003. We Have the Tombs. Who Needs the Archives? In N. Strudwick and J. Taylor (eds), *The Theban Necropolis: Past, Present and Future*. 229–43. London.

Manassa, C.M. 2013a. *Imagining the Past. Historical Fiction in New Kingdom Egypt*. Oxford.

Manassa, C.M. 2013b (ed.). *Echoes of Egypt. Conjuring the Land of the Pharaohs*. New Haven.

Manniche, L. 1988. *Lost Tombs: A Study of Certain Eighteenth Dynasty Monuments in the Theban Necropolis*. Studies in Egyptology. London.

Martin, G.T. 1989. *The Memphite Tomb of Ḥoremḥeb, Commander-in-chief of Tutʿankhamūn*. Egypt Exploration Society, Excavation Memoir 55. London.

Mathieu, B. and V. Ritter. 2008. Les sections finales du manuel scolaire Kémyt. In Ch. Gallois, P. Grandet, L. Pantallaci, *Mélanges offerts á Francois Neveu*. 193–238. Cairo.

McDowell, A. 1990. *Jurisdiction in the Workmen's Community of Deir el-Medineh*. Leiden.

Meskell, L. 2000. Spatial Analyses of the Deir el-Medina Settlement and Necropoleis. In R.J. Demarée and A. Egberts (eds), *Deir el-Medina in the Third Millennium AD*. 259–75, Leiden.

Meyer, Ch. 1982. *Senenmut: eine prosopographische Untersuchung. Hamburger Ägyptologische Studien* 2. Hamburg.

Michaux-Colombot, D. 2013. La ruralité méconnue des *Medjay* immigrés en Égypte au Nouvel Empire. *Res Antiquae* 10. 323–52.

Miller, C. 2006. On a 'man for all seasons', *Thomas More Studies*, 1, 26–9.

Moers, G. 2001. Der Papyrus Lansing. Der Lob des Schreiberberufes in einer ägyptischen Schülerhandschrift aus dem ausgehenden Neuen Reich. In O. Kaiser (ed.), *Texte aus der Umwelt des Alten Testaments. Ergänzungslieferung.* 109–42. Gütersloh.

Moers, G. 2010. New Kingdom Literature. In A.B. Lloyd, *A Companion to Ancient Egypt, Oxford, Blackwell Reference Online.* 24 September 2015: http://www. blackwellreference.com/subscriber/tocnode.html?id=g9781405155984_chunk_ g978140515598438

Montserrat, D. 2000. *Akhenaten: History, Fantasy and Ancient Egypt.* London.

Morales, A.J. 2014. Los dos cuerpos del rey: cosmos y política de la monarquía egipcia *Antiguedad, Religiones y Sociedades*, 12: 47–86.

Moreno García, J.C. (ed.). 2013. *Ancient Egyptian Administration.* Handbook of Oriental Studies. Section 1, Ancient Near East 104. Leiden.

Morenz, L.D. 1998. Sa-mut/kyky und Menna, zwei reale Leser/Hörer des *Oasenmannes*, *Göttinger Miszellen.* 73–81.

Morris, A.F. 2005. *The Architecture of Imperialism: Military Bases and the Evolution of Foreign Policy in Egypt's New Kingdom.* Probleme der Ägyptologie 22. Leiden, Boston.

Müller-Wollermann, R. 2004. *Vergehen und Strafen. Zur Sanktionierung abweichenden Verhaltens im alten Ägypten.* Probleme der Ägyptologie 21. Leiden.

Navratilova, H. 2010. Graffiti spaces. In L. Bareš, F. Coppens and K. Smoláriková (eds), *Egypt in Transition: Social and Religious Development of Egypt in the First Millennium BCE. Proceedings of an International Conference, Prague, September 1–4, 2009*: 305–32. Prague.

Navratilova, H. 2013. New Kingdom Graffiti in Dahshur, Pyramid Complex of Senwosret III: Preliminary Report. Graffiti Uncovered in Seasons 1992–2010, *Journal of the American Research Center in Egypt* 49. 113–41.

Navratilova, H. 2015a. *Visitors' Graffiti of Dynasties 18 and 19 in Abusir and Northern Saqqara. With a Survey of Visitors' Graffiti in Giza, Southern Saqqara, Dahshur and Maidum.* Wallasey.

Navratilova, H. 2015b. Ramesside Dockets on Blocks from the Pyramid Complex of Senwosret III in Dahshur, *Journal of Egyptian Archaeology*, 101, 107–16.

Newberry, P.E. 1913. Notes on the Carnarvon tablet no. I. *Proceedings of the Society of Biblical Archaeology* 35: 117–22.

O'Callaghan, R.T. 1951. New Light on the Maryannu as 'Chariot Warrior'. *Jahrbuch für kleinasiatische Forschung* 1: 309–24.

Olsen, R. 2013. The Medjay leaders of the New Kingdom. In C. Graves et al. (eds), *Current Research in Egyptology 2012. Proceedings of the Thirteenth Annual Symposium, University of Birmingham 2012.* 145–56. Oxford.

Onstine, S.L. 2005. *The Role of the Chantress (šmꜥyt) in Ancient Egypt.* Oxford.

Oppenheim A. 2011. The Early Life of Pharaoh: Divine Birth and Adolescence Scenes in the Causeway of Senwosret III at Dahshur. In M. Bárta, F. Coppens and J. Krejčí (eds), *Abusir and Saqqara in the Year 2010*. 171–88. Prague.

Oppenheim, A., Do. Arnold, Di. Arnold and K. Yamamoto. 2015. *Ancient Egypt Transformed: The Middle Kingdom*. New York.

Osing, J. 1997. School and Literature in the Ramesside Period. In: *L'impero ramesside: convegno internazionale in onore di Sergio Donadoni*. 131–42. Roma.

Papazian, H. 2013. The Central Administration of the Resources in the Old Kingdom: Departments, Treasuries, Granaries and Work Centers. In J.C.M. García (ed.), *Ancient Egyptian Administration*. 59–70. Leiden.

Parkinson, R.B. 1991. Teachings, Discourses and Tales from the Middle Kingdom. In S. Quirke, *Middle Kingdom Studies*. Malden, MA.

Parkinson, R.B. 1991a. *Voices from Ancient Egypt. An Anthology of Middle Kingdom Writings*. London.

Parkinson, R.B. 1997. *The Tale of Sinuhe and Other Ancient Egyptian Poems 1940–1640 BC*. Oxford.

Parkinson, R.B. (ed.). 1999. *Cracking Codes*. London.

Parkinson, R.B. 2002. *Poetry and Culture in Middle Kingdom Egypt. A Dark Side to Perfection*. London.

Parkinson, R.B. 2005. No One is Free From Enemies – Voicing Opposition in Literary Discourse. In H. Felber (ed.), *Feinde und Aufrührer. Konzepte von Gegnerschaft in ägyptischen Texten besonders des Mittleren Reiches*. 11–31. Leipzig.

Parkinson, R.B. 2009. *Reading Ancient Egyptian Poetry Among Other Histories*. Malden MA, Oxford, Chichester.

Parkinson, R.B., and S. Quirke, 1995. *Papyrus*. London.

Pasquali, S. 2011. *Topographie cultuelle de Memphis 1 a. Corpus. Temples et principaux quartiers de la XVIIIe dynastie*. Montpellier.

Peden, A.J. 2001. *The Graffiti of Pharaonic Egypt: Scope and Roles of Informal Writings (c. 3100–332 BC)*. Probleme der Ägyptologie 17. Leiden, Boston.

Pernigotti, S. 2005. *Scuola e cultura dell'Egitto del Nuovo Regno*. Brescia.

Pestman, P.W. 1982. Who Were the Owners, in the 'Community of Workmen', of the Chester Beatty Papyri. In R.J. Demarée and J.J. Janssen (eds), *Gleanings from Deir el-Medîna*. 155–72. Leiden.

Petersmarck, E. 2012. *Die Kemit: Ostraka, Schreibtafel und ein Papyrus*. Göttinger Miszellen, Beihefte 12. Göttingen.

Peust, C. 2006. Das Lehrstück Kemit. In B. Janowski and G. Wilhelm (eds), *Texte aus der Umwelt des Alten Testament, Neue Folge, Band 3, Briefe*. 307–13. Gütersloh.

Philips, A.K. 1980. *Besogendes Indskriften (Besucherinschriften) fra Det mellemste Rige til slutningen af Det nye Rige*. Dissertation. Kobenhavn.

Piacentini, P. 2002. *Les scribes dans la société égyptienne de l'Ancien Empire, Vol. I: les premières dynasties. Les nécropoles memphites*. Études et mémoires d'égyptologie 5. Paris.

Pinarello, M. 2015. *An Archaeological Discussion of Writing Practice. Deconstruction of the Ancient Egyptian Scribe.* GHP Egyptology 23. London.

Pinch, G. 1993. *Votive Offerings to Hathor.* Oxford.

Piquette K.E. and R.D. Whitehouse. 2013. Introduction: Developing an Approach to Writing as Material Practice. In idem (eds), *Writing as Material Practice: Substance, Surface and Medium.* 1–13. London. DOI: http://dx.doi.org/10.5334/bai.a

Polz, D. 1986. Excavation and Recording of a Theban Tomb: Some Remarks on Recording Methods. In J. Assmann, V. Davies and G. Burkard (eds). *Problems and Priorities in Egyptian Archaeology.* 119–40. London, New York.

Polz, D. 1991. Jamunedjeh, Meri und Userhat, *Mitteilungen des Deutschen Archäologischen Instituts, Abteilung Kairo* 47 (Festschrift für Werner Kaiser): 281–91.

Polz, D. 2007. *Der Beginn des Neuen Reiches. Zur Vorgeschichte einer Zeitenwende.* Berlin.

Popko, L. 2006. *Untersuchungen zur Geschichtsschreibung der Ahmosiden- und Thutmosidenzeit: 'damit man von seinen Taten noch in Millionen von Jahren sprechen wird'.* Würzburg.

Posener, G. 1951. *Catalogue des ostraca hiératiques littéraires de Deir el-Médineh* II. Cairo.

Posener, G. 1969. 'Maquilleuse' en égyptien. *Revue d'égyptologie* 21: 150–1.

Posener-Kriéger, P. 1981. Costruire une tombe á l'ouest de Mn-nfr (P. Caire 52002). *Revue d'Égyptologie* 33: 47–58.

Prada, L. 2015. Questioni di identità: un Egitto multiculturale e multilingue. In P. Giovetti and D. Picchi (eds), *Egitto. Splendore millenario: la collezione di Leiden a Bologna.* 412–19. Milano.

Quack, J.-F. 2001. Ein neuer Versuch zum Moskauer literarischen Brief. *Zeitschrift für ägyptische Sprache und Altertumskunde* 128: 167–81.

Quack, J.-F. 2009. *Einführung in die altägyptische Literaturgeschichte* III: *die demotische und gräko-ägyptische Literatur*, 2nd revised ed. Einführungen und Quellentexte zur Ägyptologie 3. Berlin, Münster.

Quirke, S. 1990. *The Administration of Egypt in the Late Middle Kingdom: The Hieratic Documents.* New Malden.

Quirke, S. 1996. Archive. In A. Loprieno (ed.). *Ancient Egyptian Literature. History and Forms.* 379–401. Leiden.

Quirke, S. 2004a. *Egyptian Literature 1800 BC Questions and Readings.* GHP Egyptology 2. London.

Quirke, S. 2004b *Titles and bureaux of Egypt, 1850–1700 BC.* GHP Egyptology 1, London.

Rabbat, N. 1997. My Life with Ṣalāḥ al-Dīn: The Memoirs of 'Imād al-Dīn al-Kātib al-Iṣfahānī. In Edebiyât: Special Issue – Arabic Autobiography (7.2). 267–87.

Rabbat, N. 2001. The Autobiography of al-'Imād al-Dīn al-Kātib al-Iṣfahānī. In D.F. Reynolds (ed.), *Interpreting the Self: Autobiography in the Arabic Literary Tradition.* 145–55. Berkeley, Los Angeles, London.

Ragazzoli, Ch. 2008. *Éloges de la ville en Égypte ancienne: histoire et littérature.* Preface R.B. Parkinson. Paris.

Ragazzoli, Ch. 2010. 'Weak Hands and Soft Mouths': Elements of a Scribal Identity in the New Kingdom. *Zeitschrift für ägyptische Sprache und Altertumskunde* 137: 157–70.

Ragazzoli, Ch. 2011, *Les Artisans du texte. La culture des scribes en Egypte ancienne d'apres les sources du Nouvel Empire.* Thése de doctorat, Université Paris-Sorbonne (unpublished).

Ragazzoli, Ch. 2013. The social creation of a scribal place: The visitors' inscriptions in the tomb attributed to Antefiqer (TT 60) (with newly recorded graffiti). *Studien zur Altägyptischen Kultur* 42: 269–316.

Ragazzoli, Ch. 2014. Un nouveau manuscrit du scribe Inéna? Le recueil de miscellanées du Papyrus Koller (Pap. Berlin P. 3043). In V.M. Lepper (ed.), *Forschung in der Papyrussammlung: eine Festgabe für das Neue Museum.* 207–39. Berlin.

Ragazzoli, Ch. 2015. 'The Pen Promoted my Station': Scholarship and Distinction in the New Kingdom Biographies. In K. Ryholt and G. Barjamovic (eds), *Problems of Canonicity and Identity Formation in Ancient Egypt and Mesopotamia.* Carsten Niebuhr Publications 43. 153–78. Copenhagen.

Ragazzoli, C. forthcoming. *La grotte des scribes à Deir el-Bahari. La tombe MMA 504 et ses graffiti.*

Ragazzoli Ch. and E. Frood. 2013. Writing on the Wall: Two Graffiti Projects in Luxor. *Egyptian Archaeology* 42, 30–3.

Rainey, A.F. 1965. The Military Personnel of Ugarit. *Journal of Near Eastern Studies* 24.1/2: 17–27.

Rainey, A.F. 1967. The Soldier-Scribe in Papyrus Anastasi I. *Journal of Near Eastern Studies* 26 (1): 58–60.

Ranke, H. 1935–1977. *Die ägyptischen Personennamen.* Glückstadt/Hamburg, New York.

Ratié, S. 1979. *La Reine Hatchepsout: Sources et Problèmes.* Leiden.

Ratié, S. 1986. Quelques problems soullevés par le persecution de Toutankhamon. In *Hommages à Francois Daumas*, vol. II. 545–50. Montpellier.

Raven, M. J. et al. 2011. *The Memphite Tomb of Horemheb, Commander-in-Chief of Tutankhamun V: The Forecourt and the Area South of the Tomb with Some Notes on the Tomb of Tia.* PALMA Egyptology: Papers on Archaeology of the Leiden Museum of Antiquities 6. Turnhout.

Raven, M. J. 2014. Pragmatics of the New Kingdom Necropolis. In M.J, Raven, R. van Walsem (eds), *The Tomb of Meryneith at Saqqara* (with contributions by W.F.M. Beex, A. Dunsmore and L. Horáčková). 323–8. Turnhout.

Redford, D.B. 1986. *Pharaonic King-Lists, Annals and Day-Books: A Contribution to the Study of the Egyptian Sense of History.* Mississauga.

Redford, D.B. 2003. *The Wars in Syria and Palestine of Thutmose III.* Leiden.

Reeves, C.N. 1988. New Light on Kiya from Texts in the British Museum. *Journal of Egyptian Archaeology* 74: 91–101.

Reeves, C.N. 1990. *The Complete Tutankhamun: The King, the Tomb, the Royal Treasure.* London.

Reeves, C.N. 2001. *Akhenaten: Egypt's False Prophet*. London.

Reisner, R.G. 1971. *Graffiti: Two Thousand Years of Wall Writing*. New York.

Richards, D.S. 1993. Imād al-Dīn al-Isfahānī: Administrator, Litterateur and Historian. In M. Shatzmiller (ed.). *Crusaders and Muslims in Twelfth-Century Syria*. 133–46. The Medieval Mediterranean 1. Leiden, New York, Köln.

Rickal, E. 2005. *Les Épithètes dans les autobiographies de particuliers du Nouvel Empire égyptien*. Thèse de doctorat inédite. Université Paris IV-Sorbonne.

Ritner, R.K. 2009, *The Libyan Anarchy: Inscriptions from Egypt's Third Intermediate Period*. Writings from the Ancient World 21. Leiden.

Robins G. 1993. *Women in Ancient Egypt*, London.

Roccati, A. 1997. Scribes. In S. Donadoni (ed.), *The Egyptians*. 61–85. Chicago, London.

Rodenbeck, J. 2010. Photography and Egypt, by Maria Golia. *Bulletin of the Association for the Study of Travel in Egypt and the Near East: Notes and Queries*, 44: 8.

Roehrig C.H. 1990. *The Eighteenth Dynasty Titles Royal nurse (mnˁt nswt), Royal Tutor (mnˁ nswt) and Foster Brother/Sister of the Lord of the Two Lands (sn/snt mnˁ n nb t3wy)*. Dissertation. University of Berkeley, California.

Roehrig, C.H. 2002. The Statue of the Royal Nurse Sitre with her Nursling Maatkare Hatshepsut. In M. Eldamaty, M. Trad (eds), *Egyptian Museum Collections Around the World*. vol. 2. 1003–10. Cairo.

Roehrig, C.H. 2005. Senenmut, Royal Tutor to Princess Neferure. In C.H. Roehrig et al. (eds), *Hatshepsut: from Queen to Pharaoh*. 112–13. New York.

Roehrig, C.H. et al. (eds). 2005. *Hatshepsut: from Queen to Pharaoh*. New York.

Ross D.M. 2002. Statue of Senenmut, no. 171. In *The Pharaohs, Venezia Palazzo Grassi*, 454. Venezia.

Rutherford, I. (ed). 2016. *Greco-Egyptian Interactions. Literature, Translation, and Culture, 500 BC–AD 300*. Oxford.

Ryholt, K. 2013. Libraries in Ancient Egypt. In J. König, K. Oikonomopoulou and G. Woolf (eds), Ancient Libraries. 23–37. Cambridge.

Rzepka, S. 2014. *Who, Where and Why: The Rock Graffiti of Members of the Deir el-Medina Community*. Warsaw.

Salvador, Ch. 2014. From the Realm of the Dead to the House of the God: the New Kingdom Appeals to the Living in Context at Thebes. In K. Accetta et al. (eds), *Current Research in Egyptology 2013: Proceedings of the Fourteenth Annual Symposium, University of Cambridge, United Kingdom, 19–22 March, 2013*: 153–67. Oxford.

Samson, J. 1979. Akhenaten's Successor. *Göttinger Miszellen* 32: 53–8

Sauneron, S. 1975. III. Les deux statues de Mentouhotep. In J. Lauffray et al., Rapport sur les travaux de Karnak. Activités du Centre franco-égyptien en 1970–1972. In *Karnak* 5: 1–42.

Schad B. 2006. *Die Entdeckung des 'Briefes' als literarisches Ausdrucksmittel in der Ramessidenzeit*, 11–40.

Schipper, B.U. 2005. *Die Erzählung des Wenamun: ein Literaturwerk im Spannungsfeld von Politik, Geschichte und Religion*. Orbis Biblicus et Orientalis 209. Fribourg, Göttingen.

Scott, G.D. 1989. *The History and Development of the Ancient Egyptian Scribe Statue*. PhD dissertation. Yale University.

Schulman, A.R. 1969–70. Some Remarks on the Alleged 'Fall' of Senmū't. *Journal of the American Research Center in Egypt* 8: 29–48.

Select papyri in the Hieratic Character from the Collection of the British Museum II, London 1842.

Shaw, G.J. 2009. The Death of King Seqenenre Tao. *Journal of the American Research Center in Egypt* 45: 159–76.

Shaw, I. (ed.). 2000. *The Oxford History of Ancient Egypt*. Oxford, New York.

Shirley, J.J. 2013. Crisis and Restructuring of the State: From the Second Intermediate Period to the Advent of the Ramesses [sic]. In J.C. Moreno García (ed.), *Ancient Egyptian administration*. 521–606. Leiden.

Shoemaker, J.S. 2002. The Nature of the Godess Qudshu in Conjunction with Min and Reshep. *Bulletin of the Egyptological Seminar* 15: 1–11.

Simon, H. 2013. 'Textaufgaben': kulturwissenschaftliche Konzepte in Anwendung auf die Literatur der Ramessidenzeit. Studien zur Altägyptischen Kultur, Beihefte 14. Hamburg.

Simpson, W.K. 1984. Senenmut, *LÄ* V. 849–51.

Simpson, W.K. 1991. Mentuhotep, Vizier of Sesostris I, Patron of Art and Architecture. *Mitteilungen des Deutschen Archäologischen Instituts, Abteilung Kairo* 47: 331–40.

Simpson, W.K. (ed.) 2003. *The Literature of Ancient Egypt: An Anthology of Stories, Instructions, Stelae, Autobiographies, and Poetry*, 3rd ed. New Haven; London.

Spalinger, A.J. 2005. *War in Ancient Egypt: The New Kingdom*. Ancient World at War. Malden MA, Oxford.

Spence, K. 1999. The North Palace at Amarna. *Egyptian Archaeology* 15: 14–16.

Spencer, A.J 1989. *British Museum Expedition to Middle Egypt: Excavations at El-Ashmunein: II: The Temple Area*. London.

Spiegelberg, W. 1921. *Aegyptische und andere Graffiti (Inschriften und Zeichnungen) aus der thebanischen Nekropolis*. Heidelberg.

Stevens, A. 2003. The Material Evidence for Domestic Religion at Amarna and Preliminary Remarks on Its Interpretation. *The Journal of Egyptian Archaeology*, 89: 143–68.

Stevens, A. 2006. *Private Religion at Amarna. The Material Evidence*, British Archaeological Reports International Series 1587. Oxford.

Stevens, A. 2012. *Akhenaten's Workers. The Amarna Stone Village Survey, 2005–2009. Volume I: The Survey, Excavations and Architecture*. Egypt Exploration Society and Amarna Trust. With contributions by W. Dolling. London. And *Akhenaten's Workers. The Amarna Stone Village Survey, 2005–2009. Volume II: The Faunal and Botanical Remains, and Objects*. Egypt Exploration Society and Amarna Trust. With contributions by A. Clapham, M. Gabolde, R. Gerisch, A. Legge and C. Stevens. London.

Stevens, A. 2015. *The Archaeology of Amarna*. Oxford Handbooks online, DOI: 10.1093/oxfordhb/9780199935413.013.3

Street, B.V. 1984. *Literacy in Theory and Practice*. Cambridge Studies in Oral and Literate Culture 9. Cambridge, New York.

Street, B.V. 1993. Introduction: The New Literacy Studies. In: B.V. Street (ed.), *Cross-Cultural Approaches to Literacy*. Cambridge Studies in Oral and Literate Culture, 23: 1–21. Cambridge, New York.

Strudwick, N. 2004. Nina M. Davies: A Biographical Sketch. *Journal of Egyptian Archaeology* 90: 193–210.

Strudwick, N. 2012. Facsimiles of Ancient Egyptian Paintings: The Work of Nina de Garis Davies, Amice Calverley, and Myrtle Broome. In: J. Green, E. Teeter and J.A. Larson (eds), *Picturing the Past: Imaging and Imagining the Ancient Middle East*. 61–70. Chicago.

Sweeney, D. 2001 *Correspondence and Dialogue. Pragmatic Factors in Late Ramesside Letter Writing*. Ägypten und Altes Testament 49. Wiesbaden.

Tait, W.J. 1988. Rush and Reed: The Pens of Egyptian and Greek Scribes. In *Proceedings of the 17th International Congress of Papyrology*. 2: 47–81. Athens.

Tassie. G.J. and L.S. Owens. 2010. *Standards of Archaeological Excavation; a Fieldguide to the Methodology, Recording Techniques, and Conventions*. London.

te Velde, H. 1986. Scribes and Literacy in Ancient Egypt. In H.L. Vanstiphout et al. (eds), *Scripta signa vocis: studies about scripts, scriptures, scribes, and languages in the Near East, presented to J.H. Hospers by his pupils, colleagues, and friends*. 253–64. Groningen.

Tefnin, R. 1979. *La statuaire d'Hatshepsout: portrait royal et politique sous la 18e Dynastie*. Monumenta Aegyptiaca 4. Bruxelles.

Thijs, A. 2003 The Troubled Careers of Amenhotep and Panehsy: The High Priest of Amun and the Viceroy of Kush under the Last Ramessides. *Studien zur Altägyptischen Kultur* 31: 289–306.

Thomas, R. 2009. The Origin of Western Literacy: Literacy in Ancient Greece and Rome. In D.R. Olson and N. Torrance (eds). *The Cambridge Handbook of Literacy*. 346–61. Cambridge.

Thompson, J. 2015. *Wonderful Things: A History of Egyptology, 1: From Antiquity to 1881*. Cairo, New York.

Toivari-Viitala, J. 2001. *Women at Deir el-Medina. A Study of the Status and Roles of the Female Inhabitants in the Workmen's Community During the Ramesside Period*. Leiden.

Tosh, J. 2009. *The Pursuit of History: Aims, Methods, and New Directions in the Study of Modern History*. London.

Traunecker, C. 1986. Les techniques d'épigraphie de terrain: principes et pratique. In J. Assmann, V. Davies and G. Burkard (eds), *Problems and Priorities in Egyptian Archaeology*. 261–98. London, New York.

Traunecker, C. 2014. The 'Funeral Palace' of Padiamenope (TT 33): Tomb, Place of Pilgrimage, and Library. Current Research in E. Pischikova, J. Budka, K. Griffin (eds). *Thebes in the First Millennium BC*. 205–34. Cambridge.

Tylor, J.J. and F.L. Griffith. 1894. *The Tomb of Paheri at El Kab*. Memoir of the Egypt Exploration Fund 11. London.

Ullmann, M. 2002. *König für die Ewigkeit- die Häuser der Millionen von Jahren: eine Untersuchung zu Königskult und Tempeltypologie in Ägypten*. Ägypten und Altes Testament 51. Wiesbaden.

Valbelle, D. 1985. *Les ouvriers de la Tombe – Deir el-Médineh á l'époque Ramesside*. Le Caire.

Vandier, J. 1954–1978. *Manuel d'archéologie égyptienne*. Paris.

Varille, A. 1968. *Inscriptions concernant l'architecte Amenhotep, fils de Hapou*. Bibliothèque d'étude 44. Le Caire.

Veldmeijer, A.J. and S. Ikram (eds). 2013. *Chasing Chariots: Proceedings of the First International Chariot Conference (Cairo 2012)*. Leiden.

Ventura, R. 1986. *Living in a City of the Dead: A Selection of Topographical and Administrative Terms in the Documents of the Theban necropolis*. Freiburg.

Verbovsek, A. 2004. '*Als Gunsterweis des Königs in den Tempel gegeben. . .'. Private Tempelstatuen des Alten und Mittleren Reiches*. Ägypten und Altes Testament 63. Wiesbaden.

Verhoeven, U. 2009, 'Die wie Kraniche balzen' – Männerphantasien zur Zeit Amenophis III. in Assiut, D. Kessler, et al. (eds), *Texte – Theben – Tonfragmente. Festschrift für Günter Burkard*. 434–1. Wiesbaden.

Verhoeven, U. 2012a. The New Kingdom Graffiti in Tomb N13.1. In J. Kahl et al. (eds), *Seven Seasons at Asyut. First Results of the Egyptian-German Cooperation in Archaeological Fieldwork*. 47–58. Wiesbaden.

Verhoeven, U. 2012b. Butehamun – Ein Nekropolenschreiber am Ende des Neuen Reiches. In S. Heimann (ed.), *Ägyptens Schätze entdecken, Meisterwerke aus dem Ägyptischen Museum Turin*. 182–3. München, London, New York.

Vernus, P. 1995. *Essai sur la conscience de l'Histoire dans l'Egypte pharaonique*. Bibliothèque de l'Ecole des hautes études. Sciences historiques et philologiques 332. Paris.

Vértes, K. 2014. *Digital Epigraphy*. Chicago.

Vike, H. 2011. Cultural Models, Power and Hegemony. In D.B. Kronenfeld et al. (eds), *A Companion to Cognitive Anthropology*. 376–92. Chichester, Malden MA, Oxford.

Vinson, S. 1995. In Defense of an Ancient Reputation. *Göttinger Miszellen* 146: 93–102.

Vinson, S. 2010. Ten Notes on the First Tale of Setne Khamwas'. In H. Knuf and D. von Recklinghausen (eds), *Honi soit qui mal y pense. Studien zum pharaonischen, griechisch-römischen und späptantiken Ägypten zu Ehren von Heinz-Josef Thissen*. 447–70. Leuven.

Vinson, S. 2011. Strictly Tabubue: The Legacy of an ancient Egyptian femme fatale. *KMT: A Modern Journal of Ancient Egypt*, 22.3: 46–57.

Walsem, R. van and M.J. Raven. 2011. New Evidence on Horemheb's Statuary. In M.J. Raven et al. *The Memphite Tomb of Horemheb, Commander-in-Chief of Tutankhamun V: The Forecourt and the Area South of the Tomb with Some Notes on the Tomb of Tia*. 375–83. Turnhout.

Welvaert, E. 1996. On the Origin of the ished-Scene. *Göttinger Miszellen* 151: 101–7.

Wente, E.F. 1967. *Late Ramesside Letters*. Studies in Ancient Oriental Civilization 33. Chicago.

Wente, E.F. 1984. Some Graffiti from the Reign of Hatshepsut. *Journal of Near Eastern Studies* 43: 47–54.

Wente, E.F. 1990. *Letters from Ancient Egypt*. Writings from the Ancient World 1. Atlanta.

Widmaier, K. 2013. Die Lehre des Cheti und ihre Kontexte: zu Berufen und Berufsbildern im Neuen Reich. In G. Moers et al. (eds), *Dating Egyptian Literary Texts*. 483–557. Hamburg.

Wildung, D. 1972. Besucherinschriften. In W. Helck and E. Otto (eds), *Lexikon der Agyptologie* I. Cols. 766–7. Wiesbaden.

Wilkinson, C.K. 1978–1979. Egyptian Wall Paintings: The Metropolitan Museum's Collection of Facsimiles. *The Metropolitan Museum of Art Bulletin (new series)* 36(4): 2–56.

Wilkinson, T.A.H. 2000. *Royal Annals of Ancient Egypt: The Palermo Stone and its Associated Fragments*. London, New York.

Winlock, H.E. 1923. Harmhab, Commander-in-Chief of the Armies of Tutenkhamon. *The Metropolitan Museum of Art Bulletin* 18 no. 10.2: 1+3–16.

Winlock, H.E. 1924. A Statue of Horemhab before His Accession. *The Journal of Egyptian Archaeology* 10.1: 1–5.

Winlock, H.E. 1932. The Museum's Excavations at Thebes: 1. Excavations at the Temple of Hatshepsut. *Bulletin of the Metropolitan Museum of Art* xxvii: 4–37.

Yoyotte, M. 2013. Ostracon figuré biface: Double portrait de Senenmout et rat (?). In G. Andreu-Lanoë (ed.), *L'art du contour: le dessin dans l'Égypte ancienne*. 274–5. Paris.

Zinn, K. 2012. Literacy, Pharaonic Egypt. In R.S. Bagnall et al. (eds), *The Encyclopedia of Ancient History*. Malden MA (online version).

Zivie, A. 2007. *The Lost Tombs of Saqqara*. Toulouse.

Zivie, A. 2009. *La tombe de Maïa: mère nourricière du roi Toutânkhamon et Grande du Harem; (Bub. I.20)*. Les tombes du Bubasteion à Saqqara 1. Toulouse

Zivie, A. 2013. *La tombe de Thoutmes, directeur des peintres dans la Place de Maât (BUB. I.19)*. Les tombes du Bubasteion à Saqqara 2. Toulouse.

Zorn, Jeffrey 1991. LÚ.*pa-ma-ḫa-a* in EA 162:74 and the role of the *Mhr* in Egypt and Ugarit. *Journal of Near Eastern Studies* 50.2. 129–38.

Žába, Z. 1956. *Les Maximes de Ptahhotep*. Prague.

Index

(pages in **bold** indicate detailed information on the subject)